PRAISE FOR
ESSENTIAL LEAD

C000095304

"A welcome reminder that all of us who aspire to lead should continue to delve and learn. I found the many relevant cases coupled with theory inspirational." **Mads Wijngaard, Senior Director, global transportation company, Netherlands**

"Practical, research-based and thought-provoking. A must-read for anyone interested in developing leaders." **Nick Petrie, Senior Faculty, Center for Creative Leadership**

"For those of us eager to improve our leadership skills but feeling overwhelmed by endless shelves with books about leadership in the bookstore, look no further. Here is a book that helps you navigate the essential leadership literature and at the same time offers a practical approach to improving your and your organization's leadership capability based on theory and practice. The book is easy to read, loaded with real-life examples and suited for all levels of leadership. I have personally seen a leadership development programme based on the framework defined in this book being implemented in a manufacturing site, resulting in a significant improvement of leadership capability." **Henk Weijers, Technology Manager, oil and gas sector, Malaysia**

"I found *Essential Leadership* compelling and extremely relevant to my role as a leader in the retail environment. This book would be an inspiration to developing leaders. I enjoyed the self-reflection activities, which got me thinking and motivated me to try something new with my team." **Lauren Clark, Store Manager, retail sector, UK**

"It is the first leadership book I have ever read, and I found it surprisingly engaging and relevant." **Alex Kirk, Senior Development Manager, transport sector, UK**

"A comprehensive, relevant and easy-to-digest overview of best-practice leadership thinking. I particularly enjoyed the section on millennial leadership." **Neil Darke, Founder and CEO of The Lifehouse.Co and former CEO of international wealth management firm, UK**

"A treasure trove of leadership reading, elegantly combining real world insights with leadership theory. No doubt I, and the managers I support, will go back to it again and again, to be challenged, supported and to keep learning." **Lindiwe Khuzwayo, HR Manager, petroleum sector, South Africa**

"Esther and Mike have done it again! Through exploring the complexities of leadership they facilitate our very own leadership journey. We all have a leadership potential, and this book will help us realize it. Based on both theory and practice, this is a must read for seasoned leaders and novices alike." **Professor Rune Todnem By, Professor of Organizational Behaviour (Staffordshire University Business School, UK), Professor II Change Leadership (University of Stavanger, Norway) and Editor-in-Chief,** *Journal of Change Management*

"This is a first-rate change leadership book that I would heartily recommend to both students and practitioners. It provides a concise summary of leadership theories and offers practical insights for both the new and experienced leader." **Michael Fekete, Head of Engagement, Digital Railway Programme at Network Rail, UK**

"For me good leadership is about using the right styles for the context and this book is a great resource to not only understand key leadership styles but to self assess and improve them. I loved the five qualities framework as a fascinating construct and a framework for self assessment. A thoroughly enjoyable read!" **Jagjivan (Judge) Matharu, Principal Portfolio Benefits Manager at Transport for London**

"A great book. *Essential Leadership* is an invaluable resource for developing leaders at all levels in today's complex business environment. I can recommend it as an excellent resource for people in leadership positions and leadership developers alike." **Dr Katja Kruckeberg, International Leadership and Organizational Development Consultant at Kruckeberg Consulting**

"I regularly use this framework with my public and private sector clients. It is highly regarded and is frequently cited by individual managers and leaders as pivotal to the progress they, and their organisations have made. It is accessible, conceptually sound and highly effective." **David Weaver, Individual and Organisational Development Consultant, DWC**

"This is a very engaging book, which would be of great practical help to anyone wrestling with the many challenges of leadership in the complex organizations of today. There are some useful categorizations of behaviour which can hold up a mirror to many of our own experiences of being managed – and led, and help us make sense of why some of those experiences were so positive, and why some of them stick with us for other reasons. The exercises in the book help embed some of the messages by offering the chance to experience the theory for ourselves. This would be a useful book to share with your coach and explore some of the ideas at a personal level in this way." **Dr Patricia Bossons, Director of Executive Qualifications at the Institute of Executive Education & Enterprise, Massey Business School, New Zealand**

"Esther and Mike have produced a valuable contribution to the field of leadership that is both rigorous and relevant. I believe that, as a reader, you will find this to be an engaging, challenging and enjoyable book." **Malcolm Higgs, Professor of Organization Behaviour and HRM, Southampton Business School, UK**

"So much leadership training fails to hit the mark. This book offers a completely fresh approach that's intuitive and immediately helpful, enabling almost anyone reading it to engage with a useful, new leadership quality and really learn something." **Howard Orme, Director General, Strategy and Resources Directorate, Civil Service, UK**

Essential Leadership

Essential Leadership

Develop your leadership qualities
through theory and practice

Esther Cameron and Mike Green

Publisher's note
Every possible effort has been made to ensure that the information contained in this book is accurate at the time of going to press, and the publishers and authors cannot accept responsibility for any errors or omissions, however caused. No responsibility for loss or damage occasioned to any person acting, or refraining from action, as a result of the material in this publication can be accepted by the editor, the publisher or the authors.

First published in Great Britain and the United States in 2017 by Kogan Page Limited

2nd Floor, 45 Gee Street	c/o Martin P Hill Consulting	4737/23 Ansari Road
London	122 W 27th Street	Daryaganj
EC1V 3RS	New York, NY 10001	New Delhi 110002
United Kingdom	USA	India

© Esther Cameron and Mike Green 2017

ISBN   978 0 7494 7740 0
E-ISBN   978 0 7494 7741 7

British Library Cataloguing-in-Publication Data

A CIP record for this book is available from the British Library.

Library of Congress Control Number

2017930849

Typeset by Integra Software Services, Pondicherry
Print production managed by Jellyfish
Printed and bound in Great Britain by CPI Group (UK) Ltd, Croydon CR0 4YY

CONTENTS

FOREWORD

Today's organizations and their leaders are operating in an environment that is characterized by volatility, uncertainty, complexity and ambiguity, and to deal with this environment they need to engage in continuous transformation. Given the poor history of organizations' ability to implement change successfully, this context presents a major leadership challenge. At the same time, organizations often struggle to find effective means of developing their leaders. The combination of these two challenges results in what some suggest is a leadership crisis.

In attempting to address these challenges, organizations and leaders are constantly seeking to find leadership solutions that are both practical and easy to implement. All too often, apparently simple solutions fail to deliver results as they are not underpinned by careful and rigorous research. Turning to examine the rigorous research, it is often found to be inaccessible and fails to deliver the 'Holy Grail' desired by the practitioners. The complexity of the phenomenon of leadership that is explored by academics is often dismissed by practitioners as being too theoretical. However, it can often be a mistake to dismiss theory, for, as Kurt Lewin is reputed to have said, 'There is nothing as practical as a good theory'.

Within the field of leadership there is indeed an abundance of research and theories. However, research is often inconclusive or contradictory and, as such, leads to the espousal of new theories for testing. This has resulted in a cycle of research that frequently dismisses existing theories and seeks to find new solutions. Rather than concentrating on finding a new 'best theory', we should reflect on what has been learned and explore how this may be reinterpreted in a new context. Indeed, the need to do this was admirably captured by Karl Weick in his book *Sensemaking in Organizations*:

> Social and organizational sciences, as opposed to physics or biology, do not
> discover anything new, but let us comprehend what we have known all along
> in a much better way, opening up new, unforeseen possibilities of reshaping,
> re-engineering and restructuring our original social environment.

At the same time, in pursuing leadership research and producing work that is of value to practitioners, perhaps academics should adhere to the advice of Neil Anderson and colleagues and ensure that their work is both rigorous and relevant (Anderson, Heriot and Hodgkinson, 2001).

In *Essential Leadership*, Esther Cameron and Mike Green have ably demonstrated an ability to build on established leadership theory and demonstrate both rigour and relevance in formulating a framework for thinking about leadership, and the development of leadership capability, in today's complex and volatile context.

The book opens with considerations of the challenge of leadership in today's context, pointing out that both the context and process of leadership are increasingly complex. Furthermore, Esther and Mike highlight the need to see leadership development as a personal journey rather than a 'quick fix'. They make the extremely good point that leadership is enacted and developed through guided reflection and experience, based on honest self-assessment, rather than learned in the classroom.

Esther and Mike provide an excellent review and critique of the major streams of leadership research and the related theories and models. In doing this they demonstrate rigour combined with relevance and make the often-complex ideas accessible through an engaging writing style. Rather than using the critical evaluation of established theories as a basis for the development of a new theory they reflect on what has been learned and, in the spirit of Karl Weick, use the reflection to make sense of previous learning in today's context. They do this through a careful mapping of existing theories and the development of five distinct themes that are underpinned by a number of leadership capabilities. These themes (or, as they refer to them, 'Archetypes') they label as: **Architect, Motivator, Connector, Implementer** and **Catalyser**. Working with these 'Archetypes' they identify related qualities that form the basis of developing leadership capability. They do not present these qualities as 'must dos' or a prescribed way of working, but rather as a map to guide leaders through a development journey and as a framework that can be adapted to meet the needs of a diverse range of challenges and contexts.

Essential Leadership makes a really useful contribution which is highly relevant to today's context. It does this by providing a sharp focus on how leaders and leadership culture can grow and mature in a way that develops capacity to handle complexity and change. A very practical self-assessment tool is also included to identify development needs and priorities, informed by the theories and models presented. Once again they reinforce the point that leadership capability is developed through guided reflection and practice. In doing so they provide a range of practical development thoughts and ideas.

Throughout *Essential Leadership*, Esther and Mike work with a strong practical and solution-focused approach to the challenges of leadership. The lessons from previous research in the field and related theories are well integrated and brought to life through the use of case studies and examples from practice. The flexible way in which they present their work provides a text that is of value to students engaging with the topic of leadership, as well as practitioners.

Overall, in *Essential Leadership*, Esther and Mike have produced a valuable contribution to the field of leadership that is both rigorous and relevant. I believe that, as a reader, you will find this to be an engaging, challenging and enjoyable book.

Malcolm Higgs
Professor of Organization Behaviour and HRM
Southampton Business School
University of Southampton

References

Anderson, N, Heriot, P and Hodgkinson, G P (2001) The practitioner – researcher divide in Industrial Work and Organizational (IWO) psychology: where are we now and where do we go from here? *Journal of Occupational and Organizational Psychology*, **74** (4), pp. 391–412

Weick, K E (1995) *Sensemaking in Organizations,* Sage, London

PREFACE

There are tens of thousands of leadership books available today, and you can get hold of anything from the densely theoretical to the inspiringly innovative to the boiled-down basic 'how to' book. Whilst this is a wonderfully rich assortment, it can also be pretty mind-boggling and leave you feeling unclear where to start your leadership journey and which books to truly trust.

What we're offering with *Essential Leadership* is a book that helps you to navigate the leadership literature, from the academic to the popular and from the historic to the current, whilst supporting you to improve the way you lead. It helps you to take responsibility for understanding the leadership territory and for finding out how to improve the quality of leadership, whatever your starting point.

With our combined experience in the academic and organizational worlds, we have attempted to merge good-quality, well-referenced theory, with proven strategies and tips for learning how to lead in practice. Most books try to do one or the other – yet we have ambitiously, and hopefully reasonably elegantly, attempted to do both!

Importantly, this book is for *anyone* interested in becoming a better leader, whatever your level of formal authority. Whether you've been leading for many years and want to bring yourself up to date, or you're only just starting out on your journey, this book enables you to understand the subject that little bit better, assess your own progress as a leader, and find out what you need to do to develop further.

Part One is fairly short and enables you to get your 21st-century bearings. Part Two guides you through the story of leadership theory and is, perhaps, to be consumed in small doses as there's a lot of information to absorb! Part Three brings in new ideas about adult development to help you to understand how you can learn and improve. Part Four supports you to self-assess and clarify your development goals and Part Five introduces an integrated leadership framework which sets out, in a clear way, all the skills and qualities that leaders need to master. The latter is practically oriented and packed with information, examples and advice about developing the various skills and qualities required. Part Six looks at leadership from an organizational perspective, and describes how 'leadership culture' forms and can be developed.

Note that if you teach leadership, there are plenty of references and exercises within the book to support your programmes. However, if you hunger for more, you can also access related resources through Kogan Page.

Our overall premise is that anyone can improve their leadership capacity if they so wish, and that this requires commitment and dedication. While this book can help you considerably, the lion's share of the job is down to you! Of course, some aspects of leading will come easier to you than others, so we advise you to be grateful for your gifts, stay acutely aware of your shortcomings and keep learning!

We wish you the very best of luck on your journey, and would love to hear from you with reports of progress, questions or any other responses!

Esther and Mike
esther@integralchange.co.uk
mike@transitionalspace.co.uk

ACKNOWLEDGEMENTS

It's a daunting task to try to thank all of those who've contributed to the production of this book, yet a pleasure to have the space to do so. One never does anything alone, and this book is definitely no exception.

We'd first like to thank our publishers Kogan Page. Anna Moss brought spark and enthusiasm to our initial thinking and Amy Minshull's dedicated editing and wise counsel along the way have been invaluable. Our own colleague Louise Overy also needs a special mention for reading absolutely everything and offering comments to a tight timescale right at the end!

We are indebted to all those whose high-quality research and thinking goes before us, and whom we credit in these pages. The opportunity to take time to read so many well-written articles and books has been rather wonderful.

We also thank, particularly deeply, those organizational leaders whom we've taught, coached, shadowed and advised. It's their responses and challenges that make our work come alive, and help us to improve and hone our own thinking. Esther is especially grateful to the leaders of Sapref in South Africa who were a joy to work with and taught her a great deal. Mike wishes to thank both the LGA's Leadership Academy for the opportunity to test out many of the ideas with real live political leaders, and the many managers he's worked with across Africa and the Middle East grappling with massive change.

Gratitude also goes to those who gave their time to participate in the Millennial Leadership research that we were involved in, and so eloquently described what it's like to enter today's organizations as a young leader and try to make your mark.

Our work colleagues have been extremely supportive during the often quite intense process of putting the book together. Esther offers profound thanks to Nick Mayhew for sharing his leadership insights over the years, offering feedback on this text and being such a stimulating and skilful business partner! Mike thanks in particular Anjali Arya, Rajwant Bains, Mhairi Cameron and David Weaver who have helped to make theory and ideas come alive in real time, again and again.

Spending time writing inevitably disrupts 'normal' life, and families and friends have been incredibly flexible and tolerant of this. Much love and heartfelt thanks goes from Esther to Duncan Cameron for his loving companionship, care and encouragement, and to her daughter Ailsa and son Ewan for their determination, humour and fresh perspectives. Mike owes a debt of gratitude to Helen Stride for advice, support, love and for hanging in there. Also to his children Lewin, Oliver and Brigit, son-in-law Christopher and daughter-in-law Amma, who have all grown into fine young people and who are now taking the lead in their own fields.

Esther would like to dedicate this book to her father, who was a leader in his own field and taught her that even big, strong men can have tender hearts.

Mike would like to dedicate the book to Helen, who is helping make the concept of responsible leadership come alive.

PART ONE
Setting the scene

Leading in a new era

In this chapter we set out the reasons why we believe this book is important for leaders right now. We describe something of the current global context and identify the leadership gap that currently exists. Readers are encouraged to use this book not just to pass exams or satisfy the boss, but to learn how to become more skilful and effective as leaders who make a positive difference. To that end we offer some tips for how to get the best out of the book and how to stick at it!

Why is leadership important now?

The Anthropocene Working Group was convened in Oslo in April 2016 to collate evidence that the world is now entering a new era. This era, known as the Anthropocene epoch, recognizes that humans are having a significant impact on planet Earth's ecosystems. One of the most crucial messages we take from this is of humankind's massive capability – with its technology, its industry, and its economic and political systems – to impact everything and everyone on the planet.

The outcomes of this new era can be tremendously positive or dramatically negative. On a macro scale, we know that alongside increases in nations' gross domestic product we also have increasing inequality. According to the 2015 Credit Suisse Global Wealth Report, global inequality is growing, with half the world's wealth now in the hands of just 1 per cent of the population. Alongside the benefits of a globalized free market we have seemingly insurmountable issues around the mass migration of people. Currently we are also consuming the equivalent of 1.6 planet Earths to give us the resources that our economies and people demand (Global Footprint Network, 2016) – clearly unsustainable.

At the organizational level, the huge advances in technologies, education and global connectivity, demographic shifts, multi-generational workforce, constant pressure to do more with less, shifting psychological employment contracts and permeable organizational boundaries require leadership of a different calibre.

As Chair of the Emergency Committee of Atomic Scientists 70 years ago, Einstein co-authored a highly prescient appeal to promote a new type of thinking:

> Our world faces a crisis as yet unperceived by those possessing power to make great decisions for good or evil. The unleashed power of the atom has changed everything save our modes of thinking and we thus drift toward unparalleled catastrophe… a new type of thinking is essential if mankind is to survive and move toward higher levels (Einstein, 1946).

It is our contention that Einstein's campaign is still desperately required. Time has moved on, but the scope, scale and challenge of the issues Einstein referred to are comparable to those we face today. We don't just need a shift in our thinking but a shift in our capacity as human beings to take responsibility, collaborate and lead. The 'wicked' issues (Grint, 2008) which are alluded to above, and described in Chapter 8, cannot be dealt with by our traditional notion of the all-singing, dancing, conquering, heroic leader who fixes everything. A type of leadership that can work to accommodate complexity and interdependence is required.

This book, *Essential Leadership*, has therefore been written to meet the above needs. We believe we bring a fresh, practical, completely up-to-date take on leadership that stimulates and provokes readers in a way that many traditional academic books don't. Uniquely, we also attempt to integrate multiple perspectives and help the reader to navigate this territory. This enables everyone to find their own, structured and yet flexible leadership recipe.

The leadership deficit

Everyone thinks of changing the world, but no one thinks of changing himself. TOLSTOY

In 2014, APQC (the world's foremost authority in benchmarking, best practices, process and performance improvement, and knowledge management) published the results of a survey into what has become known as the leadership deficit – the perception that organizations have shortages of leadership.

The key findings (APQC, 2014) suggest that organizations have a leadership deficit in the areas of strategic planning, change management, knowledge sharing, listening, and emotional intelligence. Only a fifth of respondents believed their organization had effective leadership practices, with just under half saying their organization was giving leadership development 'little or no priority'.

APQC conclude that the business environment requires a different sort of leadership, yet current leaders are resistant to adapting their style. Furthermore, HR practices which aim to attract, select, develop and reward current and future leaders are no longer fit for the purpose of ensuring the relevant leadership capacity and capability for today's world.

In some contrast, the annual UK CIPD Learning and Development Survey (2015) reported that 80 per cent of organizations intend to carry out leadership development activities over the coming year, concentrating on increasing staff performance, developing the organizational culture and equipping leaders with more strategic and future-focused skills. However, when you delve deeper, you find that yes, organizations do recognize the need to develop their leaders (Henley Business School, 2014) and yet this is coupled with employees, front-line managers and middle managers continuing to express real dissatisfaction with the state of management and leadership (CIPD, 2015). Indeed, the level of trust in our organizational leaders has been decreasing over the last two decades (Hope Hailey, Farndale and Kelliher, 2010).

This leadership deficit can be attributed to not currently having enough leaders who are effective; not having enough leaders in the pipeline; not having enough leadership capability across the organization; not recognizing that a different type of leadership is called for to meet the external business challenges of a VUCA (Volatile, Uncertain, Complex, Ambiguous) world nor a different leadership ethos to fit changing demographics, values and attitudes in the workplace; and not having effective leadership development.

Becoming a leader

In a time of drastic change it is the learners who inherit the future.
The learned usually find themselves equipped to live in a world that no
longer exists. ERIC HOFFER

Our overarching aim of this book is to equip you with a resource that doesn't just give you the theory but also opens up avenues for you to reflect upon your own leadership and then take some new steps to develop yourself and help you to deliver the outcomes required. Learning about theory is just one small part of the journey; complete adult learning takes long-term effort, practice and dedication. It also means experimenting with sharing your ideas, building relationships and taking action.

Both authors have been involved in leadership education and development over many years. We are practised in many different approaches to both and recognize some of the ways that work and many that don't, particularly in an organizational setting.

We don't really see the point of learning about leadership theory by rote, perhaps regurgitating this in an assignment on an MBA module, for example, and leaving it at that. We see leadership as something that should be felt, experienced and lived by its practitioners, making a difference in the world, in your own lives, for your teams, for your organization, for your communities and for society.

We passionately believe that being a responsible leader is one of the key factors in creating a better world and a more fulfilling workplace, and that taking responsibility for your leadership and your leadership development is one of the first steps. We think it starts with you; this book can act as your workbook or manual along the way.

How to use this book

We believe that knowing about the theory is important up to a point, to satisfy your curiosity and provide some good grounding. It also is required if you're studying at college or university. So to help you with this, we present concise, well-referenced summaries of key leadership theories in **Part Two** of this book. We also include an overall map of leadership, which sorts the theories presented into coherent clusters of essential skills and qualities.

Part Three helps you to step more fully into the 21st century by setting out what's now required of leaders. It also offers frameworks for understanding how to expand your 'mental complexity' in a way that enables you to handle increasingly 'wicked' issues and greater levels of uncertainty. You'll also find out how adults learn and what enables this – for example, lots of practice, reflection and feedback. We hope that you will find some of the ideas enlightening and useful as a springboard for action.

Then **Part Four** is all about you. It helps you to bring together your learnings from Parts Two and Three and allows you to embark on a personal stock-take and assessment of your own leadership, grounding the different theories in your own practice. It offers help and guidance on how to articulate your leadership development objectives, and how to decide what to do to move forward.

Part Five takes you into the learning zone! Having acquainted you with enough theory and reflection on leadership and how leaders learn, we introduce our Five Qualities Framework. This is an integrated leadership framework, drawn from the leadership literature presented, validated through practice, and formulated in an accessible way. Each of the Five Qualities is described in terms of the skills required and how it is demonstrated in practice. You can test yourself on each quality, read examples, reflect on case studies and choose from a myriad of different suggestions regarding how to improve your own skills and mastery.

A shift towards thinking more organizationally is introduced in **Part Six**, where the challenges of trying to change an organization's leadership culture are discussed. Our recent research into the potential impact of younger Millennial leaders on the organizations they join is also included here.

Some heartfelt tips!

Studying leadership can be dull and lack impact if it remains as theory, or as something separate from yourself and your own context. We don't want your leadership development to be dull and have tried hard to make it relevant to you. Fundamentally leadership is about how you lead your life – and most of us would like to do that with discipline, with integrity, with compassion… all these things!

We strongly believe that everyone can expand and deepen their leadership – with support. There are countless opportunities every day for you to practice leadership in different ways, for different reasons. There are also countless opportunities for you to reflect on your practice and to notice and ask for feedback or advice. This works whatever your seniority or role.

As authors, consultants and leadership developers, we have been influenced by many theorists and practitioners, some of whom are mentioned in the acknowledgements and many of whom are referred to throughout the book. Warren Bennis, and his seminal book *On Becoming a Leader* (1994), is one of those who we have both been greatly inspired by. He itemises four lessons of self-knowledge which are worth repeating here:

i) Be your own teacher: leaders assume responsibility for their own learning and treat it as a route to self-knowledge and self-expression. No one can teach them the lessons they need to learn. Stumbling blocks can be denial and blame.

ii) Accept responsibility and blame no one: do not expect other people to take charge or do things for you.

iii) You can learn anything you want to learn: leadership involves a kind of fearlessness, an optimism and a confidence.

iv) True understanding comes from reflecting on your experience: leaders make reflection part of their daily life. An honest look at the past prepares you for the future.

Leadership development requires both inner and outer work. This means being sufficiently in touch with the context and the people, as well as finding space to reflect on action and stay aware of your own mental and physical state. The inner and the outer go hand in hand. It also means having an accurate self-assessment and the flexibility to adapt your responses in line with the situation.

So as you work through this book, please take your leadership *and your leadership development* seriously. The world needs you now more than ever! That doesn't mean to say you can't enjoy it. Treat your development as an experiment and as an exploration. Like any journey, there will be excitement and pleasure as well as disappointment and occasional failure. The key is to stay curious and keep learning.

We wish you much luck and success!

References

APQC (2014) The leadership deficit, *APQC* [online] https://www.apqc.org/leadership-deficit-problem-its-causes-and-solutions-identified-apqc-research-study

Bennis, W (1994) *On Becoming a Leader*, Perseus Books

CIPD (2015) Annual survey: learning and development, CIPD [online] http://www.cipd.co.uk/hr-resources/survey-reports/learning-development-2015.aspx

Credit Suisse (2015) Global Wealth Report [online] https://www.credit-suisse.com/je/en/about-us/research/research-institute/global-wealth-report.html

Global Footprint Network (2016) World footprint: do we fit on the planet? [online] http://www.footprintnetwork.org/en/index.php/GFN/page/world_footprint/

Henley Business School (2014) Corporate learning priorities survey [online] http://www.henley.ac.uk/files/pdf/exec-ed/2015_Corporate_Learning_Survery.pdf

Einstein, A (1946) Atomic education urged by Einstein, *New York Times*, 25 May, p.13

Grint, K (2008) Wicked problems and clumsy solutions: the role of leadership, *Clinical Leader*, I (II), December, ISSN 1757-3424

Hope Hailey, V, Farndale, E and Kelliher, C (2010) Trust in turbulent times: the human cost of transformation and the consequences for intraorganizational trust, in *Organizational trust: a cultural perspective*, ed M N K Saunders, D Skinner, N Gillespie, G Dietz and R J Lewicki, Cambridge University Press

PART TWO
Leadership frameworks and research

Overview

This section is designed to give readers a good grounding in the key milestones and developments in leadership thinking over the past 100 years. We set out important theories, frameworks and research in a succinct way to enable understanding. References and reading lists are given for those wishing to explore further. This is by no means intended to be a comprehensive coverage of everything to do with leadership, but we believe that this part of the book serves well enough to give anyone who's interested an understanding of how leadership thinking has developed and what research backs it up (or not!).

The chapters take you on the same journey that the authors travelled as we sought to synthesize the leadership literature into a unifying framework. To help you stay with us on this journey, each chapter includes a description of the topic or set of frameworks, references to associated research or theoretical background, a critique, learning points and an exercise or two to help you consolidate your learning. This all builds towards an **Overall Map**, setting out the key elements of Part Two and showing how they have informed our Five Qualities leadership framework which you can read more about in Part Five. You might find it useful to skip to this map now.

In Chapter 2 on Leadership Traits and Characteristics we examine early research into what makes a good leader in terms of innate characteristics and core behaviours. This thread is carried into Chapters 3 and 4 on Contingency Theories and Situational Leadership, which set out theories and frameworks exploring how different types of leaders succeed in different contexts. The powerful idea that leaders can adapt their behaviour according to the situation is also introduced and discussed.

Chapter 5 on Psychodynamics, Power and the Shadow looks at parallel developments in the areas of psychodynamics, personality and the source of power, and explains how this work can support leaders. Approaches to understanding personality and the dynamics between individuals are identified. We also look at how power and politics arise and the ways in which these can be used well, or lead to unhealthy interpersonal and organizational dynamics. We explain some of the phenomena of the shadow or dark side of leadership too.

The question of motivation, inspiration and 'moral development' is explored in Chapter 6, which focuses on Transformational and Transactional Leadership. This chapter describes the history and evolution of this framework, sets out some of the research that has been done to explore this approach to leadership, and looks at what the critics say about the shortcomings of some applications of this framework.

Chapters 7–11 look at a wider range of perspectives from the 1990s onwards. Chapter 7 on Strategic and Innovation Leadership sets out the most important development in ideas around strategic thinking, creativity and innovation from a leadership perspective by exploring the work of Schoemaker, Mintzberg and Bossink amongst others. Chapter 8 explores the wider topic of Change Leadership, setting out the evolution of theory and frameworks in this complex and important area of leadership. We refer to Kotter, Bennis, Schein and Heifetz in particular.

The challenges of leading ethically and responsibly are explored in Chapter 9 under the heading Leadership Responsibility and Values. This sets out definitions of ethical leadership, servant leadership and values-based leadership as well as drawing on Collins' research into the type of leadership that you find in 'great' companies, which he calls 'Level 5' leadership.

Following from the notion that leadership is something enacted by leaders with respect to followers, Chapter 10 explores leadership as something that's distributed or shared across a wider system. Leadership Across Organizations and Networks describes the different ways that leadership can be enacted across boundaries and invites you to explore less traditional ways of understanding where leadership resides and what it can enable.

The last part of this section is Chapter 11, Leadership Health: Mind, Body and Spirit, which explores recent research regarding how best to support leaders to stay healthy and build personal resilience. We set out some of the implications of recent neuroscience, positive psychology and emotional intelligence findings. We also discuss important ways in which leaders can access and work with the less rational, more mysterious side of organizational life, and what can happen when they ignore or suppress this.

Leadership traits and characteristics

Introduction

Trait theory is one of the oldest theories of leadership, underpinned by the idea that leaders have particular qualities that are natural or innate: hence the notion that leaders are 'born not made'. Trait theory is sometimes called the 'great man' theory in recognition of the fact that the majority of people ascending to leadership positions at the time, in the first half of the 20th century, were male, and destined for 'greatness'.

A trait is defined as 'a distinguishing quality or characteristic' or 'a genetically determined characteristic'. The key proposition is that a leader is typically born with these characteristics, qualities or attributes. These would include personality type, temperament and values, which don't change as the individual grows and matures. However, it was later suggested that some of these attributes could be acquired through learning.

In this chapter we aim to:

- identify the objectives and results of the original research into traits;
- chart the progress and implications of this influential theory;

Description and critique

Stogdill is a key researcher in this area. He published two major studies looking at which traits distinguished people in leadership positions from others, in a variety of situations and different contexts. His analysis of research between 1904 and 1947 looked at 124 trait studies; he conducted another meta-analysis spanning 1948–1970 which looked at 163 trait studies.

Stogdill concluded that there was 'no consistent set of traits' which differentiated the two groups. Having some of these traits would not ensure that you were a leader, but did increase the probability that you would become a leader. He recognized that both the situation and the followers involved were factors influencing whether a leader with one set of traits was more likely to be effective than a leader with a different set of traits.

His first study identified intelligence, alertness, insight, responsibility, initiative, persistence, self-confidence and sociability as key traits. The second study identified traits such as drive, vigour, persistence, originality in problem solving, initiative in social situations, confidence, strong sense of self, and willingness to accept responsibility, absorb interpersonal stress and tolerate frustration. It also identified traits in social interactions such as initiative, ability to influence others and to structure the interaction to achieve a goal (Northouse 2007).

Other lists of leaders' traits include research by Lord, De Vader and Alliger (1986) into traits and the perception of leaders. They identified intelligence, masculinity, adjustment, dominance, extraversion, and conservatism.

Kirkpatrick and Locke (1991) found drive, desire to lead, honesty and integrity, self-confidence, cognitive ability and knowledge of the business to be key leadership traits.

Northouse (2007) saw that key leadership traits could be clustered around intelligence, self-confidence, determination, integrity and sociability. However, Judge, Colbert and Ilies (2004) concluded 'the relationship between intelligence and leadership is considerably lower than previously thought'.

Psychologists such as Goldberg and Saucier (1998) using the 'Big Five' personality traits (see Chapter 5) have correlated extraversion (strongest), conscientiousness (second), openness (=third) and lack of neuoroticism (=third), and finally agreeableness (weakest) with leaders. Judge *et al.* (2002) confirmed definite support for trait theory when viewed through the lens of the five-factor model.

Trait theory has face validity for many people. Whether in political, organizational or community settings, most people will say that they know leadership when they see it, that a leader stands out and is different in some way. This theory has the longest history, is one of the most researched areas of leadership and one of the most entrenched ideas in UK and US culture. No matter what other research is published, it seems this idea is very difficult to dislodge!

A big downside of the popularity of trait theory is the accumulation of endless lists of traits leaders are supposed to have. They have little regard

Figure 2.1   'Big Five' personality traits

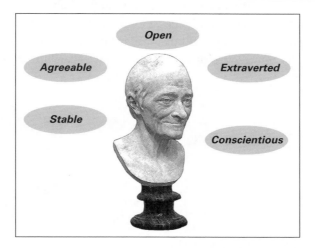

for the different situations in which leadership is exercised, day in, day out, and the different ways in which leadership can be enacted and embodied. By enacting and embodying we mean putting it into practice and giving it tangible and visible form. There is also scant regard for the people being influenced (or not) by leaders. Leadership is not only about the person of the leader, but also their behaviours in a multiplicity of situations requiring leadership, with a host of individual and collective potential followers. This might require very different traits for different people at different times.

The view of Bennis and Nanus (1985) is that leadership is multi-faceted and can be learned by all. To add more nuance, Arvey *et al.* (2007) concluded that about 30 per cent of leadership characteristics are innate and 70 per cent developed. The emergent field of neuroscience has afforded a further way of looking at traits. For example, some research has explored the link between neurological activity and inspirational leadership. It suggests that potential leaders can undertake neuro-feedback to become more inspirational. Put another way, if neurological pathways are 'malleable' through the use of neuro-feedback, it seems likely that inspirational leadership – and maybe therefore what we think of as 'charisma', for example – can be developed. This is supported by Derue *et al.* (2011), who confirmed that leaders' behaviours contribute to leadership effectiveness more than those leaders' traits.

Goleman, Boyatzis and McKee (2002) have also suggested that there is a neurological basis for emotional intelligence, which supports the view that this can be learned.

When traits were compared and combined with knowledge and skill attributes such as interpersonal and communication skills, problem solving, decision making and other managerial abilities, Hoffman *et al.* (2011) found the latter were consistent predictors of effective leadership, although their impact was 'modest overall'. Nonetheless, this does suggest that leadership can be developed.

Pause for Learning Points

The dilemma for the individual leader wanting to become a better leader is: what does one do with the evidence presented, and with the legacy of this rather entrenched view? The underpinning narrative is that you either have these leadership traits or you don't. If leaders 'should' have a trait of extroversion, what happens if you are an introvert? If you are somehow lacking in conscientiousness, or if you don't believe you're a people person, what can you do?

Maurer (2002) found evidence that those people who thought leadership characteristics or traits were innate were less likely to want to develop into leaders. This is dispiriting. Organizations and communities are in urgent need of leaders and leadership in all its forms. When individuals have the opportunity to make a difference, our observation is that they have the ability to develop the capability to step into the leadership role required. The key, perhaps, is to be open to experimenting through practice and feedback, and to allow new aspects of oneself to be revealed. Note that, as we describe in Chapter 13, Kegan and Lahey (2009) show that there are significant internal barriers to crafting a new sense of yourself or to letting go of an old self-image which can be useful to identify and work with.

So there is no need to be phony or inauthentic. The task for those of us who want or need to 'step up' and develop new traits is to identify the behaviours that we need to be a leader (eg in this situation, with these stakeholders) and create a personal development plan to practise and grow these skills and characteristics.

Stop and Reflect!

To what extent do you believe that leadership can be developed in any individual? Use examples of people you know well to support your argument. Leadership can be demonstrated in your personal, social and community life as well as in your organizational role.

Which of the Stogdill traits do you see in yourself, and which are missing? If you could develop the missing traits, how might you go about that? What difference would this make for you as a leader and in your wider life?

References and further reading

Arvey R D, Zhang, Z, Avolio, B and Krueger, R (2007) Developmental and genetic determinants of leadership role occupancy among women, *Journal of Applied Psychology*, **92** (3) pp. 693–706

Bass, B M (1990). From transactional to transformational leadership: learning to share the vision, *Organizational Dynamics*, (Winter) pp. 19–31

Bennis, W G and Nanus, B (1985) *Leaders: Strategies for Taking Charge*, Harper & Row, NY

Derue, D S, Nahrgang, J D, Wellman, N and Humphrey, S E (2011) Trait and behavioral theories of leadership: an integration and meta-analytic test of their relative validity, *Personnel Psychology*, **64** (1), pp. 7–52

Goleman, D, Boyatzis, R and McKee, A (2002) *The New Leaders: Transforming the art of leadership into the science of results*, Little Brown, London

Goldberg and Saucier (1998) What is beyond the big five? *Journal of Personality*, **66** (4), August, pp. 495–524

Hoffman, B J, Woehr, D J, Maldagen-Youngjohn, R and Lyons, B D (2011) Great man or great myth? A quantitative review of the relationship between individual differences and leader effectiveness, *Journal of Occupational and Organizational Psychology*, **84** (2), pp. 347–81

Jago, A G (1982) Leadership: perspectives in theory and research, *Management Science*, **28** (3), pp. 315–36

Judge, T A, Bono, J E, Ilies, R and Gerhardt, M W (2002) Personality and leadership: a qualitative and quantitative review, *Journal of Applied Psychology*, **87** (4) pp. 765–80

Judge, T A, Colbert, A E and Ilies, R (2004) Intelligence and leadership: a quantitative review and test of theoretical propositions, *Journal of Applied Psychology*, **89** (3) pp. 542–52

Kegan, R, and Lahey, L L (2009) *Immunity to Change: How to overcome it and unlock the potential in yourself and your organization*, Harvard Business School Publishing, Boston, Mass

Kenny, D A and Zaccaro, S J (1983) An estimate of variance due to traits in leadership. *Journal of Applied Psychology*, **68** (4), pp. 678–85

Kirkpatrick, S A and Locke, E A (1991) Leadership: do traits matter? *Academy of Management Executive*, **5** (2) pp. 48–60

Lord, R G, De Vader, C L and Alliger, G M (1986) A meta-analysis of the relation between personality traits and leadership perceptions: an application of validity generalization procedures, *Journal of Applied Psychology*, **71** (3), pp. 402–410

Maurer, T J (2002) Employee learning and developmental orientation: toward an integrative model of involvement in continuous learning, *Human Resource Development Journal*, **1**, pp. 9 – 44

Northouse, P G (2007) *Leadership: Theory and practice*, 4th edn, Sage, CA

Stogdill, R M (1948) Personal factors associated with leadership: a survey of the literature, *Journal of Psychology*, **25**, pp. 35–71

Stogdill, R M (1974) *Handbook of Leadership: A survey of theory and research*, Free Press New York

Waldman, D A, Balthazard, P A and Peterson, S J (2011) Leadership and neuroscience: can we revolutionize the way that inspirational leaders are identified and developed? *Academy of Management Perspectives*, **25** (1), pp. 60–74

Yukl, G A (2013) *Leadership in Organizations*, Pearson, Harlow

Contingency theories 03

Introduction

The contingency approach to leadership is based on the premise that a leader's success is dependent on the right match between the leader's personality and the characteristic situation.

In this chapter we aim to:

- understand the evolution of the contingency approach;
- highlight key frameworks including the Least Preferred Co-worker, Path-Goal, Leader Substitute and Decision models; and
- supply a critique to the contingency approach.

The contingency approach was a departure from the early leadership theories which attempted to find the cluster of traits or characteristics considered to be the ideal set for all leaders (as described in Chapter 2). It was therefore a movement away from a 'one size fits all' approach to leadership.

The focus was on the variables that might help or hinder task accomplishment in an organizational setting. This led to the idea that a leader needs to appreciate these other factors and respond to them by varying their leadership style – different situations required different types of leadership. A leader displaying one style may be acceptable in one situation, whereas another leader displaying a very different style could be equally successful, though in a different situation.

Researchers looked at the different factors at play in any situation requiring leadership. For example:

- the work required might vary from the relatively unambiguous, structured task through to more open-ended, less clear activities;
- the direct reports may have differing degrees of expertise or willingness to undertake the task; and

- the leader may have greater or lesser degrees of competence in this area.

  In addition it was found that:

- the leader may not have the necessary formal authority to reward or punish the direct report;
- where team working was necessary, there could be greater or lesser degrees of team cohesion and effectiveness; and
- the organizational culture ('the way things are done around here') might also help or hinder the leadership process.

The contingency approach recognizes that different leadership styles varied in their effectiveness across these different situations, and this could therefore feed into a process matching a leader with one style with an appropriate situation for that style. It also helps predict what situations a particular leader might be good in, and which leaders would be good in particular situations.

Description and critique

A number of models that were developed during the 1960s and '70s can be regarded as being part of the contingency approach.

Contingency theories

Leadership Continuum: Tannenbaum and Schmidt (1957)

Managerial Grid: Blake and Mouton (1964)

Expectancy Theory: Vroom (1964)

Least Preferred Co-worker (LPC): Fiedler (1967; 1978)

Path-Goal: Evans (1970); House (1971)

Decision Model: Vroom and Yetton (1973); Vroom and Jago (1988)

Situational Leadership: Hersey and Blanchard (1969)

Leadership Substitutes: Kerr and Jermier (1978)

Multiple-linkage: Yukl (1981; 1989)

Cognitive Resources: Fiedler (1986); Fiedler and Garcia (1987)

Fiedler developed his Least Preferred Co-worker contingency model (LPC) in the 1960s and '70s. The model was developed by the leader identifying and scoring their least preferred co-worker and through this revealing whether the leader was more relational or more task-oriented. Fiedler looked at the quality of relationship between the leader and other team member, the degree to which the task in hand was highly structured or less clear, and the degree of power and authority the leader had in that situation.

The context requiring leadership could then be categorized as being favourable or unfavourable. Good relationship, structured task, significant power was seen as favourable; poor relationship, unclear task, lesser power was seen as unfavourable. The research suggested that leaders who were more task-oriented were more likely to be effective in the most and least favourable scenarios, whereas the more relational leaders were seen to be more effective in the middle ground (where there were middling relations, variable structure and variable power).

Around the same time, at Ohio State University, the Path-Goal Theory was developed through the research of Evans (1970), House (1971), and House and Mitchell (1974). The basic premise was that a direct report would be more or less motivated towards task accomplishment if their perception of the task was positively or negatively influenced by their leader.

This was based on expectancy theory, developed by Vroom (1964), which is concerned with the degree that workers' motivation is determined by what they expect the results of their efforts to be. If the direct report has a clear idea of their role, and believes that a high level of effort is required, that the task is doable, and that there are benefits in doing it, then their performance will be better. It is therefore the leader's role to ensure that the direct report understands all these things.

More task-oriented leadership is introduced if the direct report is unsure of how they might tackle the task or is inexperienced in tackling the task. In those situations, where the direct report is anxious or liable to be bored by the task, then a more relational approach is called for.

In the Path-Goal Model, four basic leadership styles were defined, with each being appropriate in some circumstances, dependent on the characteristics of the task and the subordinate: directive leadership, supportive leadership, participative leadership and achievement-oriented leadership. When subordinates are resistant and the task unclear or difficult, then a directive style is seen to be more effective. When the subordinate needs more motivation or affiliation, and when the task is manageable, then supportive leadership behaviours work better. The participative style works if the task is not straightforward and the subordinate either desires autonomy or likes to be in control of the task. When there is a challenging and perhaps complex task, and the subordinate also has high performance standards, then an achievement-oriented approach characterized by setting high standards, with high expectations of confidence and a degree of trust, is effective.

The Leader Substitute Model was developed in the late 1970s. Kerr and Jermier's (1978) proposition was that there were factors other than the leader's behaviour (be it task- or people-oriented) that either lessened the impact of that behaviour or made it less relevant. Key elements were, not unnaturally, the abilities and attitudes of the direct reports, the nature of the task, and the organizational setting and circumstances.

For example, the clearer or easier the task, the less need for leadership intervention; the more able and motivated the subordinate, the less need for direction or leader contact; the more functional the organization, the more enabling it would be for subordinate and task accomplishment, and once again, the reduced need for leadership intervention or supervision.

A particular point of interest here is that looking at the different factors other than the leader's behaviour isn't focused on identifying which leadership style is more effective, but that the need for leadership at all is deemed greater or less.

Vroom and Yetton (1973) and later Vroom and Jago (1988) developed a model of leadership in relation to decision making. The Vroom-Yetton-Jago Normative Decision Model addresses the issue of what level of involvement a subordinate has when the leader makes a decision. They saw five types of leadership behaviour:

- Autocratic (Type One A1) where the leader has all the available information and makes the decision on their own.

- Autocratic (Type Two A2) where the leader gathers information from others and then makes the decision on their own. The issue, the reason for collecting the information and the final decision are not necessarily communicated by the leader.

- Consultative (Type One C1) where others are involved in individual discussions around the issue and ideas maybe suggested by them, though the leader makes the decision alone.

- Consultative (Type Two C2) where there are group discussions around the issue, shared understanding and options, though, once again, the leader then makes the decision alone.

- Group-based (G2) where the leader involves others, in a group setting, and the generation and evaluation of solutions leads to a decision based on group agreement.

In order to decide the specific leadership behaviour Vroom suggested asking seven questions.

Vroom states:

To determine which of these styles and processes is most appropriate, there is a series of yes/no questions that you ask yourself about the situation, building a decision tree based on the responses. There are seven questions in total:

1 Is the technical quality of the decision very important, ie are the consequences of failure significant?

2 Does a successful outcome depend on your team members' commitment to the decision? Must there be buy-in for the solution to work?

3 Do you have sufficient information to be able to make the decision on your own?

4 Is the problem well-structured so that you can easily understand what needs to be addressed and what defines a good solution?

5 Are you reasonably sure that your team will accept your decision even if you make it yourself?

6 Are the goals of the team consistent with the goals the organization has set to define a successful solution?

7 Will there likely be conflict among the team as to which solution is best?

The Situational Leadership Theory was also developed in the late 1970s. Because of its popularity amongst practitioners, we have dedicated Chapter 4 to it. Thus the contingency approach helped widen the inquiry into what effective leadership was – extending the focus beyond traits, characteristics or behaviours.

Generally, this approach is well grounded in research. Together, the various models try to map out how different situations call for different leadership styles. It is helpful in the prediction of which leadership style might work – and therefore which person might be best placed to take the lead in that situation – suggesting that forethought is a good idea!

This set of theories therefore played a role in shifting organizations towards the notion of best fitting people into roles, and identifying development gaps.

The contingency approach can be seen as a cluster of different and highly rational models; it isn't necessarily a holistic or fluid approach. However, it does enable managers to identify the variables at work in any situation where leadership is required. It therefore enables both organizations and would-be leaders to reflect upon and assess all these factors in judging the leadership style called for.

Pause for Learning Points

The contingency approach usefully suggests that the leader needs to reflect upon his or her own style, and whether this style can be flexed to better meet the requirements of the situation. At the very least a leader needs to assess whether a more task- or relationship-oriented approach is needed.

The leader needs to take account of a number of elements, which we believe need to be considered on an ongoing basis. They need to understand the organization and the immediate work environment, especially the nature of the task that needs to be completed. The clarity of the task, how structured it is, the complexity of the task, the interdependency of this task with other tasks, and the degree of urgency are all important factors.

Likewise, the characteristics of the follower or subordinate are crucial. To what degree does this person value or need autonomy or control; what general and specific experience do they have; how competent and confident are they in tackling this task; and what is their attitude towards it?

The contingency approach appears to be a very rational and scientific approach to leadership that's difficult to imagine actually doing in the moment; deciding, for example, whether I as leader need to be 'relational' and then immediately being that. However, it is no doubt useful for both reflecting and planning ahead.

In adopting this approach successfully, the leader also needs to take into account the wider system; for example, the number of co-workers involved, the inter-dependencies they have, and the level of group or team functioning. The degree to which the organization structure, culture, and systems and policies help or hinder the task accomplishment can also reduce or increase the need for leadership.

Stop and Reflect!

Pick two people who work for you, or to whom you allocate tasks, and reflect on how effective and enjoyable your relationships are with them. In each case, think about how you might improve either your task orientation or your relationship orientation.

Using Vroom's expectancy theory, look at a key responsibility or task that you need to attend to over the coming months and analyse your motivation level for doing this. What might help you or your line manager to get you more engaged in the work ahead?

References

Blake, R and Mouton, J (1964) *The Managerial Grid: The key to leadership excellence*, Gulf Publishing Co., Houston

Evans, M G (1970) The effects of supervisory behavior on the path-goal relationship, *Organizational Behaviour and Human Performance*, 5, pp. 277–98

Fiedler, F E (1967) *A Theory of Leadership Effectiveness*, McGraw-Hill, New York

Fiedler, F E (1986) The contribution of cognitive resources and leader behavior to organizational performance, *Journal of Applied Psychology*, **16** (6), pp. 532–48

Fiedler, F E and Garcia, J E (1987) *New Approaches to Leadership, Cognitive Resources and Organizational Performance*, John Wiley and Sons, New York

Hersey, P and Blanchard, K (1969) Life cycle theory of leadership, *Training and Development Journal*, **23** (5) pp. 26–34

House, R J A (1971) Path-goal theory of leader effectiveness, *Administrative Science Quarterly*, **16**, pp. 321–39

House, R J and Mitchell, T R (1974) Path-goal theory of leadership, *Contemporary Business*, **3** (Fall) pp. 81–98

Kerr, S and Jermier, J M (1978) Substitutes for leadership: their meaning and measurement, *Organizational Behavior and Human Performance*, **22**, pp. 375–403

Tannenbaum, R and Schmidt, W (1957) How to choose a leadership pattern, *Harvard Business Review*, **32** (2), pp. 95–101

Vroom, V H (1964) *Work and Motivation*, Jossey-Bass, San Francisco, CA

Vroom, V H and Jago, A G (1988) *The New Leadership: Managing participation in organizations*, Prentice-Hall, Englewood Cliffs, NJ

Vroom, V H and Sternberg, R J (2002) Theoretical letters: the person versus the situation in leadership, *The Leadership Quarterly*, **13**, pp. 301–23

Vroom, V H and Yetton, P W (1973) *Leadership and Decision Making*, University of Pittsburgh Press, Pittsburgh, PA

Yukl, G (1981) *Leadership in Organizations*, Prentice-Hall, Englewood Cliffs, NJ

Situational leadership

Introduction

Situational Leadership was developed by Hersey and Blanchard during the latter half of the 20th century (Hersey and Blanchard, 1969). As the name implies, this framework examines the type of leadership required in response to different situations, and is predominately about adjusting your leadership approach to match the maturity of each follower. The situations are categorized in terms of the subordinate's level of competence and confidence, or motivation, to carry out the work required of them. This is a clear movement away from looking at the traits of the leader and towards a focus on the needs of the subordinate and the leadership behaviours that enable the subordinate to deliver outcomes.

This chapter aims to:

- describe and critique the Situation Leadership model;
- identify the core styles suggested;
- discuss the implications for managers and leaders.

Descriptions and critique

Four assumptions underpin Situational Leadership theory. The first assumption is that no one leadership style is appropriate to all situations. Indeed, each situation, judged and evaluated by the leader, requires different characteristics of leadership.

The second assumption is that leadership is primarily a combination of two styles – more or less directive, and more or less supportive – and given different situations, a calibrated balance between supportive and directive styles is needed.

The third assumption is that each follower will have different degrees of competence to complete the task, and different levels of commitment to carrying out the task.

The fourth assumption is that as a follower becomes more competent and confident (or 'mature'), he or she will require different types of leadership to enable success and growth, culminating in low levels of direction and low levels of support.

The Situational Leadership framework therefore suggests:

- the leader's style is based on exercising high or low levels of direction and high or low levels of support:

   a. high direction, low support is labelled Directing;

   b. high direction, high support is labelled Coaching;

   c. low directive, high support is labelled Supporting;

   d. low direction, low support is labelled Delegating.

- these four styles are clusters of conscious leadership behaviours based on the follower's competence and commitment;

- the more competent the individual, the less direction required;

- the more confident and committed the individual, the less support required.

Directive behaviour involves telling the person what to do and perhaps how to do it. Supportive behaviour is more person-oriented and involves behaviours such as listening, involving the person in finding a solution, etc.

Directing involves the leader telling the subordinate what to do and perhaps how to do it. This is required if the subordinate doesn't have the knowledge, skills or experience needed to complete the task, and the leader does.

Coaching can be performed by the leader when there is still the requirement to direct what needs to be done, but there is more supportive behaviour and the subordinate has some confidence and some competence.

Supporting behaviour from the leader is indicated when the subordinate has the ability to complete the task but perhaps variable levels of commitment or confidence.

Delegating occurs when the subordinate is both competent and committed and thus little or no direction or support is required.

Hersey and Blanchard's work draws together different themes from the history and development of other leadership theories, for example Reddin's 3D Leadership Model (1967) and also resonates with later notions of adult learning, developed, for example, by Malcolm Knowles (1955).

Reddin's work built on the Ohio State Studies (1957) and Michigan Leadership Studies (Katz and Kahn, 1952) which identified two independent

Figure 4.1 Situational leadership

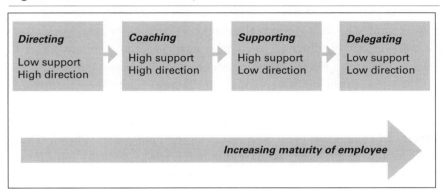

axes of leadership – focus on the task, and focus on the relationship. He added a further axis of effectiveness – focusing in on 'how and when each style is effective'.

Situational Leadership can be seen as a subset of the contingency approach (see Chapter 3), in which Hersey and Blanchard recognized the requirement for the leader to attend not only to the task but also the person.

Although well established as a leadership development training intervention and used as a common language amongst many managers and management developers, there has been relatively little academic research into this model's validity. In our experience, the proprietary training in Situational Leadership has been marketed very successfully. Many managers we have encountered have been taught the basic tenets of this approach.

Situational Leadership represents a practical and pragmatic approach to leadership which less experienced managers tend to find attractive, useful and implementable. It seems especially to appeal to those with a structured or technical mindset – once people are placed on a grid, clear guidance is offered!

The framework opens managers' minds to the idea that as a manager or leader one has to assess any given situation and those in the situation, to enable a judgement to be made as to what is the most effective style of leadership. It also highlights to the manager the need to fully understand the strengths and motivations of his or her staff, which will vary according to the different challenges that arise, either as a result of organizational imperatives or from the manager's decisions and consequent actions.

Additionally, it brings into the manager's awareness the concept of employee development and some of the behaviours required by the manager to support that development, allowing a graduated path towards mastering the specific behaviours required.

However there has been only limited research to attest to its use in practice. It focuses on a one-to-one, leader-follower relationship and ignores the more complex issues surrounding a manager's need to manage, say, a group of individuals with different levels of competence and commitment or to lead a team with a similar disparity of competence and commitment.

The need for the manager to make judgements about the situation and also about the employees' levels of competence and commitment can be quite subjective. Similar (low) levels of commitment in two employees may be for entirely different reasons and the needs of those employees may therefore vary dramatically. People may also have different levels of maturity for different tasks, so the process for deciding the type of leadership can get quite complex, indeed more complex than is suggested by the Situational Leadership model.

Blanchard has suggested that levels of commitment are a summation of confidence and motivation, though the theoretical basis of this is thin. Confidence (in one's ability to do the task) and motivation (one's inclination to do it) are different concepts, and the manager needs to evaluate them both and develop interventions accordingly.

Pause for Learning Points

As mentioned above, Situational Leadership does have face validity; our experience is that many managers have found the concepts, and the associated training, very useful. This has tended to be useful for leaders and managers in the early stages of their professional development where a task focus is more common. As leaders progress and take on more complex work, they start to realize that:

a) they need to delegate tasks to direct reports;

b) relationships matter;

c) different people may need a different approach.

This realization can, in itself, increase managerial effectiveness. The development needs arising for both the manager and the direct report – if actioned – can bring about increased organizational capability and capacity.

Stop and Reflect!

Using the theories and ideas set out in this chapter, review the style(s) of three different leaders you know well. Is it true to say that the more effective leaders adopt a variety of styles with their subordinates, in line with the person's maturity?

References and further reading

Halpin, A W and Winer, B J (1957) A factorial study of the leader behavior descriptions, in *Leader Behavior: Its description and measurement*, ed R M Stogdill and A E Coons, Bureau of Business Research, Ohio State University, Columbus, OH

Hersey, P and Blanchard, K (1969) Life cycle theory of leadership, *Training and Development Journal*, **23** (5) pp. 26–34

Katz, D and Kahn, R L (1952) Some recent findings in human relations research, in *Readings in Social Psychology*, ed E Swanson, T Newcombe and E Hartley, Holt, Reinhart and Winston, New York

Knowles, M S and Knowles, H F (1955) *How to Develop Better Leaders*, Association Press, New York

Reddin, W J (1967) The 3D management style theory, *Training and Development Journal*, **21** (4) pp. 8–17

Vecchio, R and Boatwright, K (2002) Preferences for idealized style of supervision, *Leadership Quarterly*, **13**, pp. 327–42

Psychodynamics, power and the shadow

05

Introduction

This chapter looks at leadership from the psychodynamic and power perspectives, including the shadow or dark side of leadership.

The chapter aims to explore and explain:

- the key elements of the psychodynamic approach to leadership;
- the relationship between power and leadership; and
- the impact of the shadow side of leadership from an individual, team and organizational perspective.

The psychodynamic perspective on leadership concerns the psychology of leadership and in particular the role that the personality of the leader plays and the theory behind this. It also concerns the impact that the leader's personality has on followers and other parties, and the interplay between leader and followers.

Underpinning much of the leadership theory is the notion of power. In recent times, this concept has been renamed as 'influence', perhaps in an attempt to sanitize it. However, this chapter explores more directly the role that power has to play in the exercising of leadership.

The chapter concludes with an exploration of the shadow or dark side of leadership, what Tate (2005) describes as 'the disagreeable, messy, crazy and opaque side of leaders and organizations'. An understanding of the shadow side relies heavily on the psychodynamics of relationships and how power can be used in a dysfunctional way.

Description and critique

The psychodynamic approach to leadership

Psychodynamics is the study of the psychological processes that form the basis of human life – feelings, emotions, thoughts and behaviours. These processes can happen either at conscious or unconscious levels. The psycho-dynamic approach starts with the premise that we are all human beings, each with a personality. The inquiry is into what happens when human beings with certain personality types become leaders. Followers with different personalities will react in a variety of ways to leaders demonstrating different traits, and whole teams of people interact in a more complex way. Thus group psychodynamics play out via leaders and within and between teams throughout the organization.

Alongside the development of management and leadership theory during the 20th century there co-existed the development of theories and practices focused on understanding the human mind. This set of theories and practices principally included on the one hand an understanding of the human psyche and unconscious processes pioneered by Freud and later Jung via psychoanalysis and analytical or depth psychology, and on the other hand the study of the interface between mind and body, human behaviour, mental processes such as perception, thinking, learning and human relationships.

Kets de Vries and Cheak (2014) describe the fundamental principles of the psychodynamic approach:

- There is a logical explanation to every act, however seemingly irrational.
- Much of our mental life is outside our conscious awareness.
- How an individual regulates their emotions is central to who they are.
- Everyone is a product of their past experiences.

From the 1950s onwards, this therapeutic approach was developed into a set of ideas which focused more on the development of human potential. The field of psychodynamics and leadership has been enriched by the cross-fertilization of these various fields of inquiry into unconscious processes, human behaviour, motivation, leadership, etc. For example, the Tavistock Institute of Human Relations, established in 1946 in the UK, drew on psycho-dynamic and psychoanalytic techniques to study group and organizational behaviour. Key figures included Jaques, Bion and Trist. The Tavistock was influenced by other social scientists, notably Lewin in the United States, who is considered to be the founder of the Organizational Development movement.

By way of illustration, we describe below three approaches to better understanding personality and in particular its relationship to leadership.

Transactional Analysis

We have all heard stories of or experienced the overly critical boss, or the patronizing boss, or the boss who throws their toys out of the pram. Likewise, we've heard about or observed the helpless employee or the rebellious employee. These dynamics can play out at both individual and team levels.

Transactional Analysis is a technique for analysing human behaviour and interpersonal communications developed by Eric Berne in the 1960s. He suggested that all human beings bring to any situation the memories of early childhood experiences – many of which are configured around notions of hierarchy, from the original family configuration. In particular, Berne identified three 'ego states' (Parent, Adult, Child) which we can inhabit, and described the multiple types of interaction that we can have with other people from these different states.

According to the theory, we all bring with us experiences from our past which push us into certain ego states, resulting in behaviour which isn't mature and can be sub-optimal. Understanding the nature of these transactions – where the other person is coming from and which ego state you respond from – aids understanding and enables a different set of conversations and behaviours. Learning how to stay in an Adult-Adult connection with others is very important work for leaders; Parent-Child or Child-Child dynamics either way can be counter-productive and even destructive.

Myers-Briggs Type Indicator

The Myers-Briggs Type Indicator (MBTI®) is one of the most widely used personality profiles in the world today. Based on initial work by Jung in the early part of the 20th century, the MBTI was devised by Katharine Briggs and her daughter Isabel Myers and has been well documented and researched over the past 65 years (www.capt.org)

MBTI identifies four different personality dimensions (giving eight preferences) that we all use at different times. Each person will have a preference for one combination over the other combinations. This generates 16 different personality 'types'.

In exploring leadership, what is of interest to us is that different personality types tend to approach, step into and respond to leadership in different ways. Each type has its strengths and pitfalls. Leaders can be found across all sixteen types, and the theory doesn't suggest a better or worse type for a leader.

Developmental in focus, the MBTI literature is full of helpful suggestions for leaders to enable them to become more self-aware and to develop the skills and capacities that their personality structure can make difficult to access.

While the statistical and test validity of the MBTI has been questioned, the extensive use of the instrument suggests that it has immense face validity.

Five Factor Model

The Five Factor Model of personality has its origins in the early trait research conducted in the late 19th century by Galton, and developed in the first half of the 20th century by Allport and Odbert (1936), and Cattell (1983). In the second half of the 20th century, Goldberg amongst others reduced these factors down to what become known as the 'Big Five'. Goldberg and Saucier (1998) stated that nearly all clusters of personality-relevant adjectives could be subsumed under the Big Five (see Chapter 2). These five are:

- Extraversion (gregarious, assertive, active, talkative, affectionate).

- Agreeableness (trusting, lenient, frank, good-natured, compassionate).

- Conscientiousness (conscientious, confident, organized, hardworking, goal-orientated).

- Neuroticism (anxiety, anger, temperamental, self-conscious, vulnerable).

- Openness to experience (imaginative, curious, creative, original, open to emotion).

Judge *et al.* (2002) suggest that the Big Five dimensions of extroversion and conscientiousness show the most consistently positive impact on leadership effectiveness, whereas the impact of openness, neuroticism and agreeableness varies more with the setting and context. Judge's research also says that measuring the Big Five factors can predict to some degree the emergence of leadership within an individual and also effectiveness of that leadership. However, there is some scepticism about this claim, given how difficult it is to measure accurately the effectiveness of leadership, and how few studies appear to do this accurately.

The major criticism is that there is no fundamental theory behind this approach – it is merely the result of clustering of the different factors, and therefore the causes of these phenomena are not known. However, because of its apparent predictive capability, it is often used in recruitment.

Power dynamics underpinning leadership

Power is the capacity or ability to direct or influence the behaviour of others or the course of events in accordance with your intent. Power is implicitly embedded in the majority of leadership theories, and explicitly addressed in a few.

Definitions of power

Collinson (2011) suggests that mainstream approaches to leadership can underestimate issues around power and control due to an assumption that leaders and followers are working toward common organizational aims:

> typically mainstream studies define leadership in terms of 'influence' (positive), and distinguish this from power (negative). In so doing they fail to appreciate that the former may be one aspect of the latter.

Collinson goes on to remind us that Burns (1978) saw leaders as people who mobilized others, whereas people who held power and wielded it were not actually leaders, which somehow has removed discussions around power from a central place in leadership theory. This is evidenced by the great reliance on the word 'influence' rather than 'power' in leadership texts. Power is about influence, and influence in the process of leadership is composed of the dynamic between the leader, the follower(s) and the context. The power, or perceived power, of the leader, is therefore just one part of the leadership process, albeit a crucial part. Power is a key element, not least when it is seen to be exercised in a negative or destructive manner. Of course, the power of the potential follower or target of the leader can be just as important.

In his writings on the nature of bureaucracy, Weber (1922) saw that a leader possessed power by virtue of his position, whereas Follett (1940) saw that 'participatory management' was exercising power *with* as opposed to power *over*. Barnard (1938) stated that power was the ability of a superior to influence the behaviour of direct reports and persuade them to follow a particular course of action.

Sources of power

French and Raven (1959) identified what have become the key distinctions of where power emanates from. They distinguished between a leader's Positional Power and their Personal Power.

Positional Power can come from three bases:

- Legitimate Power, which comes from the position or rank the person holds in an organization, the job role and place in the hierarchy and the status of that role;
- Reward Power, which comes by means of the ability to control promotion, salary increases and current and future role activities; and
- Coercive Power, which comes from the ability to penalize, punish, compel someone to do something and withhold rewards.

Later writers (Pettigrew, 1972; Tushman and O'Reilly, 1996) have added two more Positional Power bases:

- Information Power, which is the power to access and control dissemination of data and information, and indeed access or denial of access to important others; and
- Ecological Power, which is the power to determine physical, technological and organizational infrastructure matters.

Personal Power comes from two bases:

- Expert Power – comes from the person possessing more in-depth or broader knowledge, skills, understanding, competence and/or experience of the task, activity or business area; and
- Referent Power – comes from the fact that direct reports can identify, like and/or respect the leader.

Figure 5.1 Power bases

There is evidence (Yukl, 2013) that in general the more effective leaders are the ones who tend to rely on the Personal Power bases of Expert and Referent as well as the exercising of a moderate use of Positional Power. It is also important to note that it is not necessarily the actual power the leader has that has the effect of influencing people, but the perceived power that others see in them. It's also interesting to note that Fiedler, O'Brien and Ilgen (1969), in the Contingency Theory of Leadership, recognized that the Positional Power of the leader was a favourable factor in determining leader effectiveness.

However, Coercive Power and Personal Power need to be used with care. Goleman's research into the six leadership styles that get results (2000), underpinned by the concept of emotional intelligence, identified the Coercive ('do as I say') and Pacesetting ('do as I do, now') leadership styles as having their place, but ultimately having a negative impact on the climate of the organization if habitually used over long periods.

The power of push and pull

This is supported by Dent and Brent's (2009) description of the Push and Pull influencing styles, with the Push style seen as being directive with persuasive reasoning, and the Pull style as collaborative and visionary. The Push style works best when you have Positional Power, although it can clearly be used to great effect by others, given practice. Push is useful to address things in the short term, or to ask for things than can be fairly easily delivered. In more tricky situations, Push may need emotional back-up or enforcement to be effective; overuse tends to elicit compliance rather than commitment from people. The Pull style works when you haven't necessarily got positional power, and tends to be more effective in maintaining relationships and securing buy-in over the longer term.

In their article 'Power is the great motivator' (2003) McClelland and Burnham reached the conclusion that:

> the top manager of a company must possess a high need for power – that is,
> a concern for influencing people. However, this need must be disciplined and
> controlled so that it is directed toward the benefit of the institution as a whole
> and not toward the manager's personal aggrandizement. Moreover, the top
> manager's need for power ought to be greater than his or her need to be liked.

An interesting perspective on power is Hawkins and Smith's (2013) model of developing confidence in order to achieve outcomes. They suggest a leader requires Authority (derived from what, or who, you know, or what you've done in the past), Presence (the ability to be fully present and develop relationships quickly) and Impact (being able to shift the direction of a meeting, conversation or situation).

The impact of the shadow side of leadership

Power tends to corrupt, and absolute power corrupts absolutely. Great men are almost always bad men. LORD ACTON (1887)

The above sections have explored the psychodynamics at play between leaders and followers, and power as a key factor in how leaders influence others. This section looks at leadership dysfunction: how personality impacts and is impacted by people stepping into leadership positions, and what can happen when they exercise their power. Interesting phenomena begin to appear when people take on the reins of power. Sometimes it's due to their own personalities; sometimes it's the psychodynamics between followers and leaders, perhaps influenced by wider systemic forces.

The very traits that help people become leaders can be the traits which later derail them. Bolden (2011), in reviewing the work of Maccoby, said:

> Larger-than-life leaders are almost inevitably driven by a need for recognition, power and self-promotion that is key to their success, and occasionally their downfall. Such leaders tend to express a clear vision, and are capable of inspiring followers through their charisma and communication abilities. On the negative side, however, they are often sensitive to criticism, shun emotions, are poor listeners, lack empathy, have a distaste for mentoring and development, and are intensely competitive.

Many have written on the various manifestations of conscious and unconscious dysfunctional leadership behaviour (including Argyris, Gemill and Oakley, Conger, Maccoby, and Kets de Vries). We touch on some of this wide body of literature here.

Argyris (1990) suggests that 'organizational defensive routines make it highly unlikely that individuals, groups, inter-groups and organizations will detect and correct the errors that are embarrassing and threatening' because the fundamental rules are often to:

- bypass the errors and act as if they were not being done;
- make the bypass undiscussable; and
- make its undiscussability undiscussable.

He says, 'To challenge the undiscussable feels like a very high-risk strategy, even at the best of times, but when uncertainty prevails during times of change, the risks can be even higher.' Fear about discussing the undiscussable is palpable in many organizations facing change. Often it's difficult for people to speak up; by being insensitive to this, and unwilling to create the safety levels required, leaders can become deluded about the success they are having and the level of buy-in that exists.

Kets de Vries and Balazs (2011) identified various dysfunctional patterns in leadership such as conflict avoidance, tyrannizing subordinates, micromanagement, inaccessibility and folie a deux ('shared madness'). In particular, Kets de Vries (1989) describes leadership situations which can lead to aggressive behaviour, paranoid reactions, depression, substance abuse, schizoid-like thinking and self-defeating behaviour.

In any team or small group situation, not only do we all bring our respective individual shadows, but we can and will often display even more seemingly non-rational behaviour as the team shadow manifests itself. W R Bion (1961) suggests that various phenomena can be observed. For example, the group starts to look towards one person to solve all their problems (the messiah), or they exhibit fight or flight behaviours, either way avoiding the task in hand. Another common example is that people will scapegoat one person, either in or outside of the group, and blame them for any failures or difficulties. And because there are power and politics at play (beneath the surface) there can be all sorts of 'hidden agendas' which bear little resemblance to the agenda on the table. Sometimes a team will 'park the elephant' in the corner – that is, they've recognized there is an issue which needs addressing, but no one has the appetite to address it.

In addition to the cited work of Argyris and Kets de Vries, a useful practical source of information is Egan's *Working the Shadow Side* (1994).

Overall critique

The main criticism of the psychodynamic approach is that it focuses almost exclusively on the personality structures of the leader and their followers. They do not explicitly take into account the context in which they work. However, some approaches recognize that different personalities will be more or less better equipped to deal with certain situations.

Some psychodynamic approaches claim to be able to predict leadership behaviours and outcomes, whilst others acknowledge that they don't necessarily say much about leadership, just about individuals who happen to be leaders.

Different psychological tools have different uses – recruitment, development and increasing self-awareness and social awareness. Sometimes these uses get muddled up, for example the MBTI being used to recruit people, for which it was never intended and is not appropriate.

Using an understanding of psychodynamics as an investigative tool to spot dysfunction via the shadow side is useful. However, it is just one lens through which to see leadership and organizational dynamics. This subject area tends to be favoured by analytic or reflective types and may go unnecessarily deep when what is actually needed is a pragmatic decision or a simpler 'surface' approach to resolving issues.

Through getting too interested in problems and dysfunctions and how to categorize them, one could miss offering quick, solution-focused support; spotting what is working is sometimes more liberating and useful than spotting what or who is wrong.

Pause for Learning Points

In terms of leadership and power we have seen a shift over the last 20 years from the 'command and control' type of leadership towards more collaborative and consensual forms. This is due, in no small part, to societal shifts towards a more egalitarian and equitable society, coupled with research that points to the need for more relational forms of leadership. Today's organizations are increasingly characterized by being:

- flatter and less hierarchical;
- more permeable and sometimes ill-defined boundaries;
- with revolutionary ways of communication both vertically and laterally;
- part of the knowledge economy with the continued ascent of the knowledge worker; and
- with new generations arriving with radical perspectives on authority.

This suggests that there is plenty of need for continued movement towards the Expert and Referent and (Personal) Power as a way of exercising leadership with impact.

Looking at the shadow side of leadership can be quite difficult – painful and taxing. Argyris (1990) points out we cover up certain things and then cover up the cover, ie there are things in this organization we don't discuss and we don't discuss the fact that we don't discuss them. This is particularly true when we openly discuss (or don't discuss) our leaders. For those people who are intent on developing effective leaders within healthy, productive organizations looking at the shadow side of leadership is important and indeed key to understanding where there may be dysfunction. Argyris (1990) and Egan (1994) have much good advice to offer.

We believe that an understanding of leader-follower psychodynamics can add tremendously to leader effectiveness. Understanding yourself and others through a process of self-reflection, aided by psychometric or personality profiles, can allow you the opportunity to become aware of your personality patterns, your inner life and how you present to others, and how you can better manage those relationships.

In exercising leadership, you need to be aware of what type of power you can draw upon in order to achieve your aims, and what and whom those aims are serving. Understanding the basis of your authority is important when going into any situation. Indeed, by having an understanding of the situation and of the people involved (for example, the stakeholder groups to be influenced) you should be able to decide which power base to access to gain maximum impact. Do not forget about power; it is usually present in every situation, often not explicitly. Becoming conscious of power dynamics is an important factor in being a leader or influencer in your organization and community.

Whether alone or with others, we are all a complex mix of past, present and future. We bring with us into any situation baggage from the past. Our personality tendencies can cause us to react to different types of communication and put us and others under stress in different ways. All these things can happen below the level of awareness, and are usefully surfaced and considered through self-reflection or coaching.

The purpose of understanding the concept of the shadow side of leadership is in discovering where your blind spots are, by increasing your self-awareness and by checking out how you interact with others and where you tend to come into conflict with them.

Stop and Reflect!

If you haven't already taken a personality questionnaire, ask your HR department to help you do this, or find one independently online. Having taken one, what does it say about you and your leadership style? What are the implications for how you deal with co-workers different to you?

How much power and influence do you feel you have in your organization? What is the basis of that power at the moment, and what new or different ways might you be able to use it to increase your power or authority? If you are not in paid employment, then choose a club or a community organization – you could even reflect upon your family.

Consider an organization you know well and look at whether there are 'dysfunctional' departments or teams. If so, what is the usual response from managers and employees? Drawing on this chapter, what advice would you give someone leading that department or team about how to help people to speak up more bravely about what's going wrong?

References and further reading

Allport, G W and Odbert, H S (1936))Trait names: a psycho-lexical study, *Psychological Monographs*, **47**

Argyris, C (1990) *Overcoming Organizational Defenses: Facilitating organizational learning*, Allyn and Bacon, MA

Barnard, C I (1938) *The Functions of the Executive*, Harvard University Press, Cambridge MA

Berne, E (1964) *Games People Play*, Penguin, London

Bion W R (1961) *Experience in Groups*, Basic Books, NY

Bolden, R (2011) distributed leadership in organizations: a review of theory and research, *International Journal of Management Reviews*, **13**, pp. 251–69

Burns, J M (1978) *Leadership*, Harper & Row, NY

Cattell, R B (1983) *Structured Personality-Learning Theory: A wholistic multivariate research approach*, Praeger, New York, pp. 419–57

Collinson, D (2011) Critical Leadership Studies in *The SAGE Handbook of Leadership*, ed A Bryman, D Collinson, K Grint, M Uhl-Bien and B Jackson, Sage, London

Conger, J (1990) The dark side of leadership, *Organizational Dynamics* **19** (2), pp. 44–55

Dent, F E and Brent, M (2009) *Influencing Skills and Techniques for Business Success*, Palgrave, London

Egan, G (1994) *Working the Shadow Side*, Jossey Bass Wiley, CA

Fiedler, F E, O'Brien, G E and Ilgen, D R (1969) The effect of leadership style upon the performance and adjustment of volunteer teams operating in successful foreign environment, *Human Relations*, **22** (6), pp. 503–14

Follett, M P (1940) *Dynamic Administration: The collected papers of Mary Parker Follett*, ed E M Fox and L Urwick, Pitman Publishing, London

French, J R and Raven, B (1959) The bases of social power, in *Studies in Social Power*, ed D Cartwright, Institute for Social Research, Ann Arbor, MI

Galton, F (1869) *Hereditary Genius*, Appleton, New York

Gemmill, G and Oakley, J (1992) Leadership: an alienating social myth? *Human Relations*, **45** (2), pp. 113–29

Goleman, D (2000) Leadership that gets results, *Harvard Business Review*, March/April

Goldberg, L R and Saucier, G (1998) What is beyond the big five? *Journal of Personality*, **66** (4), pp. 495–524

Hawkins, P and Smith, N (2013) *Coaching, Mentoring and Organizational Consultancy: Supervision, skills and development*, OUP, London

Jaques, E (1989) *Requisite Organization: The CEO's guide to creative structure and leadership*, Cason Hall, MA

Judge, T A, Bono, J E, Ilies, R and Gerhardt, M W (2002). Personality and leadership: A qualitative and quantitative review, *Journal of Applied Psychology*, **87**, pp. 765–80

Kets de Vries, M F R (1989) Leaders who self-destruct: the causes and cures, *Organizational Dynamics*, **17** (4), pp.5–17

Kets de Vries, M F R and Balazs, K (2011) The Shadow Side of Leadership, in *The SAGE Handbook of Leadership*, ed A Bryman, D Collinson, K Grint, M Uhl-Bien and B Jackson, Sage, London

Kets de Vries, M F R and Cheak, A (2014) Psychodynamic Approach, INSEAD Working Paper 2014/45/EFE

Lewin, K (1951) *Field Theory in Social Science: Selected theoretical papers*, ed D. Cartwright, Harper & Row, New York

Maccoby, M (2003) *The Productive Narcissist: The promise and peril of visionary leadership*, Broadway Books, New York

McClelland, D C and Burnham, D H (2003) Power is the great motivator, *Harvard Business Review*, January

MBTI, https://www.capt.org/mbti-assessment/isabel-myers.htm [accessed 18 August 2016]

Pettigrew, A M (1972) Information control as a power resource, *Sociology* 6 (2) pp. 187–204

Tate, W (2005) Working with the shadow side of organisations, *Developing HR Strategy*, May

Trist, E L *et al.*, (1997) *The Social Engagement of Social Science: A Tavistock Anthology Volume 3: The socio-ecological perspective*, University of Pennsylvania

Tushman, M L and O'Reilly, C A (1996) The ambidextrous organization: managing evolutionary and revolutionary change, *California Management Review*, 38, pp. 1–23

Weber, M (1922) *Economy and Society* (this version published in 1978) University of California Press, Berkeley

Yukl, G A (2013) *Leadership in Organizations*, Pearson

Transformational and transactional leadership

06

Introduction

The ideas behind 'Transactional and Transformational Leadership' were initially introduced by Burns (1978) and later developed by Bass (1985). Although leadership thinking has evolved considerably since this framework was introduced, there is no doubt that it has been and continues to be extremely influential in current leadership discourse about what successful leadership looks like and how leaders should be developed. Many believe that this is due to its strong intuitive appeal, the breadth of the model and its focus on follower impact.

In this chapter we aim to:

- explain how Transactional and Transformational Leadership arose as a way of thinking about leadership;

- set out definitions of these styles, and the associated leadership behaviours;

- explore and summarize the results of research into the effectiveness of these styles;

- set out the key criticisms of this approach to thinking about leadership and measuring its effectiveness.

Description and critique

Transformational Leadership represents a style of leading that is said by many to have a positive impact on follower satisfaction and productivity. At best, this style is said to transform individual attitudes and the team or organizational culture. Much work has been done to both define and test the impact of this style.

Transactional leadership complements, or offers a complete contrast to, transformational leadership – depending on your perspective. This style is said to focus on rewards and rules, and to be suited to preserving the status quo rather than creating change.

Behavioural definitions of these two central concepts can be summarized below.

Transformational Leadership (sometimes known as the 'four I's'):

- provides a role model for ethical behaviour, instills pride, gains respect and trust (Idealized Influence);
- articulates an appealing vision in an engaging way, challenges with high standards, communicates optimism (Inspirational Motivation);
- challenges assumptions, invites creativity, encourages people to think independently (Intellectual Stimulation);
- attends to each follower in a different way, is empathetic, gives advice, acts as mentor (Individualized Consideration).

Transactional Leadership:

- exchanges rewards for effort and achievement (Contingent Reward);
- searches for and corrects deviations from rules and standards (Management by Exception – Active);
- intervenes only if standards are not met (Management by Exception – Passive);
- abdicates responsibilities and avoids making decisions (Laissez-faire – Non-transactional).

The early, more rational or scientific thinking on leadership described in Chapters 2–4 was characterized by studies of traits and a series of quests to find the 'best' leadership approach in any given context. This eventually led to a realization that there was new territory still to be explored, which included human emotions, needs, values and yearnings, and the role of inspirational and charismatic leadership. This was the start of a new interest in how leaders enable change and difference through motivating and stimulating their followers.

The German sociologist Weber (1864–1920) wrote about charisma as part of an exploration into the legitimacy of power beyond the rational and traditional. Although his conclusions are complex, the questions that he raised about the desirability of charisma in the organizational world started a train of thought.

Over 50 years later, Burns (1978), a political historian, worked with similar themes and wrote an influential book about what makes great leaders different. He undertook descriptive research into the histories of a range of powerful political leaders, and through drawing on the theories of Freud, Maslow and others he reached a number of significant conclusions. He proposed that leadership was either 'transactional' or 'transforming', and he also suggested that leadership was 'distributed' rather than in the hands of a few (see Chapter 10).

Transforming leadership, he claimed, is what's happening when 'leaders and followers help each other to advance to a higher level of morale and motivation'. It is practised by those who choose to focus on changing the culture for the better and are motivated to deliver benefits for the team, organization or community, rather than just for themselves. Transactional leadership, he proposed, lacks enduring purpose and is practised by those who focus on a generalized 'give and take' equation, with no intention to change or develop the individual or the culture. Burns also asserted that the two approaches are mutually exclusive.

Figure 6.1   Transformational and Transactional Leadership

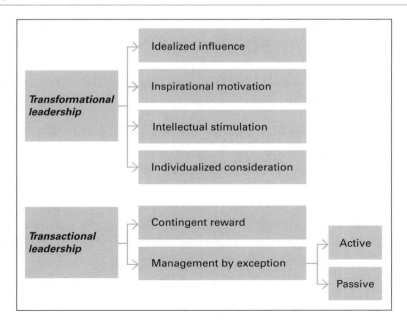

The Multi-factor Leadership Questionnaire

This work was extended by Bass (1985, 1990), an industrial psychologist and researcher. He mapped out the behaviours associated with transactional leadership and the newly named 'transformational' leadership after interviewing executives about leaders who had inspired them to higher goals or to deliver greater service to the organization. Bass sought to measure transformational leadership and its impact on people's motivation and performance, and to this end, developed an instrument called the Multi-factor Leadership Questionnaire (MLQ). The MLQ has since been used extensively in researching this topic (and in leadership development), as have other similar tools such as Podsakoff's Transformational Leadership Inventory (TLI), though to a much lesser extent. The results and their implications have led to much debate and many academic articles over the last 20–30 years, reaching beyond academics into government, education and health sectors.

Bass and Alvolio (1995) claimed their studies indicated that although every leader displays a combination of transactional and transformational leadership, those who are more successful and satisfying as leaders are more transformational than transactional. These leaders transcend self-interest and are concerned with something larger than themselves. Bass and Alvolio supported the notion that although transactional leadership is necessary to establishing leadership basics, the addition of transformational leadership is the lever that enables inspiration, development and change in followers. This is an echo of the distinction drawn by Bennis and Nanus (1985) and then Kotter (1990) between management and leadership.

Evidence of a positive impact

There have been many, many studies into the impact of transformational leadership. There is considerable evidence from empirical research that transformational leadership in its various forms – with and without transactional elements added – has a positive influence on follower behaviour, enabling greater loyalty and respect for the leader and a drive to do more work than originally expected. For instance, Bass's own research in 1998 (using MLQ data) indicates positive effects on followers. Yukl (1999) in his even-handed, critical paper on the topic, cites Lowe, Kroeck and Sivasubramanian's 1996 research which looked at 39 studies using the MLQ and found that key elements of transformational leadership correlated with follower satisfaction and performance (as did contingent reward – a transactional element – though more weakly).

More recently, Jung and Wu (2003) found a positive link between transformational leadership behaviour in Taiwanese senior leaders and organizational innovation, while Tims, Bakker and Xanthopoulou (2011), in their study of 42 Dutch participants, found a positive link between transformational leadership and levels of engagement and optimism in followers.

Even more interesting perhaps, given the environmental and economic challenges of the times we live in, Zhu *et al.* (2011) brought a focus to examining the impact of 'authentic' transformational leadership (ATL) on individual and group ethics or morals, with a focus on impacting 'end values' such as security, equality, justice and community. However, the results were inconclusive.

Weaknesses of this approach

Although transformational leadership has such wide and popular appeal, it has also been found to have serious weaknesses, some of which are listed below:

i)   The definitions of the various components of transformational leadership appear too diverse and imprecise to some, and could potentially include all sorts of behaviours which end up being correlated with each other (Yukl, 1999; Tracey and Hinkin, 1998).

ii) Some say that key leadership behaviours are missing from the MLQ (see above), such as empowering people, negotiating roles and responsibilities, building teams and thinking strategically (Yukl, 1999).

iii) The model appears to cast leaders as 'heroes' by implying that follower behaviours are wholly dependent on the leader's actions and modes of relating. There's an implication too that leadership is unidirectional and there's no scope for the follower to challenge and co-create a way forward. The model also assumes that the leader's influence is the dominant factor, whereas organizational and group processes, the prevailing culture as well as follower capability and drive also have considerable impact.

The dangers of 'heroic' leadership are further highlighted by Meindl and Ehrlich (1987) who warn of an over-valuing of leadership as the root of an organization's success. This can lead to organizational leaders successfully using symbolic actions and the management of meaning-making to look better and more powerful than they are, often for reasons of self-interest.

iv) The MLQ neglects the original 'moral' or 'ethical' focus that Burns included in his early proposals, thus leaving the possibility open for leaders to use this type of leadership in a coercive or otherwise negative way. This has been written about extensively and persuasively by Tourish (2013). Note that Tourish and Vatcha (2005) cite the Enron scandal as an example of a context where non-ethical transformational leadership was used to eliminate dissent.

v) There has not been sufficient research on the impact of transformational leadership in different contexts. For example, the impact of this type of leadership might increase significantly in a time of instability or crisis (Yukl, 1999).

vi) As the world becomes ever more interconnected and complex, organizational structures become flatter and high levels of responsibility-taking more commonplace, it could be said that this model, with its notion of a 'higher moral authority' and its slightly 'parental' feel, is becoming outdated.

Links to other authors/frameworks

Charismatic leadership

There are strong links between studies of 'charisma' and the emergence of the transformational leadership model. Charismatic leadership was originally explored by Weber (1947) and then Willner (1984). Burns (1978) also referred to charismatic leaders, as did House (1977) who was interested in behaviours and effects. Bass then extended this work to include more factors, with 'charisma' originally being the label for 'Idealized Influence',

Engaging leadership

Studies into the level of employee engagement and the willingness of employees to put in discretionary effort became a topic of discussion and investigation in the early 2000s. This followed Yukl's (1999) critique of transformational leadership and two or three significant studies by HR consultancies which indicated there were significant performance gains to be made through increasing engagement levels within organizations. These levels were thought to be influenced by many factors, one of which was the presence of engaging leadership, at first referred to as 'nearby transforming leadership' (Alban-Metcalfe and Alimo-Metcalfe, 2000). This less heroic, more distributed version of transforming leadership was taken up by a number of organizations in the UK as their core model (Macleod and Clarke, 2009).

Emotional intelligence

It's generally accepted that the components of emotional intelligence have an important connection with an individual's ability to lead. Several studies have been carried out to investigate the links between Emotional Intelligence (EQ) components such as self-awareness, self-regulation, empathy, motivation, social skills and the component of transformational leadership (TL). This correlation looks convincing, but more research is required to make the argument sufficiently robust (Polychroniou, 2009; Hunt and Fitzgerald, 2013).

Management versus leadership

Bennis and Nanus (1985) shared their descriptive interviews of dozens of world leaders in their popular book. They proposed the distinction between management and leadership, very aligned to transformation and transactional leadership, that is still informing training courses and provoking discussion today. This is further illuminated in Chapter 8.

Project management

Projects are increasingly used by organizations as the preferred way of securing resources, building new products or services, making internal changes, and implementing new ways of working. The traditional skills of project management are an extension of the core understandings of transactional leadership, and began with the use of software planning tools in the 1980s. Recent research indicates that project management approaches need revision to accommodate for increased complexity, the importance of social processes and the importance of creating value rather than simply creating the 'right' product (Cameron and Green, 2015).

Pause for Learning Points

The transformational and transactional leadership model and the MLQ tool are useful provocations for those aspiring to lead. However, the MLQ measure and the evidence for the effects of transformational leadership have to be well understood before coming to any conclusions about how best to act. Our advice would be to assume that it's just not that simple, and it really does depend on the context!

Critics of the model say that the definitions of transformational leadership are too diverse. They argue that the model is missing important elements of leadership, is all about leaders and ignores the input of followers to success, and doesn't include a check on whether such leadership is ethical.

Our experience indicates that training people to use the various behaviours associated with transformational leadership may bring some benefits; the downside comes if those learning how to lead start to believe that leadership is all about vision, influence, and the power of personality, rather than about bringing a wider variety of intelligences and sensitivities to bear in a way that's highly attuned to the context.

Stop and Reflect!

Reflect on your own leadership at home and at work over the past two weeks. Rate yourself across the transactional and transformational leadership behaviour criteria given above. What conclusions can you draw from the research results mentioned here about your effectiveness as a leader? How does this resonate or not with your own gut feel about your performance?

How would you describe the culture of leadership in your organization or department, using transactional and transformational leadership as your reference framework? What's the balance between these two modes, how do you think the culture got that way, and is it fit for purpose? What, if anything, needs to change?

References and further reading

Alban-Metcalfe, R J and Alimo-Metcalfe, B (2000) An analysis of the convergent and discriminant validity of the Transformational Leadership Questionnaire, *International Journal of Selection and Assessment*, **8** (3), September, pp. 158–75

Barling, J, Slater, F and Kelloway, K (1980) Transformational leadership and emotional intelligence: an exploratory study, *Leadership and Organization Development Journal*, **21** (3), pp. 157–61

Bass, B M (1985) *Leadership and Performance Beyond Expectations*, Free Press, New York

Bass, B M (1990) From transactional to transformational leadership: learning to share the vision, *Organizational Dynamics*, 18 (3) pp. 19–31

Bass, B M (1998) *Transformational Leadership: Industrial, military and educational impact*, Lawrence Erlbaum Associates Inc., Mahwah, NJ

Bass, B M and Alvolio, B J (1995), *Multifactor Leadership Questionnaire*, Mind Garden, Redwood City, CA

Bennis, W and Nanus, B (1985) *Leaders: The strategies for taking charge*, Harper and Row, New York

Burns, J M (1978) *Leadership*, Harper and Row, New York

Cameron, E and Green, M (2015) *Making Sense of Change Management*, Kogan Page, London

House, R J (1977) A 1976 theory of charismatic leadership, in *Leadership: The cutting edge*, ed J G Hunt and L L Larson, Southern Illinois University Press

Hunt, J G and Fitzgerald, M (2013) The relationship between emotional intelligence and transformational leadership: an investigation and review of competing claims in the literature, *American International Journal of Science*, **2** (8)

Jung, D I, Chow, C C and Wu, A (2003) The role of transformational leadership in enhancing organizational innovation, *Leadership Quarterly*, **14**, pp. 525–44

Kotter, J P (1990) What leaders really do, *Harvard Business Review*, **68** (3), pp 101–11

Lowe, K B, Kroeck, K G and Sivasubramanian, N (1996) Effectiveness correlates of transformational and transactional leadership: a meta-analytic review of the MLQ literature, *Leadership Quarterly*, 7, pp. 385–425

Macleod, D and Clarke, N (2009) *Engaging for Success*, UK Government Report

Meindl, J R and Ehrlich, B (1987) The romance of leadership and the evaluation of organizational performance, *The Academy of Management Journal*, **30** (1), pp. 99–109

Polychroniou, P V (2009) Relationship between emotional intelligence and transformational leadership of supervisors: the impact on team effectiveness, *Team Performance Management*, **15** (7/8) pp. 343–56

Tims, M, Bakker, A B and Xanthopoulou, D (2011) Do transformational leaders enhance their followers' daily work engagement? *Leadership Quarterly* **22** (1) pp. 121–31

Tourish, D (2013) *The Dark Side of Leadership*, Routledge, Abingdon, UK

Tourish, D and Vatcha, N (2005) Charismatic leadership and corporate cultism at Enron: the elimination of dissent, the promotion of conformity and organizational collapse. *Leadership*, **1** (4) pp. 455–80

Tracey, J B and Hinkin, T R (1998) Transformational leadership or effective managerial practices? *Group and Organization Management*, **23** (3), 220–36

Weber, M (1947) The Methodology of the Social Sciences, Freepress of Glencoe, Illinois

Willner, A R (1984) The spellbinders: charismatic political leadership, *Science Quarterly*, **99** (4)

Yukl, G A (1999) An evaluation of conceptual weaknesses in transformational and charismatic leadership theories, *Leadership Quarterly*, **10**, pp. 285–305

Zhu, W, Avolio, B J, Riggio, R E and Sosik, J J (2011) The effect of authentic transformational leadership on follower and group ethics, *Leadership Quarterly*, **22**, pp. 801–17

Strategic and innovation leadership

07

Introduction

Throughout this book, we have tended to define leadership as the ability to influence people towards the organization's outcomes. This chapter looks in closer detail at the sort of leadership required to define those outcomes and how leaders shape strategy and build the sort of organization that can deliver these intended outcomes. Organizations may need to refresh and reinvent themselves when the time is right – for some this may be quite frequently. They also need to approach core issues innovatively and use ideas and resources creatively. We want to understand the role of the leader in these processes of creativity and innovation.

This is against a backdrop of a VUCA world; the pace of change is ever increasing, and the speed of technological and social media advancements make it imperative that leaders respond to drivers for change by:

- listening to the deeper forces at play;
- understanding technology (and social media in particular);
- becoming adept at facilitating and managing the human side of change.

The objectives of this chapter are to:

- explore strategy and particularly the role of leadership in strategy formulation and implementation;
- understand the relationship between leadership and an organization's capacity for creativity and innovation; and

- discover the role that leadership plays in creating a learning organization which itself enables strategy formulation and implementation and creativity and innovation to flourish.

We will look specifically at the leadership of change in Chapter 8.

Key frameworks, research and critique

Strategic leadership

Strategic leadership can be defined as the leadership ability to 'anticipate, envision, maintain flexibility, think strategically, and work with others to initiate changes that will create a viable future for the organization' (Ireland and Hitt 1999).

Whittington, (2001:39) described the evolution of strategic thinking through four different schools and Alagirisamy (2016) highlighted the leadership required for each school:

- Classical – focused on planning (Chandler; Ansoff; Porter) with decisions and implementation undertaken by top management.
- Processual – focused on learning (Cyert and March; Mintzberg; Pettigrew), collective with both vertical and lateral organizational input.
- Evolutionary – focused on efficiency (Hannan and Freeman; Williamson) which requires a resource focus.
- Systemic – focused on social sensitivity (Granovetter; Whitely), needing to be sociologically sensitive.

Probably the most well-known strategy theorist is Mintzberg, who has written many academic and practical books on strategy. In 1987 he described strategy from five different perspectives, which he termed the 5 Ps of Strategy. These perspectives saw strategy functioning as:

- a Planning function;
- a Ploy (an intervention to deter or disarm competitors);
- a Pattern (looking at the pattern of how you have managed the business in the past as an indication of what is and isn't potentially successful going forwards);
- a Position (strategic positioning of the company, product or service in relation to others' offerings and positions);

- a Perspective (the mindset which has become ingrained within the organization and in some ways then repeats itself automatically, in being risk-averse or risk-taking, for example).

In terms of strategic leadership, each of the 5Ps draws upon different qualities in the leader, from being a more rational, longer-term thinker through to being a more political, responsive, externally focused player; from seeking to understand what has made the organization successful, to challenging the assumptions which inform the decision-making process.

Schoemaker, Krupp and Howland (2013) researched the essential skills for thinking and acting strategically, which are listed below. Although there is nothing fundamentally new in this list, they argue that to demonstrate effective strategic leadership one needs to exhibit these in concert with one another – enacting the skills in a holistic and integrative manner.

- **Anticipate**: the ability to scan the operating environment and beyond; interpret and make sense of trends; pick up weak signals and filter out noise; and be in communication with all stakeholders. Learning from past and present customers, competitors, trends inside and outside the immediate business context.

- **Challenge**: the ability to challenge the status quo, one's own underlying assumptions and those of others, including the business model; ensure someone is playing the 'devil's advocate' and that role is treated seriously; be open-minded, ensure multiple perspectives are seen, and encourage real dialogue and out-of-the-box thinking.

- **Interpret**: making sense of the data at a deep level requires challenging the assumptions one is making in the problem-solving process and challenging the interpretations of the data; seeing the data from at least three viewpoints; seeing the bigger picture and overarching context as well as zooming in on the specifics, noting that both God and the devil are in the detail; joining the dots and making connections between.

- **Decide**: leadership is naturally about making decisions; operational ones which can dramatically impact the enterprise and the wellbeing of employees, and strategic ones with incomplete information that are an even tougher call. This requires you to be open to more options than perhaps you're considering; to recognize where you are in the decision-making process (divergent or convergent thinking); to think both fast and slow (á la Kahneman, 2011); and to recognize that a solution may not be a 100 per cent yes or no, but perhaps a partial solution or a pilot.

- **Align**: this requires connecting up the wants and needs of multiple stakeholders and aligning towards one's own objectives. Schoemaker, Krupp and Howland suggest that this depends on 'proactive communication, trust building and frequent engagement'. In order to do this, the strategic leader needs to utilize stakeholder mapping, tailored two-way communication and ongoing monitoring of any shifting positions or dynamics.

- **Learn**: strategic leadership, innovation and learning are inextricably linked. Strategic leadership requires individuals, teams and the organization to learn from the way they strategize, implement, create success and make mistakes. A culture of learning is required and this is incubated from the top, with leaders role-modelling how they spot when a mistake has been made and how they learn from it.

A key consideration that Hitt and Ireland (2002) emphasize is the need to 'continuously evaluate, change, configure and leverage human capital and social capital'. Human capital – the aggregated value of the organization's intellectual capital of knowledge, skills, experience, etc – is important

Figure 7.1   Strategic leadership skills (Schoemaker, Krupp and Howland, 2013)

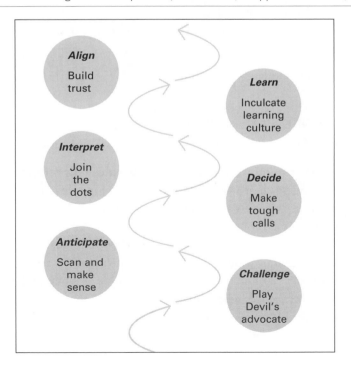

because in today's environment knowledge workers can be a critical factor in every organization's core competence. Social capital is also critical. Defined by the OECD as 'networks together with shared norms, values and understandings that facilitate co-operation within or among groups', the network of internal relationships and external relations is key to both the efficient and effective functioning of the enterprise and enables organizations to learn.

We believe the Schoemaker framework requires a higher level of leadership maturity, working in a more interdependent, collaborative way (see Part 3 for a discussion of leadership maturity). Leaders at earlier levels of maturity will inevitably prefer to focus more narrowly on goal setting, planning, and controlling.

Leading innovation

Tushman and Nadler wrote a seminal paper on organizing for innovation in 1986 in which they regarded the most important leadership task as the 'sustained management of innovation and change'. They recognized the need for organizations to be effective at learning, and identified the capacity to be self-critical as a key component. An organization also needs to balance stability with the drive and initiative to change. They suggested that, to ensure innovation, focus was needed across four key organizational dimensions:

- the work to be done;
- the people;
- the formal structure and systems; and
- the more informal cultural element of the way things get done.

They noted that naturally there is never a 100 per cent fit between the strategy and the business environment, thus the leadership role is always to work on bringing these two into alignment or 'congruence', through the adaptation of the four dimensions.

In particular they highlight the need for both formal and informal networks of communication to engender organizational learning and thus foster innovation. Within these networks, people – both managers and employees – are needed who will generate ideas, champion those ideas to fruition, and link people across both internal and external boundaries. All of this requires a cadre of sponsors, coaches and mentors who provide support, resource and protection.

O'Reilly and Tushman (2007) describe the concept of 'ambidexterity' as a key 'dual' capability for the innovation leader. This is the two-sided ability, on the one hand to exploit what currently is, with all the competencies that entails, and on the other hand to explore new ideas, products and markets, with the different set of competencies that requires. In some ways leaders need to work in the business and work on the business, or to paraphrase Pascale (1990) they need to be making happen not only what should be happening, but also making happen what otherwise wouldn't happen.

Bel (2010) supports this view by claiming that organizations need both to encourage individuals to be innovative and to evolve an organizational culture that enables innovation to occur. The process of innovation itself can be broadly divided into two parts – the generation of the idea, and the transformation of the idea into implemented reality. Clearly leaders have a role in encouraging individuals, developing a culture of innovation, being creative and also bringing enough discipline to see it through. Bel stresses the need for leaders to be both creative and disciplined and that 'a good innovation leader is not so much the one who knows the key success factors but the one who handles risks successfully. And guiding an organization for innovation implies accepting this uncertainty but also learning from failures.' Encouraging a culture of allowing mistakes and learning from them is a key element in this process.

Deschamps (2005) identified six distinctive characteristics of innovation leaders:

- combining and balancing creativity and a disciplined process;
- accepting risks and failures but learning from the latter;
- being able to acknowledge when to stop a project, knowing when to continue and when not to;
- investing in developing successful teams and attracting and retaining creative people;
- being open to new ideas and technologies and willing to experiment; and
- passionate about creating something new and imbuing others with that passion.

In his review of leadership styles for sustainable innovation, Bossink (2007) highlights the research on four effective innovation leadership styles which align with Deschamps' characteristics of innovation leaders:

- Charismatic – 'communicates an innovative vision, energizes others to innovate and accelerates innovation processes'.

- Instrumental – 'sets goals, establishes standards, and defines roles and responsibilities. It creates systems and processes to measure, monitor and assess results, and to administer corrective action'.

- Strategic – 'strategically commits to innovation, makes bold decisions despite the uncertainty of their outcomes and invests in innovation, even when faced with decreasing profit margins'.

- Interactive – 'empowers employees to innovate and to become innovation leaders themselves... supports the conclusion that an interactive innovation leadership style concentrates on individualized consideration when providing support, coaching and guidance'.

Schweitzer (2014) then broadens the discussion by looking at innovation within strategic alliances, and concludes that there is a 'positive relationship between transformational leadership and the development of innovation and operational capabilities.' However, he also recognizes that transactional leadership behaviours contribute to both ongoing business and innovation capability development, concluding that innovation leaders need to display a range of leadership styles when in strategic alliances. (See Chapter 6 for definitions of transformational and transactional leadership).

Lichtenstein *et al.* (2006), looking at complex adaptive systems, argue that leadership doesn't reside in any one individual or team. It is about the outcomes that result from the interactions within a system-wide network of interactive and interdependent agents, which produce tensions that directly lead to 'emergent learnings, capabilities, innovations, and adaptability'. Aligned to systemic and distributed leadership (see Chapter 10), innovative leadership within complex adaptive systems is about enabling everyone to step into a leadership role by having constructive, creative conversations in a collaborative manner. In the words of Lichtenstein *et al.*:

> Complexity leadership theory provides a clear and unambiguous pathway for driving responsibility downward, sparking self-organization and innovation, and making the firm much more responsive and adaptive at the boundaries.

In contrast, Soken and Barnes (2014) identify some of the potential barriers to innovation as a result of leadership action or non-action:

- fear and punishment dampen risk taking;
- lack of vision and understanding;
- no communication of the part you as an employee can play;
- focus on what doesn't work rather than success stories;

- resentment and frustration produced by lack of recognition and appreciation;
- lack of autonomy;
- internal fighting across individuals and departments;
- distraction due to fire-fighting and other operational 'busy-ness';
- reinforcement of the status quo and obstacles to experimentation;
- lack of flexibility and openness to new opportunities;
- lack of an enabling environment (physical, social, cultural).

They conclude that 'innovation requires people to change and move beyond the status quo. Vision, motivation, focus, perseverance, and leadership guidance are required to achieve success.'

Shelton (2016) provides a description of five types of behaviours that assist in building an innovation culture:

- Build collaboration across your ecosystem – recognizing and encouraging the free flow of information, ideas and collaboration vertically, horizontally, and diagonally across the organization and beyond.
- Spot, motivate and measure the 'intrapreneurs' within the organization.
- Focus on and encourage speed and agility.
- Think like a venture capitalist – generate and focus on the big ideas and then ask the questions:
  - What are the challenges we need to address to achieve the breakthrough?
  - Which of those could kill the idea?
  - How will we mitigate them?
- Balance operational excellence with innovation – apply disciplined attention to rigorous innovation processes coupled with the experimentation mindset.

Leadership and the learning organization

Peter Senge's work on the learning organization contributed to the growing belief that competitive advantage resided in people and the route to success was through organizational learning and development. His seminal book *The Fifth Discipline* (1993) suggested five learning disciplines which would enhance an organization's creative capabilities:

- **Personal mastery**: self-awareness and sensitivity to strengths and weaknesses in consciously applying the principles and values most important for achieving personal goals.

- **Mental models:** the judgements and perceptions from past experiences that influence what we hear and say, as well as how we react to others.

- **Building shared visions:** using the collective capability of a team or an organization to create and realize a vision in which the sum of the whole is greater than the parts.

- **Team learning:** applying this to the first three disciplines allows people who work well together to learn and accomplish more than they could by themselves.

- **Systems thinking:** looking at the organization not as a set of isolated functions or tasks but as interdependent parts, each of which influences the performance of the whole.

Senge *et al.* (1999) suggest that successful change and innovation don't come from the top of an organization but from within, developing communities of interdependent leaders across the organization. In our book *Making Sense of Change Management* (2015) we describe the three types of leadership role that Senge believes are required.

- Local line leaders: overcoming obstacles, showing commitment and energy at the front line; executive leaders and network leaders who create infrastructure and connect them to others.

- Executive leaders: developing governing ideas; designing infrastructure for reward, performance management and learning; teaching and mentoring local line leaders; serving as role models.

- Network leaders: guides, advisors, active helpers and accessors (resources from elsewhere); working in partnership with line leaders.

(Senge *et al.*, 1999).

Freeflow of communication and feedback loops is also key. Torbert (2004) describes three levels of organizational feedback required in learning organizations (see Part 6 Chapter 24).

Bass (2000) stresses that the dimensions of both transactional and transformational leadership styles are required and enhance the development and sustainability of the learning organization. However, Caldwell (2011) criticizes the concept of the learning organization as it fails to incorporate notions of power and indeed how specifically and in practice change is initiated within a learning organization.

Pause for Learning Points

The traditional way of looking at strategic leadership focuses on the need for a strategic alignment and fit between the external environment and the internal organization. This requires leadership which scans the external environment and assesses opportunities and threats whilst assessing whether the organization is fit for purpose.

In more mature organizational cultures (see Part 6), it is about enabling everyone to step into a leadership role by having constructive, creative conversations in a collaborative and learning-oriented manner.

Key skills for strategic leadership include the ability to:

- Anticipate: scan the environment, pick up trends, project yourself forward.
- Challenge: question the status quo, your assumptions about reality and about your decision-making process.
- Interpret: be able to make sense of data and information, surface assumptions, pick up weak signals, filter out noise.
- Decide: have a robust and inclusive problem-solving and decision-making process.
- Align: ensure coherence across the strategy and alignment within the organization.
- Learn: foster a culture of learning from one's own and others' actions, mistakes, failures, successes.

Innovation leadership enables the organization to refresh and reinvent itself when required, due to external or internal factors, or both. Innovation leadership is concerned with developing the creative and innovative processes which allow this to happen.

Innovation leadership can be concerned with unlocking the talent of individuals and teams and/or creating a culture of innovation. It requires both operational (innovation process) excellence balanced with an innovation mindset (experimentation).

Leadership behaviours which enable innovation in organizations include allowing higher degrees of autonomy and levels of risk-taking, learning from mistakes and failures, enabling communication and learning to take place across the organization. Innovation leadership is not about control or micro-management; it is about orchestration of a culture of open-mindedness, exploration and experimentation within set boundaries.

Stop and Reflect!

Use a framework from strategic planning (such as PESTLE or SWOT) to identify the key drivers for change in an organization you know well. Build a business case for changing your organization's business operating model or strategic direction. Be mindful of any assumptions you are making – in terms of your assessment of the business environment or your choice of model. Construct a number of future scenarios, evaluate each and discuss your ideas with one or more colleagues and elicit their views.

How innovative is your organization? List the top five obstacles you see in making it even more innovative. Commit to coming up with one innovative idea over the coming week and consider how you might get this idea implemented. Stay sensitive to any obstacles and construct a strategy to get any necessary approvals and work it through to completion. Work out how you can do this even with some organizational resistance.

References and further reading

Alagirisamy,G (2016) Henry Mintzberg on Strategic Management, *Academia* [online] https://www.academia.edu/4913544/Henry_Mintzberg_on_Strategic_ Management [accessed 21 July 2016]

Amabile, T M (1998) How to kill creativity, *Harvard Business Review*, 76 (9), pp. 77–87

Bass, B M (2000) The future of leadership in learning organizations, *Journal of Leadership & Organizational Studies*, 7 (3), pp. 18–40

Bel, R (2010) Leadership and innovation: learning from the best, *Global Business and Organizational Excellence*, 29 (2), pp. 47–60

Bossink, B A G (2007) Leadership for sustainable innovation, *International Journal of Technology Management and Sustainable Development*, 6 (2)

Caldwell, R (2011) Leadership and learning: a critical reexamination of Senge's learning organization, *Systemic Practice and Action Research*, 25 (1), pp. 39–55

Carmeli, A, Gelbard, R and Gefen, D (2010) The importance of innovation leadership in cultivating strategic fit and enhancing firm performance, *The Leadership Quarterly*, 21 (3), pp. 339–49

Deschamps, J-P (2005) Different leadership styles for different innovation strategies, *Strategy & Leadership*, 33 (5), pp. 31–38

Hamel, G (2000) *Leading the Revolution*, Harvard Business Review Press, Boston

Hitt, M A and Ireland, R D (2002) The essence of strategic leadership: managing human and social capital, *Journal of Leadership and Organizational Studies*, 9 (l)

Ireland, R D and Hitt, M A (1999) Achieving and maintaining strategic competitiveness in the 21st century: the role of strategic leadership, *Academy of Management Executive*, 13 (l)

Kahneman, D (2011) *Thinking, Fast and Slow* Farrar, Straus & Giroux

Lichtenstein, B B *et al*. (2006) Complexity leadership theory: an interactive perspective on leading in complex adaptive systems, *Emergence: Complexity and Organization* 8 (4) pp. 2–12

Mintzberg, H 1987 The strategy concept: Five Ps for strategy, *California Management Review*, 30 (1), pp. 11–24

O'Reilly, C A and Tushman, M (2007) Research Paper No. 1963 Stanford Graduate School of Business

Pascale, R (1990) *Managing on the Edge*, Penguin, Harmondsworth

Schoemaker, P J H, Krupp, S and Howland, S (2013) Strategic leadership: the essential skills, *Harvard Business Review*, Jan–Feb

Schweitzer, J (2014) Leadership and innovation capability development in strategic alliances, *Leadership & Organization Development Journal*, 35 (5)

Senge, P (1993) *The Fifth Discipline*, Century Business London

Senge, P M, Kleiner, A, Roberts, C, Ross, R B and Smith, B J (1994) *Fifth Discipline Fieldbook*, Doubleday, New York

Shelton, R (2016) These five behaviors can create an innovation culture, *Strategy + Business* [online]http://www.strategy-business.com/blog/These-Five-Behaviors-Can-Create-an-Innovation-Culture?gko=85549&utm_source=itw&utm_medium=20160721&utm_campaign=resp [accessed 30 June 2016]

Soken, N H and Barnes, B Kim (2014) What kills innovation? Your role as a leader in supporting an innovative culture, *Industrial and Commercial Training* 46 (1)

Tobert, B and Associates (2004) *Action Inquiry*, Berrett-Koehler, San Francisco

Tushman, M and Nadler, D (1986) Organizing for innovation, *California Management Review*, 28 (3), pp. 74–92

Whittington, R (2001) *What is Strategy – and Does it Matter?* Cengage, London

Change
leadership

08

Introduction

Over the last 20 years or so the concept of change leadership has emerged as a key area of discussion, particularly within the community of practising managers. Kotter's seminal *Harvard Business Review* paper 'Leading Change: why transformation efforts fail' (1995), further developed in his book *Leading Change* (1996), explored leadership in the context of an organizational change process. Until then this type of leadership hadn't really been separated out as a distinct topic.

In this introduction, as a way of understanding the frameworks and research underpinning this territory, we address these questions:

- What differentiates change leadership from other forms of leadership?
- Is change leadership merely leadership in one specific type of situation or context?
- What is the difference between managing change and leading change?
- Which theoretical frameworks help effective change leadership?
- What are some of the key qualities associated with effective change leadership?

Management and leadership

Many of the leadership theories of the 20th century do not explicitly differentiate between management and leadership. The majority (eg traits, contingency and situational) treat leadership as managing in a steady state environment, although Chapter 6 does touch upon this in the frame of transactional and transformational leadership.

However, some authors, notably Zaleznik (1977), Bennis (1989) and Kotter (1990) draw clear distinctions between the functions of a manager and those of a leader. Although some have argued this to be a false distinction (Jaques, 1997), there is a growing body of literature which focuses on the specific qualities needed in a leader when leading change in an organization.

Pascale, in *Managing on the Edge* (1990), defined the difference thus:

> Managing is helping to make happen what is supposed to happen anyway; leadership is making happen what isn't going to happen anyway.

And in that definition we can see how leadership can be aligned with effecting change. Bennis (1989) teased out more distinctions, as outlined below.

A manager	A leader
Administers	Innovates
Is a copy	Is an original
Maintains	Develops
Focuses on systems and structure	Focuses on people
Relies on control	Inspires trust
Has a short-range view	Has a long-range perspective
Asks how and when	Asks why
Has his eye on the bottom line	Has his eye on the horizon
Imitates	Originates
Accepts the status quo	Challenges the status quo
Classic good soldier	His own person
Does things right	Does the right thing

Kotter (1996) echoes the ideas of Bennis. He says: 'we have raised a generation of very talented people to be managers, not leader/managers, and vision is not a component of effective management. The management equivalent to vision creation is planning.' He says that leaders are different from managers: 'They don't make plans; they don't solve problems; they don't even organize people. What leaders really do is prepare organizations for change and help them cope as they struggle through it.' He identifies three areas of focus for leaders and contrasts these with the typical focus of a manager:

1 setting direction versus planning and budgeting;

2 aligning people versus organizing and staffing; and

3 motivating people versus controlling and problem solving.

Zaleznik recognized the need to innovate, Bennis the need to have a long-range perspective, challenge the status quo and develop a guiding vision. In order to do this there is a requirement to focus on people (rather than systems and structure) and inspire trust. Tichy and Devanna (1986) also saw leaders as essentially agents for change, consciously and deliberately paying attention to what's not working and setting out to move the organization on.

This is very similar to Kouznes and Posner (2003) who saw that the focus for the leader was to inspire a shared vision, challenge the current process, enable others to act, model the way, and encourage the heart.

The separation of management from leadership is useful for those wishing to take on more of a leadership role, although it is sometimes interpreted as downplaying the important role of a good manager in organizational life. Most managers have to undertake both roles.

Leading in times of change

... there is no more delicate matter to take in hand, nor more dangerous to conduct, nor more doubtful in its success, than to set up as a leader in the introduction of changes. For he who innovates will have for his enemies all those who are well off under the existing order of things, and only lukewarm supporters in those who might be better off under the new.
MACHIAVELLI, 1469–1527

The ever-increasing amount of literature on change and change leadership can, perhaps, be attributed to three factors:

- the current external context in which leadership is now required to function;

- the growing sense that organizations and organizational change are becoming increasingly complex; and

- a broad acknowledgement that change management and change leadership are different things.

As mentioned in Chapter 1, we are now living in a VUCA world. This concept was developed by the US Army War College in response to the cataclysmic events surrounding 9/11. It begins to describe a world that requires a different type of leadership. Horney, Pasmore and O'Shea (2010) characterize this as a world of:

Volatility – the nature, speed, volume, magnitude and dynamics of change;

Uncertainty – the lack of predictability of issues and events;

Complexity – the confounding of issues and the chaos that surround any organization; and

Ambiguity – the haziness of reality and the mixed meanings of conditions.

These factors suggest a different type of leadership is required. Grint's (2010) work on 'wicked' issues also underscores this. Wicked issues are complex, messy, often intractable challenges that can probably rarely be totally eliminated. There are often multiple or partially understood causes, and there may be no known solutions. Climate change, the refugee crises and the rise of ISIS are three current wicked issues.

Snowden and Boone's work (2007) on tackling complex problems, where the outcomes are unclear and cause and effect not known, also suggests a different type of leadership. This approach is one that values diversity of view, including dissent; exploring the views of internal and external stakeholders more thoroughly; and experimentation and other emergent practices, such as encouraging self-organization and supporting amplification/dampening strategies.

The leadership required in these more complex and uncertain situations and contexts include the need to:

- establish shared agendas and priorities across organizational boundaries;
- develop shared narratives;
- build trust and share risk;
- be courageous and have robust discussions;
- spot talent and enable it to act;
- understand the new skills mix and mindsets required to provide strategic leadership in this context;
- exchange information and resources;
- spot opportunities as they unfold;
- create new knowledge;
- enable, facilitate and coach.

A useful summary template produced by Green (2007) highlights the need to focus on the task of change, the process of change and the people involved in the change. Active management and leadership of the change is required through:

- a clear rationale and compelling reason to change;
- a clear direction, end point and motivation for change;
- a clear sense of how the process will be managed;

- ongoing visible sponsorship;
- demonstrable engagement with stakeholders, enabling them to go through transition;
- a credible effective dedicated change management team;
- a well-planned and organized approach;
- ongoing, focused, tailored communication of direction and progress;
- attention to Task, Process and People.

For more extensive information on individual change psychology and team leadership and dynamics, our book *Making Sense of Change Management* (2015) provides a comprehensive set of frameworks and suggestions.

Key frameworks, research and critique

This section looks at some of the key change leadership frameworks and understandings which have been developed over the last 20 years or so.

We have selected:

- an overarching change leadership framework (Kotter);
- a way of looking at leadership behaviour necessary for cultural change (Schein);
- an approach to understanding and staying agile with some key leadership tasks (Heifetz and Laurie); and
- academic research on the best approach to change (Higgs and Rowland).

Kotter was one of the first to set out a framework for leaders to follow when leading transformational efforts. His eight-step framework (see Box 8.1) was based on his research into the success and (mainly) failure of over 100 change initiatives, and built on his initial distinction of what leaders do – setting direction, aligning people and motivating people.

Recently (Kotter, 2012), having continued his observations of scores of organizations undergoing change, and working in-depth with eight companies, adapted his earlier framework to accommodate changing organizational cultures, increased global turbulence and the exponential nature of change. He recognizes that the original methodology was somewhat linear and more useful for 'episodic' change; that the guiding coalition needn't be just a small powerful core but can be more networked and extensive; and the requirement now is to be more fleet of foot, agile and adaptable. The original framework appeared very much top-down; he now advocates having many change

Box 8.1

Establish a sense of urgency.

Form a powerful guiding coalition.

Create a vision.

Communicate the vision.

Empower others to act on the vision.

Plan for and create short term wins.

Consolidate improvements and produce still more change.

Institutionalize the new approaches.

(Kotter, 1995).

agents and using volunteers – individuals who bring energy, commitment and genuine enthusiasm. In his 'Accelerate' template, Kotter argues for a different type of change leadership: 'The game is all about vision, opportunity, agility, inspired action, and celebration – not project management, budget reviews, reporting relationships, compensation, and accountability to a plan.'

This goes some way to address the perceived criticism of its linearity. Cameron and Green (2015), in line with a number of organizations they have worked with, have adapted it with continuous management attention and stakeholder feedback loops for it to be a continuing cycle.

Schein (1992), Professor Emeritus at the MIT Sloan School of Management, has written extensively on leadership, in particular in regard to organizational culture and culture change. He suggests that organizational culture is formed and determined by how people think about and how they act when following the organization's strategy.

Box 8.2: Schein's embedding mechanisms

Primary embedding mechanisms:

- what leaders pay attention to, measure, and control on a regular basis;
- how leaders react to critical incidents and organizational crises;
- how leaders allocate resources;

- deliberate role modelling, teaching, and coaching by leaders;
- how leaders allocate rewards and status;
- how leaders recruit, select, promote and excommunicate.

Secondary articulation and reinforcement mechanisms:

- organizational design and structure;
- organizational systems and procedures;
- rites and rituals of the organization;
- design of physical spaces, facades, buildings;
- stories about important events and people;
- formal statements of organizational philosophy, creeds and charters.

(Schein, 1992).

When this is successful, the way things are done gets reinforced and becomes self-sustaining. It is only when the strategy changes that the organization might then need to shift its culture. Schein realized that leaders play a pivotal role in this change. He described a number of ways in which the actions of the leader can help embed a new culture (see Box 8.2)

Ronald Heifetz, Harvard professor, has been researching and teaching leadership for over 30 years. He focuses on the challenge of building the adaptive capacity of organizations and societies and the development of future leaders. In his book *Leadership Without Easy Answers* (1994), Heifetz highlights what he calls the adaptive challenge and describes how leaders need to approach this. He says:

> Leadership is a razor's edge because one has to oversee a sustained period of social disequilibrium during which people confront the contradictions in their lives and communities and adjust their values and behaviour to accommodate new realities.

Heifetz suggests that the leader needs to be focused on the adaptive rather than mere technical challenges (see Fig 8.1). These are more difficult or complex changes requiring shifts in people's values, beliefs and approaches to work.

Figure 8.1 Technical problems versus adaptive challenges (Heifetz and Laurie, 1997)

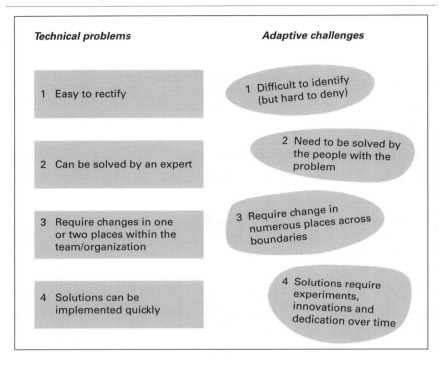

Box 8.3

Get on the balcony.

Identify the adaptive challenges.

Regulate distress.

Maintain disciplined attention.

Give the work back to the people.

Protect the voices of leadership from below.

(Heifetz and Laurie, 1997).

Heifetz and Laurie's advice to leaders (see Box 8.3) is to take an overview, spot what it is that needs addressing and recognize that in change people will experience some pain, and that it is the leader's role to ensure that it is managed within acceptable limits. They also recognize that once started, you need to follow it through to the end, and you also need to empower people and listen to their feedback.

Higgs and Rowland (2005) mapped different conceptions of managing change onto two axes. One axis represented change from uniform to disseminated, and the other axis from simple to complex. They investigated the success rates of each change approach and what leadership behaviours tend to be associated with the effective approaches. They found that change leadership behaviours could be clustered around the three themes of shaping behaviours, framing behaviours and creating capacity (see Box 8.4). Importantly, the findings suggest that the more complex the change, the more an emergent approach to change should be adopted, albeit within a structured framework. The framing behaviours associated with change leadership were also seen as the behaviours which correlated most with change success.

Box 8.4: Change leadership behaviours

Shaping behaviours:

- act as a catalyst;
- adopt new approaches;
- reveal beliefs;
- express emotions and thoughts;
- role model new behaviours;
- make others accountable.

Framing behaviours:

- identify and use multiple sources of change;
- articulate direction and principles;
- journey design and orchestration;
- articulate and work with culture and values.

Creating capacity:

- help others learn about change;
- provide feedback and coaching;
- create networks and alliances;
- keep people informed;
- adapt structures, processes and systems.

(Higgs and Rowland, 2005).

Pause for Learning Points

Change leadership can be viewed as a particular form of leadership which also includes elements of 'change management'.

It is important for organizational leaders, and all those responsible for initiating, implementing and integrating change, to be able to understand the current context.

A structured framework for the change process is often an important component of change leadership and management. This is sometimes referred to as 'framing leadership'.

Kotter advocates setting direction, aligning and motivating people as core change leadership activities. More recently, he advises that less top-down, more agile and networked approaches tend to work better.

Given the correlation between leadership behaviour and corporate culture, the leader and the leadership team need to be aware that their activities will reinforce the development of a particular culture as change progresses.

Any pain or disturbance triggered by change needs to be kept within acceptable limits.

In a VUCA world, complex problems with unknowable solutions require different, new forms of leadership, sometimes referred to as 'emergent leadership'.

Stop and Reflect!

Think of a recent organizational change that you have experienced, and assess the effectiveness of it when mapped onto Kotter's eight steps. With hindsight, what could have been done differently? Are there any aspects of the change that Kotter's model fails to address?

Review the different models and frameworks in this chapter and build your own checklist for change leaders. Then look at your leadership style (or that of someone you have witnessed leading change) and note down what has worked, and where your or their change leadership can be improved.

References and further reading

Bass, B M and Avolio, B J (1990) Developing transformational leadership, *Journal of European Industrial Training*, **14** (5)

Bennis (1989) *On Becoming a Leader*, Addison Wesley, New York

Cameron, E and Green, M (2008) *Making Sense of Leadership*, Kogan Page, London

Cameron, E and Green, M (2015) *Making Sense of Change Management*, Kogan Page, London

Green, M (2007) *Change Management Masterclass*, Kogan Page, London

Grint, K (2010) Wicked problems and clumsy solutions, in *The New Public Leadership Challenge*, ed S Brookes and K Grint, Palgrave Macmillan, New York

Heifetz, R (1994) *Leadership Without Easy Answers*, Harvard University Press, Boston

Heifetz, R and Laurie, D (1997) The work of leadership, *Harvard Business Review*, **75** (1), pp 124–34

Higgs, M and Rowland, D (2005) All changes great and small, *Journal of Change Management*, **5** (2), pp 121–51

Horney, N, Pasmore, B and O'Shea, T (2010) Leadership agility: A business imperative for a VUCA world, *People & Strategy*, **33** (4)

Informal Networks [online] http://informalnetworks.co.uk/ [accessed 5 June 2016]

Jaques, E (1997) Requisite Organization: Total system for effective managerial organization and managerial leadership for the 21st century, Gower, London

Kail, E G (2010/2011) Leading in a VUCA environment, *HBR Blog Network* [online] www.hbr.org

Kotter, J P (1990) What leaders really do, *Harvard Business Review*, **68** (3), pp 101–11

Kotter, J P (1995) Leading change: why transformation efforts fail, *Harvard Business Review*, **73** (2), pp 59–67

Kotter, J P (1996) *Leading Change*, Harvard Business School Press, Boston

Kotter (2012) Accelerate, *Harvard Business Review*, **90** (11), pp. 43–58

Kouzes, J M and Posner, B Z (2003) *The Leadership Challenge*, 3rd edition, Jossey-Bass, San Francisco

Machiavelli (1513), *The Prince*, (this edition 2015) Wisehouse Classics, Sweden

Pascale, R (1990) *Managing on the Edge*, Penguin, Harmondsworth

Schein, E (1992) *Organizational Culture and Leadership*, 2nd edn, Jossey-Bass, San Francisco

Snowden, D J and Boone, M (2007) A leader's framework for decision making, *Harvard Business Review*, **85** (11), pp. 69–76

Tichy, N M and Devanna, M A (1986), *The Transformational Leader*, Wiley, New York

Zaleznik (1977), Managers and leaders: are they different? *Harvard Business Review*, May–June, pp. 67–78

Leadership responsibility and values

09

Introduction

Leadership of organizations has come under immense scrutiny due to the litany of corporate scandals that have occurred over the past two decades. This has led to a debate as to whether leaders should be socially responsible as well as seeking the maximization of shareholder value. Human action is underpinned by a set of values, and leaders are no different to other human beings. We have, however, seen how different leadership theories suggest that leaders can flex their behaviours according to the situation or according to the behaviours of their followers. This pragmatic approach to leadership can be seen as distinct from a more principles-driven form of leadership (Gosling *et al*. 2012).

This chapter therefore looks at leadership and values from a number of different perspectives and aims to understand:

- what it means to be a responsible, ethical leader;
- what underpins values-based leadership;
- the key characteristics of servant leadership;
- how you can become an authentic leader;
- the implications of the components of Jim Collins' 'Level 5' leadership.

Key frameworks, research and critique

Ethical leadership

Trait theory included the observation that personal integrity has a positive impact on leadership effectiveness, and according to Yukl (2013), integrity consistently comes high in studies on effective leadership characteristics across all cultures. Authors such as Kirkpatrick and Locke (1991), Kouzes and Posner (1995), Posner and Schmidt (1992), McAllister (1995) and Dirks and Ferrin (2002) have made the links, in their research, between leadership effectiveness and ethical attributes such as dependability, honesty, integrity, professionalism, trustworthiness.

Box 9.1: Unethical leadership

Falsifying information.

Stealing assets for personal use.

Blaming others for one's own mistakes.

Provoking unnecessary hostility and distrust amongst others.

Divulging secrets to competitors.

Showing favouritism in exchange for bribes.

Reckless behaviour liable to endanger others.

Exploiting subordinates.

Box 9.2: Ethical leadership

Care about others.

Care about broader society.

Dependability.

Fairness.

Honesty.

Trustworthy.

Personally ethical.

Principled.

Professional.

Professionally ethical.

Proactively influence others' ethical and unethical behaviour.

However, there are some inherent difficulties in looking at ethical or moral leadership. For example, is it ethical if the leader acts consistently in line with their own values, but the values themselves are dubious? Who is to be the judge of this? Another example: is it acceptable to manipulate people into agreeing to something when it is against their best interests either as an organization or as individuals, recognizing that these elements might also be in opposition to each other? Typical indicative unethical and ethical leadership behaviours are itemized in Boxes 9.1 and 9.2 respectively.

Brown and Trevino (2006) identified two aspects to the ethical leader – as moral people adhering to a set of moral principles, and as moral managers, in that they actively seek to influence subordinates by behaving in an ethical manner.

How ethical leaders become influential in their organizations or with followers can be understood by looking at Bandura (1986)'s Social Learning Theory. Followers tend to observe and seek to emulate their leaders, especially in regard to the leader's espoused and practised set of attitudes, values and behaviours and the role-modelling of them. The leader's inherent positional power and status assist this process.

Seidman (2010) suggests that today's leaders are equipped only to navigate, not to guide. He uses Barack Obama as an example of a leader willing to guide through his efforts on ethics and criminal justice reform as a State senator, and his quiet demeanour as President. This can be contrasted with the apparent willingness of some politicians to lie blatantly to achieve their aims. For example, Presidential candidates in the United States, and some of those who campaigned to take the UK out of the European Union, have been accused by some of lying (Freedland, 2016).

Seidman says:

> Ethical leaders distinguish themselves by doing that which is inconvenient, unpopular, and even temporarily unprofitable in the service of long-term health and value. They view the world as interconnected and develop multidisciplinary solutions to address complex problems that crop up every day.

He suggests that leaders should not be asking themselves whether an action is wrong but instead asking if it is the right thing to do.

Values-based leadership

...your leadership must be rooted in who you are and what matters most to you. When you truly know yourself and what you stand for, it is much easier to know what to do in any situation. H M J Kraemer Jr (2011)

Schwartz (1994) suggests that a person's values motivate that person to action, give them both direction and purpose and engender passion. Allport (1961) identifies them as a 'dominating force'. We also know how the alignment or otherwise between leaders' espoused values and values-in-practice (ie what leaders say they believe versus what underpins their actions) contributes to organizational culture (Schein, 2004; Cameron and Green, 2015). Higgs (2006) highlights research that indicates 60 per cent of organizational performance can be attributed to culture and 80 per cent of culture is down to leadership behaviour. Collins and Porras (1994) discuss how truly sustainable companies ('built to last') are created by values-based leaders. Fernandez and Hogan (2002) concluded that there was more of a correlation between CEOs' effectiveness and the alignment between their values and those of the organization than their level of industry knowledge.

Box 9.3: The value-based leader characteristics

Bob McDonald, previously president and CEO of Procter & Gamble, suggested 10 key characteristics of a 'values-based leader'. These can be understood via the 10 questions we pose below:

1 Do you lead your life guided by purpose?

2 Do you let yourself assume that everyone wants to succeed?

3 Do you put employees in jobs where they can bring their strengths?

4 As a leader, do you have integrity and take responsibility for your mistakes?

5 Do you bring diverse groups of people together to encourage new ideas to emerge?

6 Do you enable your people to build a high-performance organization rather than tolerate ineffective strategies, processes and culture?

7 Do you take action when there is not a good match between the employee and the company?

8 Do you make space and time for the organization to renew itself?

9 Do you make recruitment and talent management a priority?

10 Do you understand that the test of your leadership is what happens once you leave?

(Farell, 2009)

Values-based leadership (see Box 9.3) is demonstrated by being able to motivate people towards the organization's objectives by connecting with their values. By establishing a strong organizational culture based on values which contribute to the organization's success, employees are motivated to learn how to behave in accordance with those values. This requires employees to have alignment between their individual values and those of the organization and, importantly, requires the organization's leaders to communicate and role-model the organization's values (Stride, 2011).

In order to be an effective values-based leader, Kraemer (2011) identified four core elements:

- Self-reflection – knowing what you stand for.

- Balance – seeing the situation from 'multiple perspectives and differing viewpoints to gain a much fuller understanding'.

- Self-confidence – confidence in your abilities, acknowledging strengths and deficits and recognizing that that is who you are.

- Humility – being modest, humble, not vain or proud, accepting that others may have a better solution.

Servant leadership

Servant leadership is also underpinned by values – around ensuring basic human needs are met (to live); to engender trusting relationships (to love); to be open to developing and maximizing everyone's potential (to learn); and to build and ensure sustainability (to leave a legacy) (Spears, 1998).

Greenleaf coined the term 'Servant Leadership' in 1970 and although popular in some boardrooms (Bass and Bass, 2008) and with some seminal management authors (Block, 1993; Covey, 1990; Senge, 1990; Wheatley, 2005), it hasn't been subjected to too much academic scrutiny. This is partly attributable to the original contextualizing of servant leadership as more a way of life than a theory of leadership. Greenleaf stressed the importance of the motivation to serve, which was an intrinsic motivation and, he suggested, a lifelong journey.

Greenleaf's original definition of servant leadership dwells on this calling to serve:

> It begins with the natural feeling one wants to serve, to serve first. Then conscious choice brings one to aspire to lead. That person is sharply different from one who is a leader first... The difference manifests itself in the care taken by the servant first to make sure that other people's highest priority needs are being served. The

best test, and difficult to administer, is this: Do those served grow as persons? Do they, while being served, become healthier, wiser, freer, more autonomous, more likely themselves to become servants? And, what is the effect on the least privileged in society? Will they benefit or at least not be further deprived?

Spears (1998) identified 10 characteristics of servant leaders from Greenleaf's writings:

1   Listening automatically: responding to any problem by receptively listening to what is said, which allows them to identify the will of the group and help clarify that will.

2   Empathy: striving to accept and understand others, never rejecting them, but sometimes refusing to recognize their performance as good enough.

3   Healing: recognizing as human beings they have the opportunity to make themselves and others 'whole'.

4   Awareness: strengthened by general awareness and above all self-awareness, which enables them to view situations holistically.

5   Persuasion: relying primarily on convincement rather than coercion.

6   Conceptualization: seeking to arouse and nurture their and others' abilities to 'dream great dreams'.

7   Foresight: intuitively understanding the lessons from the past, the present realities, and the likely outcome of a decision for the future.

8   Stewardship: committing first and foremost to serving others' needs;

9   Commitment to the growth of people: nurturing the personal, professional and spiritual growth of each individual.

10 Building community: identifying means of building communities among individuals working within their institutions, which can give the healing love essential for health.

Laub (1999) defined servant leadership simply as the leader placing the needs of others above his own. He went on to develop an organizational leadership assessment which links servant leadership to organizational health. Key elements are:

● valuing people through believing, serving, and non-judgmentally;

● listening to others;

● developing people through providing learning, growth, encouragement and affirmation;

● building community through developing strong collaborative and personal relationships;

- displaying authenticity through being open, accountable, and willing to learn from others;
- providing leadership through foreseeing the future, taking initiative, and establishing goals;
- sharing leadership through facilitating and sharing power.

(Laub's Organizational Leadership assessment: http://www.olagroup.com)

Authentic leadership

Since the turn of the Millennium and the many business scandals there has been an increasing focus on how much leaders need to be authentic and act authentically (Luthans and Avolio, 2003; George *et al.*, 2007; Cashman, 1998, 2003).

The key realization is that just because something isn't unlawful doesn't make it right. The notion that leaders have to have a moral compass, ie a values base, is taking hold. One way of acting with integrity is acting authentically.

Authenticity has four key elements:

1 Awareness – knowledge and trust in one's thoughts, feelings, motives and values;

2 Unbiased processing – objectivity about and acceptance of one's positive and negative attributes.

3 Behaviour – acting based on one's true preferences, values and needs rather than merely acting to please others, secure rewards or avoid punishments.

4 Relational orientation – achieving and valuing truthfulness and openness in one's close relationships.

(Kernis 2003; Kernis and Goldman, 2006)

When applied to leadership, we can expand the definition somewhat. An authentic leader can be seen as one who:

1 is self-aware, humble, always seeking improvement, aware of those being led and looks out for the welfare of others;

2 fosters high degrees of trust by building an ethical and moral framework; and

3 is committed to organizational success within the construct of social values.

(Whitehead, 2009)

Walumbwa *et al.* (2008) undertook a review of writings on authentic leadership and identified some distinctive and unifying characteristics:

- Self-awareness: an ongoing process of reflection and re-examination by the leader of his or her own strength, weaknesses and values.
- Relational Transparency: open sharing by the leader of his or her own thoughts and beliefs, balanced by a minimization of inappropriate emotions.
- Balanced Processing: solicitation by the leader of opposing viewpoints and fair-minded consideration of those viewpoints.
- Internalized Moral Perspective: a positive ethical foundation adhered to by the leader in his or her relationships and decisions that is resistant to outside pressures.

One of the leading proponents of authentic leadership is Bill George. He criticizes much of the leadership theory literature, suggesting that would-be leaders try to imitate what the various theories say are the characteristics and behaviours of effective leaders. As we have seen above, authentic leadership takes a different view. George *et al.* (2007) take the stance that leadership is based on trust, and trust is engendered by being authentic. To be an authentic leader you need to demonstrate a passion for your purpose, practise your values consistently, and lead with your heart as well as your head.

In order to become an authentic leader one needs to have an understanding of one's own leadership journey; how you came to be the person you are, through all the trials and tribulations. Knowing oneself is clearly an important attribute, and to ensure this, authentic leaders tend to have a network of trusted colleagues who can provide timely and honest feedback. They tend to be more intrinsically motivated rather than seeking financial reward or status. And their focus is predominately on longer-term outcomes and building sustainable organizations.

Level 5 leadership

Jim Collins wrote two seminal business books – *Built to Last: Successful habits of visionary companies* (1994) with Jerry Porras and *Good to Great: Why some companies make the leap... and others don't* (2001a). Because of their focus on the values of leaders in sustainably successful companies, these books chimed with business people and business schools alike.

Box 9.4: Seven characteristics of a Good to Great company

- Get the right people on board (and the wrong people out).
- Confront the brutal truth of the situation, and don't give up.
- Enact the 'Hedgehog' concept, combining passion, competence and profitability.
- Culture of discipline.
- Technology accelerators.
- 'Flywheel' of many small initiatives.
- Level 5 leadership.

(Collins, *Good to Great*, 2001)

Collins identified seven characteristics of a 'Great' company, one of which was the leadership that was displayed. Collins named this 'Level 5 Leadership'. Level 1 to Level 4 leadership covers the range of highly capably individuals, contributing team members, competent people, task-oriented managers and effective leaders who can motivate individuals and groups towards a compelling vision. Level 5 leadership 'builds enduring greatness through a paradoxical combination of personal humility plus professional will' (Collins, 2001). Personal humility encompasses modesty, quiet determination and ambition for the organization, not for one's self, and others are recognized and appreciated for their contributions.

Professional will encompasses the drive for outstanding results, a perseverance and persistence in pursuing those results, setting and maintaining the highest standards and taking responsibility for any difficulties or mistakes along the way.

Collins cites examples of a number of companies who, with Level 5 leadership, have outperformed their comparators. Although his research methodology and conclusions have sometimes been questioned (for example, Levitt (2008) points out that some of the original Good to Great companies are now underperforming), there is little doubt that on a practical and pragmatic level his ideas have had enduring value.

Pause for Learning Points

There are clearly many overlaps between the characteristics of Ethical, Values-based, Servant, Authentic and Level 5 leadership. They all embody a type of leadership which is less focused on traits or on consciously matching different behaviours to different situations.

The learning points for each of us include:

- Be true to yourself by being clear about what values you hold dear, and embodying them with integrity.
- Connect with your true purpose and passions.
- Ask yourself – whom do you serve as a leader?
- Develop your self-awareness and social awareness.
- Balance being humble with a strong drive for organizational outcomes.

Stop and Reflect!

List your core values and identify behaviours that accompany them. Then assess your modelling of these behaviours over the last 12 months.

Think of a couple of moments when your values have been compromised in organizational life, for example maybe you have been asked to do something that you didn't agree with. What did you do, and how did you manage your inner feelings and your behaviour? What does this tell you about the match between your values and those of the organization?

Select one of the leadership frameworks in this chapter and picture how you might fully develop into embodying that kind of leader.

References and further reading

Allport, G (1961) *Pattern and Growth in Personality,* Harcourt College Publications

Bandura, A (1986) *Social foundations of Thought and Action: A social cognitive theory*, Prentice Hall, Englewood Cliffs, NJ

Bass, B M and Bass, R (2008) *The Bass Handbook of Leadership*, Simon & Schuster, CA

Block, P (1993) *Stewardship: Choosing service over self-interest*, Berrett-Koehler Publishers, San Francisco

Brown, M E and Trevino, L K (2006) Ethical leadership: a review and future directions, *The Leadership Quarterly*, **17**, pp. 595–616

Cameron, E and Green, M (2015) *Making Sense of Change Management*, Kogan Page, London

Cashman (1998) *Leadership from the Inside Out*, Berrett-Koehler, San Francisco

Cashman (2003) *Awakening the Leader Within*, John Wiley & Sons, New Jersey

Collins, J (2001) *Good to Great*, William Collins, USA

Collins, J and Porras, J (1994) *Built to Last*, Random House, New York

Covey, S (1990) *The 7 Habits of Highly Effective People*, Information Australia Group, Melbourne

Dirks, K T and Ferrin, D L (2002) Trust in leadership: meta-analytic findings and implications for research and practice, *Journal of Applied Psychology* 87 (4), pp. 611–628

Farrell, R (2009) Principles of 'value-based leadership': drawing upon his experiences at P&G, President and CEO Bob McDonald outlines 10 characteristics of a great leader, *Kellog School of Management* [online] http://www.kellogg.north-western.edu/news_articles/2009/bob_mcdonald.aspx [accessed 13 July 2016]

Fernandez, J E and Hogan, R T (2002) Values-based leadership, *Journal for Quality and Participation*, **25** (4), (Winter) pp. 25–27

Freedland, J (2016) Post-truth politicians such as Boris Johnson and Donald Trump are no joke, *Guardian*, 13 May

Gardner, W L, Cogliser, C C, Davis, K M and Dickens, M P (2011) Authentic leadership: a review of the literature and research agenda, *Leadership Quarterly*, **22**, pp. 1120–45

George, B, Sims, P Mclean A, Mayer (2007) Discovering your authentic leadership, *Harvard Business Review*, February

Gosling, J, Jones, S and Sutherlands, I, with Dijkstra, J (2012) *Key Concepts in Leadership*, Sage, London

Greenleaf, R K (1970) *The Servant as a Leader*, Greenleaf Center, Indianapolis, IN

Higgs, M (2006) Course material prepared for Henley Management College

Kernis, M H (2003) Toward a conceptualization of optimal self-esteem, *Psychology Inquiry*, **14**, pp. 1–26

Kernis, M H and Goldman, B M (2006) A multicomponent conceptualization of authenticity: theory and research, *Advances in Experimental Social Psychology*, **38**, pp. 283–357

Kirkpatrick, S A and Locke, E A (1991) Leadership: do traits matter? *Academy of Management Executive*, 5 (2) pp. 48–60

Kouzes, J M and Posner, B Z (1995) *The Leadership Challenge: How to keep getting extraordinary things done in organizations*, Jossey-Bass, California

Kraemer Jr, H M J (2011) *From Values to Action: The four principles of values-based leadership*, Jossey-Bass, California

Laub's Organizational Leadership assessment, *OLA Group* [online] http://www.olagroup.com/ [accessed 20 October 2016]

Levitt, S (2008) From good to great… to below average, *Freakonomics* [online] http://freakonomics.com/2008/07/28/from-good-to-great-to-below-average/ [accessed 14 July 2016[

Luthans, F and Avolio, B J (2003) Authentic leadership: positive developmental approach, in *Positive Organizational Scholarship*, ed K S Cameron, J E Dutton and R E Quinn, Berrett-Koehler, San Francisco, pp. 241–61

McAllister, D J (1995) Affect- and cognition-based trust as foundations for inter-personal co-operation in organizations, *Academy of Management Journal*, **38** (1) pp. 24–59

Parris, D L Peachey, J W (2013) A systematic literature review of servant leadership theory in organizational contexts, *Journal of Business Ethics*, **113**, pp. 377–93

Posner, B Z and Schmidt, W H (1992) Demographic characteristics and shared values, *International Journal of Value-Based Management*, **5** (1) pp. 77–87

Schein, E (2004) *Organizational Culture and Leadership*, 3rd edn, Jossey Bass, San Francisco

Schwartz, S H (1994) Are there universal aspects in the structure and contents of human values? *Journal of Social Issues*, **50** (4), pp. 19–45

Seidman, D (2010) Ethical Leadership: an operating manual, *Bloomberg* [online] http://www.bloomberg.com/news/articles/2010-12-17/ethical-leadership-an-operating-manual [accessed 12 July 2016]

Senge, P (1990), *The Fifth Discipline: The art and practice of the learning organization*, Doubleday, NY

Spears L C, ed (1998) *Insights on Leadership*, John Wiley, New York

Stride, H (2011) Personal and organizational values, in *Leadership and Personal Development*, ed Kruckeberg *et al.*, IAP, Charlotte NC

Walumbwa, F O, Avolio, B J, Gardner, W L, Wernsing, T S and Peterson, S J (2008)
Authentic leadership: development and validation of a theory-based measure, *Journal of Management*, **34**, pp. 89–126

Wheatley, M (2005), *Finding Our Way: Leadership for an uncertain time*, Berrett-
Koehler, San Francisco

Whitehead, G (2008) Adolescent Leadership development: building a case for
an authenticity framework, *Educational Management Administration &
Leadership*, 37 (6)

Yukl, G A (2013) *Leadership in Organizations*, Pearson

Leading across organizations and networks   10

Introduction

Leadership is often conceived as something which happens at the very top of an organization. Although, of course, people readily refer to the senior executives as the 'leadership team', managers of specific groups are also given the title of 'team leader'; these leaders are often managing employees at the front line of the organization's operations.

In addition, we note the breaking down of organizational boundaries, with partnering and outsourcing in the private sector; complex supply chains everywhere; multi-agency working and shared services in the public sector; and, increasingly, 'public-private partnerships'.

Add to this mix the growth in home working; the rise in innovative SMEs with teams from around the globe where they rarely meet, if at all, and whose leaders might be considered 'virtual leaders'.

Considering the changing nature of organizations and leadership within these organizations, this chapter aims to answer the questions:

- Where does leadership reside in an organization?
- What are the different ways we can describe leadership when it doesn't reside solely with just one individual at the very top of the organization?

To answer these questions, we explore the notions of shared leadership, distributed leadership, systemic leadership and collaborative leadership. Each of these approaches for leading across boundaries differs in terms of the types of task and the organizational span they can readily be applied to. This is set out in Figure 10.1.

Key frameworks, research and critique

Shared leadership

The concept of 'shared leadership' reflects the idea that problem solving and decision making are conducted in a shared manner across a team, with collective responsibility. It is therefore implicit in shared leadership that the interactions between people within the system or traditional leadership team can have leadership elements flowing in all directions (Pearce and Conger, 2003). As well as sharing leadership, an individual will exhibit an element of autonomy in demonstrating leadership with peers, downwards and upwards, and, naturally, across projects and other shared endeavours. A key differentiator from delegated leadership is that shared leadership can flow both ways in equal measure.

And of course the behaviours which accompany this shared leadership concept need to be congruent with that concept. So if you are technically above someone in the organizational hierarchy, a key challenge is to avoid slipping into a traditional top-down leadership style. Pearce and Manz (2005) suggest that in this situation, you need to: avoid authoritarian control; not over-rely on any one person to take the lead; relinquish the role of being the heroic top-down leader; allow power and influence to circulate freely; allow others' views to be articulated before yours; and ask others for input through engagement and dialogue. Contracting and continuous dialogue are key too, in the form of peer-to-peer influencing.

Shared leadership can manifest in different forms. For example, accountability can be shared for the delivery of a policy or project; or the leadership of a team can be rotated dependent on the needs of the situation and, for example, the skills, knowledge and experiences of the team. Pearce (2004) suggests that some of the indicators of the need for shared leadership are when high levels of interdependence and creativity are called for, and the task or situation is complex.

However, Pearce also suggests that vertical and shared leadership are not incompatible. Indeed, he sees the role of the vertical manager in designing the team (for example team purpose, recruitment, roles, operating processes, etc.) and setting the team boundaries as being a key enabler to encourage shared leadership, for example amongst a leadership team. Additionally, he sees the need for a watching brief from the manager – spotting any gaps or misalignment, and making interventions to sustain momentum – as also the responsibility of the vertical leader.

Distributed leadership

Whereas shared leadership is often seen as more of a horizontal phenomenon, distributed leadership could be conceived as power and authority being distributed across the organization vertically, horizontally and diagonally. However, in the same way that shared leadership doesn't just mean allocation of different leadership segments to different individuals adding up to one whole, distributed leadership isn't just the component parts of a leadership task distributed across the organization.

Bennett *et al.* (2003) reinforce this view – it is not delegation, it is not dissemination of tasks; distributed leadership is a 'group activity that works through and within relationships, rather than individual action'. Uhl-Bien (2006) builds on this by saying it is a 'collective social process emerging through the interactions of multiple actors'.

Bolden (2011) charts the history of distributed leadership back to Mary Parker Follett's (1942) work on reciprocal influence and Benne and Sheats' (1948) work on the diffusion of leadership functions within groups. Various writers (Pearce and Conger, 2003; Lipman-Blumen, 1996) highlight a range of factors that have contributed to the emergence of distributed leadership including changing nature of teams, the massive increase in information flow, the increasing complexity of roles (within organizations) and globalization and issues around diversity. All of these have contributed to the emergence of distributed leadership.

He reiterates Bennett *et al.*'s (2003) three premises of distributed leadership that seem to be shared by most authors. Distributed leadership:

- emerges as a consequence of the interactions between individuals belonging to a group or network;

- does not have closed boundaries;

- has differing expertise which is distributed across the network or group.

Bolden (2011) also highlights the many ways in which distributed leadership can manifest. He cites MacBeath, Oduro and Waterhouse's (2004) list of the different types of distributed leadership (see Box 10.1).

Distributed leadership is a relatively under-developed and under-researched concept, and as such there is little evidence of a positive correlation between distributed leadership and organizational performance. In the same way that some animals and insects have multiple brains or brains spread throughout their bodies, the idea of distributed leadership may well be suited to helping organizations become more agile in an ever more complex and changing world.

Box 10.1: Different types of distributed leadership

Formal distribution: through a process of delegation or devolution.

Pragmatic distribution: different individuals take on different roles and responsibilities through a process of discussion and negotiation.

Strategic distribution: when the organization requires leadership by someone internal or external who hasn't previously been required to exhibit it.

Incremental distribution: as part of a developmental or capability-increasing process.

Opportunistic distribution: when leadership is given or taken on an ad hoc basis.

Cultural distribution: when it is organizationally customary to distribute leadership across and around.

Figure 10.1   Leadership across organizations and networks – calibrating your approach

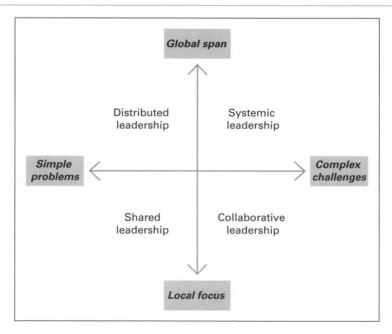

Systemic leadership

Traditional leadership theory has accentuated the use of power and influence in order to get individuals or groups to achieve a particular objective. Given the increasing levels of complexity within and without organizations, systemic leadership can be viewed as leadership that sees the organization, its past and future and its environment as a whole, evolving system or perhaps a cluster of interconnected sub-systems. The role of leadership is therefore an enabling function to facilitate the organization to achieve its objectives within the current, evolving context.

Pinnow (2011) sees the leader as part of a system; he or she needs to understand their part in the system as well as see the whole system, acknowledging that the whole system will have elements which may not be wholly visible. These invisible aspects of organizational culture are discussed by Stam (2006). He sees systemic leadership as a deep process of supporting an organization to understand the way its history, patterns of inclusion, exchange habits and leadership structures all influence organizational health and success (see Box 10.2).

Box 10.2

The systemic way of thinking and looking at the world helps us to become aware of the mechanisms and dynamics that are at work in systems that we normally never notice. These are the dynamics that can, in one moment, give us wings to fly and in another moment, hold us paralysed and unable to act. (Stam, 2006)

The need for systemic leadership can be best illustrated when exhibited in complex adaptive systems. The authors have discussed elsewhere (Cameron and Green, 2015) how some organizations can be seen as complex adaptive systems and how in their capacity to change and learn from experience, they can produce coherence, continuity and transformation in the absence of any external blueprint or nominated designer.

The control of a complex adaptive system is highly dispersed and decentralized. The whole system's behaviour appears to arise from competition and cooperation among the local agents in the system, coupled with sensitivity to amplifying or dampening feedback (see Box 10.3).

Box 10.3: Characteristics of complex adaptive systems

There is no central control.

There is an inherent underlying structure within the system.

There is feedback in the system.

There is nonlinearity; things do not happen in a cause and effect manner.

Emergence is an outcome of the system. This happens without planned intent.

The system is non-reducible. This means that you cannot understand the system's behaviour by looking at one part. It is necessary instead to look at a representative slice of all of the parts.

(Cameron and Green, 2015)

Pinnow suggests that there needs therefore to be a shift from believing one can lead the organization, to a state where one is asking: how can I assist the system to lead itself? This can be done by endeavouring to create the optimal conditions and incentives for people, and also to enable an environment where the system can learn about and develop its capacity and capability for learning and developing! Van Velsor, Taylor and Leslie (2006) stress that this is also a continuing learning and development process for systemic leaders themselves. Pinnow (2011) concludes that the systemic leader needs to focus on eight key behaviours (see Box 10.4).

Box 10.4

1. Self-knowledge
Understanding yourself and your motivations, the limits to your competence and the impact you have on others.
Being authentic by having an inner moral compass which guides decisions and direction.

2. Communication
Enabling free flow of information across the system.
Connecting the right people to the right issues.
Seeking feedback.

3. Being able to let go
Delegating and distributing tasks and responsibilities within a framework of clear goals, responsibilities and priorities.

4. Withstanding conflicts
Allowing conflict and tensions to emerge and engaging people in weighing alternatives and balancing change with stability.

5. Dealing with change
Change management should be embedded within the system and draw on best practice (stakeholder engagement, good communications, etc.).

6. Conferring meaning
Conferring meaning through providing context, point and purpose to decisions and necessary actions.

7. Having power
Exerting influence from a base of relational power and expertise.

8. Providing guidance and making decisions
Role modelling, example setting and taking difficult decisions even when uncertain of the outcomes.

(Pinnow, 2011)

Collaborative leadership

There are two situations where collaborative leadership is required:

- When there is a coming together of different entities for a common purpose – a coalition (eg in politics); a consortium (eg for a complex project or product development); a partnership (eg between two complementary private sector businesses); multi-agency working (eg between various public sector bodies to tackle a cross-cutting theme).

- When no single individual has the wherewithal to take ultimate leadership responsibility, and it is shared around the group, based on criteria such as skills set. Examples might be self-managing teams on a car assembly production line, or a group of MBA students placed together in a learning team to achieve module objectives.

In her 1994 *Harvard Business Review* article 'Collaborative advantage', Rosabeth Moss Kanter (1994) highlighted the notion of collaborative leadership across organizations (see Box 10.5). Specifically, she identified those situations which involved critical business relationships '… that cannot be controlled by formal systems but require a dense web of interpersonal connections…'

Box 10.5: Characteristics of effective collaborations across organizations

Individual organizational excellence.

Strategic importance.

Interdependence – the need for each other.

Investment of time, effort, resources.

Information sharing and data flow.

Integration – shared operating processes.

Institutionalization – formal status of the collaboration.

Integrity – development of a trustworthy relationship.

(Kanter,1994)

Chrislip and Larson (1994), researching in the public sector, suggest collaborative leaders can 'safeguard the process, facilitate interaction and patiently deal with high levels of frustration'. They go on to say that collaborative leadership can be employed in many situations, but they see more evidence in the public sector and in communities. It is most useful when there is no one person or stakeholder group 'in charge' with formal authority, and for situations or issues which are exceedingly complex. They underscore the point that collaborative leadership doesn't mean there is no responsibility or accountability; this needs to be discussed, worked through and agreed.

Chrislip and Larson see the key elements of collaborative leadership as:

- there is collaborative problem solving and decision making;
- the decision-making process is a collective one with an open process; and
- there is leadership of the process, not of the individuals or the group.

Collaborative leadership helps the collaborative process work to bring together multiple agendas towards a common purpose, but does not have the aim of leading people towards a given objective through charisma or persuasion.

Pause for Learning Points

This chapter has brought together a number of leadership theories or perspectives which challenge the notion of leadership being embodied in just one person, with the objective of the leader being to move people, however artfully, into a particular direction or towards a particular decision.

Shared leadership expands the notion of leadership away from the personality and behaviours of just one person towards a situation where there is more of a collective responsibility and accountability.

Distributed leadership focuses on the idea that, once again, leadership is not the sole prerogative of those at the top, but can manifest in all parts of the organization. This approach might lead towards a more coherent culture of leadership (see Part 6).

Systemic leadership is about acting as steward of and for the system, with the belief that with the right enabling interventions from the leader, the system acts as a complex adaptive system, and will organize itself towards its own chosen outcomes.

Finally, collaborative leadership – with similarities to shared and systemic leadership – is focused on a process of leadership which supports a broad, joint intent, agreed priorities and plans.

Stop and Reflect!

Reflect upon where leadership sits in your organization and how you would describe it – does it reside within one person; within the top team; is it shared amongst the top 100 leaders; or maybe continually distributed across the organization?

How shared is the leadership in your organization? What would be the advantages and disadvantages of moving closer to this framework in your department or between departments you know well?

What would be the benefits if there was more collaborative leadership in your organization and with partner organizations?

In what ways could you become a more systemic leader? What ways of thinking and new behaviours would you need to adopt in relation to that system, and what might this enable?

References and further reading

Benne, K D and Sheats, P (1948) Functional roles of group members, *Journal of Social Issues*, **4**, pp. 41–49

Bennett, N, Wise, C, Woods, P A and Harvey, J A (2003) *Distributed Leadership*, National College of School Leadership, Nottingham

Bolden, R (2011) Distributed leadership in organizations: a review of theory and research, *International Journal of Management Reviews*, **13** (3), pp. 251–69

Cameron, E and Green, M (2015) *Making Sense of Change Management*, Kogan Page, London

Chrislip, D and Larson, C (1994) *Collaborative Leadership*, Jossey-Bass, San Francisco

Follett, M P (1942/2003) *Dynamic Administration: The collected papers of Mary Parker Follett*, Routledge, London

Kanter, R M (1994) Collaborative advantage: the art of alliances, *Harvard Business Review*, **72** (4) pp. 96–108

Lipman-Blumen, J (1996) *Connective Leadership: Managing in a changing world*, Oxford University Press, Oxford

MacBeath, J, Oduro, G K T and Waterhouse, J (2004) *Distributed Leadership in Action: A study of current practice in schools*, National College for School Leadership, Nottingham

Pearce, C L (2004) The future of leadership: combining vertical and shared leadership to transform knowledge work, *The Academy of Management Executive*, **18** (1), pp.47–59

Pearce, C L and Conger, J A (2003) *Shared Leadership: Reframing the hows and whys of leadership*, Sage, London

Pearce, C L and Manz, C C (2005) The new silver bullets of leadership: the importance of self- and shared leadership in knowledge work, *Organizational Dynamics*, **34** (2), pp. 130–40

Pinnow, D F (2011) *Systemic Leadership in Leadership and Personal Development: A toolbox for the 21st-century professional*, IAP, Charlotte NC

Senge, P and Kaufer, K H (2000) Communities of leaders or no leadership at all, in *Cutting Edge: Leadership*, ed B Kellerman and L R Matusak, James Macgregor Burns Academy, College Park, MD

Spillane, J P (2006) *Distributed Leadership*, Jossey-Bass, San Francisco

Stam, J J (2006) *Fields of Connection*, Uitgeverij Het Noorderlicht

Uhl-Bien, M (2006) Relational leadership theory: exploring the social processes of leadership and organizing, *The Leadership Quarterly*, **17** (6)

Van Velsor, E, Taylor, S and Leslie, J (2006), An examination of the relationships among self-perception accuracy, self-awareness, gender, and leadership effectiveness, *Human Resource Management*, **23**, pp. 249–63

Leadership health: mind, body and spirit

Introduction

With recent advances in neuroscience and popular interest in 'positive psychology' (the study of happiness and personal growth) there's now increased interest within leadership circles in the physical and psychological processes that impact the quality of human functioning at work. Much of this interest, and therefore associated research, tends to focus on the links between people's mental, emotional and physical states and their capacity to perform. The intent is to find out what personal or organizational interventions can support continued health and happiness.

The prevalence of stress and anxiety at work, the increased competitiveness and vulnerability of many organizations, and the worrying rise of mental health issues in many geographies makes this an extremely important subject. Personality type can affect an individual's vulnerability to stress and anxiety (see Big Five personality dimensions, Chapter 5), and of course some leaders are more capable than others at building their own and others' capacity to ride the waves of change and build their own resilience (see Heifetz, Chapter 8).

In this chapter we give a flavour of what enables leaders to thrive and to create an environment that their teams can thrive in. This means building trust, being able to handle setbacks, making good decisions, engaging others and bringing their own creativity.

We also touch on the deeper and far less tangible topic of the 'human spirit'. Given the stresses and strains of the organizational world, and the enormous potential than human beings have for creativity and expression, we discuss how leaders can make sure this aspect of our nature is healthily embraced, and what happens when it is suppressed.

The aims of this chapter are therefore to:

- identify some of the implications of recent neuroscience research for leaders and HR professionals;

- show what recent neuroscience research appears to indicate about achieving sustained high performance and resilience at work;

- find out whether the ability to manage emotions and build relationships can be learned, and if this actually makes a leader more effective;

- discover ways in which leaders can stay healthily connected to their 'human spirit', and what can happen if they don't.

Key frameworks, research and critique

Lessons from neuroscience

Neuroscience is the study of the brain and associated nervous systems which examines how these systems are structured and what they do. While this study began as a branch of biology, it now involves mathematicians, linguistic experts, engineers and many more disciplines. Advances in brain imaging in particular have great appeal for those who yearn for scientific proof of the effectiveness of different leadership strategies, although the interpretation of such images is still very much in its infancy and the results need to be treated with caution.

The attraction of neuroscience for leaders and HR professionals is that it can start to give hard evidence to support training and advice for leaders on how to build good relationships, make good-quality decisions and enable employees to learn and grow.

A crucial understanding emerging from neuroscience is that the brain and body are inextricably interconnected via the nervous system, through neurotransmitters and hormones. An individual's experience of emotions can be observed in a rudimentary way via brain scans, and we know that particular chemicals in the body are involved. The science is new and fast-moving, so lessons for leaders are tentative at present, although some writers are already rushing to assumptions. Here are some of the latest highlights.

Trust and fear

Trust is a key area of exploration for neuroscience, and an important concept for leaders, particularly given that recent Gallup studies into employee loyalty and engagement point to the importance of a trusting relationship with the immediate line manager. Without trust, it's difficult to inspire and motivate people. It appears that oxytocin, a calming neurotransmitter used by the brain, underpins trust and bonding behaviour (Brown, Swart and Meyer, 2009). This chemical is released when we sense psychological support, and tends to lead to a reduction of fear, a relaxation of boundaries, and a movement towards the source.

Fear, alongside trust, is also deeply seated in the 'feeling and reacting' part of our brain, known as the limbic system. It is known as a 'survival' emotion, alongside anger, disgust, shame and sadness which all lead to forms of avoidance and complex behaviours. Neuroscience research tells us that feelings of fear can restrict the brain's ability to do anything but focus on this, thus dampening creativity, innovation, learning, relationship building, etc. (Brown, Swart and Meyer, 2009) Thus the threat of being sacked or demoted, or leaders who focus on what's wrong in an aggressive or non-empathetic way, are not likely to be motivating in any positive sense, and more likely to trigger compliance and/or avoidance (see Chapter 7 for effects on creativity).

Making decisions

Decision making can be complex and exposing for leaders in today's organizations. Small-scale studies cited in Swart, Chisholm and Brown (2015) show that it's important to be calm, hydrated and adequately resourced with bodily energy. Similarly, bias can be created by one's emotional state, recent events, beliefs and values, affectionate memories or favourite processes. These need to be held in awareness and counter-balanced by a combination of good-quality, probing research and taking the space to ponder and sense into deeper 'gut' feelings by, for example, going on a walk in the woods.

Learning agility

Neuroplasticity is an exciting new concept arising from neuroscience, which indicates that the brain's structure changes over time with learning. New neurons and neural connections can be formed and existing connections strengthened throughout our lives. Factors such as focus, practice and reward impact this learning in various ways, and it's now clear that lack of repetition and practice leads to a reversion of this (Swart, Chisholm and Brown, 2013).

This discovery has all sorts of possibilities in the education and health arenas as it offers good-quality evidence of the need for adult learners to practise and get feedback, and to be rewarded somehow for progress. It is important news for leaders too: learning agility is becoming more important as leaders and their teams are increasingly required to adapt to new business models, work across cultures and generations, tackle multiple projects and learn to work more collaboratively. This research points to how learning can be properly embedded and helps leaders to accept that without at least some real-world practice and good-quality feedback, people are unlikely to change their behaviours.

What supports sustained performance and overall resilience?

Where neuroscience meets positive psychology, referred to above, is in the area of sustaining high performance and building resilience. Both are areas of great interest to leaders. In the quest for sustained high performance, neuroscience points to factors such as sleep, nutrition and exercise, which all have a positive impact.

Lack of sleep can temporarily lower your IQ and deny your brain the opportunity to flush out potentially neurotoxic waste products. Deeper REM sleep, only experienced after 4–6 hours of sleep, helps perform essential information-sorting activities and embeds learning (Connolly, Ruderman and Leslie, 2014).

In addition to sleep, healthy nutrition, hydration, exercise and oxygenating your brain via deep breathing are prerequisites for sustained high performance at work. For instance, significant cardiovascular exercise helps produce the neurotransmitter serotonin, which can be similar to the effects of an anti-depressant and may boost productivity. Hydration is also important, and research shows that if it drops, it can impact memory and concentration (Cian *et al.*, 2000). The avoidance of caffeine and alcohol, and the introduction of various vitamins, teas and oils is also supported by multiple pieces of research.

Resilience, defined as the ability to pick yourself up after a setback, or to keep going despite multiple difficulties, is a human quality sought by many organizations. Can people build their resilience, and if so, how?

Martin Seligman, known as the father of positive psychology, refers to the importance of emotional, social, family, spiritual and physical fitness to overall resilience. He believes that individuals can learn to manage emotions in a more positive way, and to be more optimistic about their lives (Duckworth, Steen and Seligman, 2005) such that this positively impacts their resilience.

Other recent studies (see Big Five, Chapter 5) indicate that certain characteristics such as conscientiousness, openness and lower levels of anxiety all contribute to greater resilience. Of course, these are often enabled through childhood by secure parenting, living in a stable society, access to education and sufficient economic resources.

The question of how to build and strengthen resilience as a leader is partly answered exactly as the above high performance question, ie sleep, nutrition and exercise. In addition, recent studies indicate that the factors below can have a powerful impact over the longer term:

- regular journaling, which helps release or rebalance the negative effects of the 'survival' emotions mentioned above by taking a more objective look at one's own performance;

- coaching that's informed by psychology and neuroscience can help to build more positive responses to difficulties, and help develop new patterns of thinking and acting

- meditation and mindfulness, over time, can train the mind to focus and be calm, thus reducing the reactivity of the limbic system to negative triggers (Tang, Holzel and Posner, 2015).

Figure 11.1 Building blocks of resilience

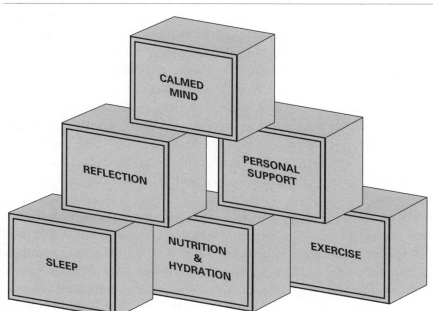

Managing emotions and building relationships

Since the 1960s, academics have tried to define a set of skills and capacities that represent an individual's ability to work well with emotions and relationships. Supporters of this work say that these skills, referred to as 'EQ', have just as much, if not more impact than IQ on people's levels of success and happiness. Claims have been made that EQ is correlated with psychological well-being, performance at work and leadership effectiveness, although studies of these causal links give mixed results.

Daniel Goleman (1995, 1998) popularized the notion of 'emotional intelligence' and was the first to establish a working model and apply it to the world of leadership (others have followed with similar models). The five core domains of Goleman's definition of emotional intelligence or EQ are:

- knowing your emotions;
- managing your own emotions;
- motivating yourself;
- recognizing and understanding other people's emotions;
- managing relationships.

This range of skills is said to enable an individual to be aware of their own emotions, manage these, understand and work with the territory of emotions, build satisfactory relationships and navigate the wider, social environment. Various instruments have been designed to measure this intelligence, for example the Emotional Competency Inventory (ECI) or the Mayer-Salovey-Caruso Emotional Intelligence Test (MSCEIT).

Goleman's framework represents a set of capabilities that he claims are twice as important as cognitive intelligence and technical skills to a leader's capacity to deliver organizational outcomes. Although this claim has been contested by others (Brown, Bryant and Reilly, 2006) and the model itself has been criticized by psychologists for being unscientific (Eysenck, 2000), it remains extremely influential in the fields of leadership and personal development.

The notion of EQ is supported by positive psychology research which indicates that people *can learn* to influence both their own emotions and their own level of happiness or satisfaction, which in turn is likely to impact their ability to build good-quality relationships with high levels of mutual trust. As the neuroscience work above indicates, the ability to build good relationships with high levels of trust is fundamental to leadership success. However, developing these skills in adults is takes sustained, focused work over time.

A crisis of leadership spirit?

It would seem odd to have a chapter on 'Mind, Body and Spirit' that doesn't refer in some way to our inner depths, our yearnings, our desires and our wider potential as human beings, which some call 'spirit'.

Although much of the discourse and research on leadership appears rational and logical, the reality of our lives and the impact that leadership can have on us is much more mysterious and wide-reaching. The subject of leadership is a good deal more emotional and irrational than we may be willing to admit. Some would argue that leadership is more of a humanities or arts subject than a science, but perhaps it's actually all of these!

Human potential and depth

In this section we're interested in encouraging leaders to open up to this area of human potential and mystery, and exploring the dangers of denying or ignoring this deeper side of our nature. Too much rationality and order can be problematic. When there is change and a loosening of the usual rules, leaders need to be able to tolerate chaos and disorder within their deeper psyches, making them more like artists or creative thinkers (Zaleznik, 2004).

Myths and stories

One way of exploring this potential is through myths and stories. If a leader tells a story, or uses a particular image, this can impact followers deeply and in quite a different way to a series of arguments backed up by data. In his book about narrative leadership, Geoff Mead (2014) explains how important it is for leaders to master the art of imaginative storytelling, particularly in complex change contexts. He says, 'Our ability to change ourselves, our organizations and the world depends on our capacity to re-imagine them: nothing changes unless the story changes.' This is about tapping into the deeper 'meaning-making' capacities that humans have and realizing that the meaning we make of our own lives can influence significantly the way our lives turn out.

Although people are alert to the possibility of being manipulated through leadership 'spin' and narrative, we can all think of examples of leaders who tell stories about themselves (true or false) that encourage us to believe in their potency and to support them. You may be able to think of examples of this in politicians you know well. Despite our rational society in the United States, the UK and beyond, we are still prone to being impacted by this, which can be wonderfully positive and liberating, or terribly dangerous and destructive depending on the leader's intentions. A more skillful and valuable leadership art is to lead in a way that begins to build an imaginative, credible story that unites and engages people from all sorts of backgrounds and loyalties.

Inner lives of leaders

To be able to be imaginative while delivering outcomes in a high-pressure, complex context demands capacity, and requires a healthy creative spirit and inner life.

The inner lives of leaders is a subject that is often left out of leadership programmes or MBA studies. Self-awareness is one thing, but finding the space to discover and keep in good contact with our own depths is more difficult, and may be painful or uncomfortable for some. It requires spending time alone, processing one's thoughts and digesting one's experiences. This can pave the way to capacities such as imaginative and/or strategic thinking, creative problem solving, or collaborative working, without having to actively work on specific issues or problems.

The kind of inner space and imaginative capacity that effective leaders need can be opened up in a variety of ways: examples are books or films, meditating, journaling, walking, mindfulness, and yoga. Increasingly, leaders are warming to the possibilities of this territory via some of the above practices, often supported by executive coaching from those experienced in adult development and depth psychology (Schuster, 2014).

Stress and crisis

Given the amount of stress that many leaders are under and the difficulty of dealing with this, a crisis may occur at some point in a leader's life. This may be a crisis of confidence, or meaning, or a more suppressed inner crisis that's hard to fathom. Symptoms vary and may include difficulty in concentrating and sleeping. Depth psychologists might say that a crisis happens when a leader is not able to face up to the reality of their lives and their own limits, and is somehow avoiding the extremely difficult process of fully growing up.

If a crisis of this type is suppressed or ignored, and not given space to be attended to (eg through talking about it to a good friend, doctor or coach) destructive events may start to occur: an extra-marital affair, bouts of aggression, various forms of self-medication, impetuous or risky behaviour, health problems, depression and even thoughts of suicide.

Some will deny the existence of such patterns and phenomena, arguing that life is unpredictable and these crises don't necessarily mean anything (Atkins, 2016). The writings of Thomas Moore, James Hillman and Ginette Paris make good starting points if you're interested in finding out more about the psyche and challenging yourself to develop your human potential and inner life at a deeper level.

Pause for Learning Points

Neuroscience is an emerging field with many possible applications for leaders, most of which are yet to be fully understood and worked through. This chapter offers insights into:

- the debilitating effects of 'survival' emotions on learning and creativity and how leaders need to counteract this by building trust and safety;
- the positive effects of good nutrition, exercise, hydration, sleep and breathing on decision making and sustained performance;
- the danger of biases and complexity in decision making;
- how neuroplasticity shows that it's possible for people to learn new ways of thinking and acting later on in life, with effort.

Resilience is enhanced by the same factors as sustained performance and decision making, as well as learning how to manage your own emotions. In leaders, it can be enhanced by regular journaling, good-quality coaching, meditation and mindfulness.

Emotional intelligence, as defined by Goleman (1995) is a powerful model, used to help people develop their ability to be more emotionally aware and more attuned in their interactions. For leaders, this is likely to impact trust levels at work, enhance the morale of teams and deliver more successful organizational outcomes.

Rather than being a wholly logical, rational science, leadership can be highly affecting in mysterious ways, both for followers and for the leaders themselves. Many leaders face a crisis of some sort in their leadership lives, particularly given the levels of anxiety experienced, and maybe suppressed, in today's society. It is important that this type of crisis is given space and attention.

Stop and Reflect!

How is trust built or damaged in your organization or an organization you know well? What psychological supports are present at an individual, team and organizational level which enable employees to speak up about important issues, and what threats are present that get in the way of this? What behaviours would you want to both appreciate and suggest to i) your line manager and ii) your line manager's line manager?

Think about your own level of resilience to setbacks and pressure. How would you rate yourself out of 10? Whatever your score is, note down all the ideas you can gather from this chapter about building and sustaining your resilience. List three simple aims which you can stick to over the coming month. Share them with a colleague and ask him or her to follow up in four weeks' time.

References and further reading

Atkins, R (2016) Ex-Zurich chief's suicide highlights executive stress, *Financial Times*, 31 May

Brown, F W, Bryant, S E and Reilly, M D (2006) Does emotional intelligence as measured by the EQI influence transformational leadership and/or desirable outcomes? *Leadership and Organizational Development Journal*, **27** (5), pp. 330–51

Brown, P, Swart, T and Meyer, J (2009) Emotional intelligence and the amygdala: towards the development of the concept of the limbic leaders in executive coaching, *Neuroleadership Journal*, **2** pp. 1–11

Cherniss, C, Extein, M, Goleman, D and Weisberg, R P (2010) Emotional intelligence: what does the research really indicate? *Educational Psychologist*, June

Cian, C *et al.* (2000) Influence of variations in body hydration on cognitive function: effect of hyperhydration, heat stress, and exercise-induced dehydration, *Journal of Psychophysiology*, **14**, pp. 29–36

Connolly, C, Ruderman, M and Leslie, J B (2014), *Sleep Well, Lead Well*, Center for Creative Leadership, NC

Cranston, S and Keller, S (2013) Increasing the meaning quotient of work, *Mckinsey Quarterly*, January

Delgado, M (2008) To trust or not to trust: ask Oxytocin, *Scientific American*, July

Duckworth, A L Steen, T and Seligman, M E P (2005) Positive psychology in clinical practice, *Annual Review of Clinical Psychology*, 1, pp. 629–51

Eysenck, H (2000) *Intelligence: A new look*, Transaction Publishers, New Jersey

Goleman, D (1995) *Emotional Intelligence*, Bantam Books, New York

Goleman, D (1998) What makes a leader, *Harvard Business Review*, 76, November–December, pp. 93–102

Goleman, D and Boyatzis, R (2008) Social intelligence and the biology of leadership, *Harvard Business Review*, September

Guthrie, T (2016) Taboos within business about mental illness need challenging, *Financial Times*, 1 May

Hillman, J (1997) *Kinds of Power*, Doubleday, New York

Jacobs, E (2016) The managers who hold the line on workplace stress, *Financial Times*, 2 February

Korn, C (2012) The neuroscience of looking at the bright side, *Scientific American* [online] http://www.scientificamerican.com/article/neuroscience-looking-bright-side/

Lyubomirsky, S (2008). *The How of Happiness: A scientific approach to getting the life you want*, Penguin Press, New York

Mann, A and Harter, J (2016), The worldwide employee engagement crisis, *Gallup Business Journal* [online] www.gallup.com

Mead, G (2014) *Telling the Story*, John Wiley & Sons

Moore, T (2009) *A Life at Work*, Piatkus, London

Paris, G (2016) *Wisdom of the Psyche, Beyond Neuroscience*, Routledge, Abingdon

Petrie, N (2014) *Wake Up! The surprising truth about what drives stress and how leaders build resilience*, Center for Creative Leadership, NC

Ruderman, M N, Clerkin, C and Connolly, C (2014) *Leadership Development Beyond Competencies: Moving to a holistic approach*, Center for Creative Leadership White Paper

Satel, S and Lillenfied, S (2015) *Brainwashed: The seductive appeal of mindless neuroscience*, Basic Books

Swart, T, Chisholm, K and Brown, P (2015) *Neuroscience for Leadership*, Palgrave, Basingstoke

Schuster, J (nd) Therapy, depth psychology and executive coaching [online] http://www.johnpschuster.com/wp-content/uploads/2014/05/Coaching-and-Therapy-Article-Layout.pdf [accessed 18 August 2016]

Tang, Y Y, Holzel, B K and Posner, M I (2015) The neuroscience of mindful meditation, *Neuroscience*, 16, pp. 213–25

Tang, Y Y *et al.* (2007) Short-term meditation training improves attention and self-regulation, *Proceedings of the National Academy of Sciences*, **104** (43) pp. 17152–56

Zaleznick, A (2004) Managers and Leaders, Are they Different? (2004), *Harvard Business Review* **82** (1) pp. 74–81

An overall map of leadership

Creating an integrated framework

Chapters 2–11 set out what we believe to be the most significant elements of research and thinking about leadership over the past 100 years. Here we demonstrate how we have synthesized and distilled this accumulated wisdom into an integrated framework for 21st-century leaders.

The aims of this section are to:

- explain how and why we created this integrated framework;
- describe the key clusters of skills and qualities that arose, and how they relate to the theory;
- introduce the Five Leadership Qualities Framework in summary form.

Chapters 2–11 are likely to have been stimulating for you in various ways. Some frameworks may have been affirming of your existing knowledge, ideas or approaches, whereas others may have been more challenging or harder to grasp. Maybe you have found one element particularly provocative and wish to focus on that; or another that you have wanted to push away for some reason and don't wish to return to. Whatever your response, most people start to yearn for an overall map of the territory with some useful signposts!

In meeting this need for a map, we sought significant clusters amongst all these models of leadership, and turned these into a succinct set of leadership qualities for 21st-century organizations. Our sense was that these qualities needed to offer sufficient structure and form, whilst encouraging growth and development through improving skills, developing capacities and learning how to weave deft combinations of the qualities. In essence, we wanted to distil essential leadership archetypes that guide leaders as they gain experience and mature.

We also wanted this new set of roles to cover horizontal and vertical leadership. This means embracing all the important fundamental skills and competencies, as well as giving headroom for leaders to expand from individual influencer, to team leader, to entrepreneur, right through to CEO. We also wanted the qualities to be readily accessible, yet open enough for people's imaginations to fill them in.

Growing your own style

We're not wishing to predict or recommend a natural leadership style for any one person, or to pin leadership down to a set of competencies. We're not saying that everyone should have a particular leadership style. What we do strongly believe is that if you are serious about developing yourself as a leader, all Five Qualities that we are about to describe are open to you to master. Some will be a lot easier for you to develop than others. Leadership is something you need to grow into, and your own particular 'recipe' will emerge and mature over time. However, as you'll see in Part Three, this takes work and you need to be sufficiently motivated and supported to do this. Help is available in Part Four!

How the leadership clusters emerged

We spent many months in 2007 digesting a very wide selection of leadership literature, much of which is referred to in this book. We entered into deep dialogues around this material and our own experiences of good practice in organizations, and from this we started to see clusters of leadership qualities emerging, which were gathered around key areas of leadership focus described below. The relationship between the contents of Part Two and these clusters is explained in the summaries below, plus there is a comprehensive table at the end of this section that sets out the significant connections by chapter.

Archetype 1: The Architect

Focusing on design, the Architect crafts seemingly disparate ideas and information into a well-thought-out, structured way forward and continually scans the environment for patterns and feedback.

This archetype combines the following theoretical and research elements:

- how cognitive ability supports leaders to see patterns and possibilities (Kirkpatrick and Locke, 1991);
- the importance of stepping back and reflecting on your leadership (Hersey and Blanchard, 1969);
- the use of aspects of Personal Power (Yukl, 2013);
- the need to stimulate followers intellectually (Bass, 1985);
- the importance of ideas generation (Bel, 2010);
- how various strategic skills need to be mastered (Schoemaker *at al.*, 2013).
- how gaining a clear picture and being able to frame this for others is a key leadership skill (Heifetz and Laurie, 1997; Higgs and Rowland, 2005);
- the need for leaders to reflect, take space, contact their inner guidance and depths (Swart, Chisholm and Brown, 2015; Schuster, 2014).

Archetype 2: The Motivator

Focusing on buy-in, the Motivator taps into their own and other people's passions, articulates a compelling picture or vision of the future, motivates and inspires people to engage in the way ahead.

This archetype combines the following theoretical and research elements:

- the link between extraversion, self-confidence and leadership success (Saucier and Goldberg, 1998; Northouse, 2007);
- the importance of expectation-setting (Vroom and Jago, 1988);
- use of supporting and coaching skills to increase commitment (Hersey and Blanchard, 1969);
- how leaders influence via push and pull, and aspects of transformational leadership (Dent, 2009; Bass, 1985);
- the importance of inspiring a shared vision, modelling the way, and encouraging the heart (Kouznes and Posner, 2003);
- the role for leaders in managing emotions, recognizing and understanding other peoples' emotions (Goleman, 1995, 1998);
- imaginative storytelling (Mead, 2014).

Archetype 3: The Connector

Focusing on connectivity, the Connector reinforces what's important, establishes a few simple rules, connects people and agendas, brings care to process and establishes safety in a measured way.
This archetype combines the following theoretical and research elements:

- the link between sociability, integrity and leadership success (Northouse, 2007; Yukl, 2013);
- the importance of focusing on relationship 'in the middle ground' (Fiedler, 1967; Bennett *et al.*, 2003);
- use of 'supporting and coaching' skills to increase confidence (Hersey and Blanchard, 1969);
- how leaders influence through the use of 'pull', including questioning and listening (Dent and Brent, 2009);
- the importance of 'Individualized Consideration' through mentoring advice giving, empathy (Bass, 1985);
- how interactive leadership supports innovation through, for example, empowerment (Bossink, 2007; Kouznes and Posner, 2003);
- successful outcomes in a complex system result from high-quality interactions and collaboration (Lichtenstein *et al.*, 2006; Chrislip and Larson, 1994);
- significance of servant leadership, personal humility, care about others, trust (Laub, 1999; Collins, 2001; Brown and Trevino, 2006; Brown, Mayer and Swart, 2009);
- how good leaders manage their emotions and their relationships (Goleman, 1995, 1998).

Archetype 4: The Implementer

Focusing on delivery, the Implementer drives and reviews the plan, holds people to account, leads by delegating and follow-up with tenacity and rigour.
This archetype combines the following theoretical and research elements:

- the link between drive, conscientiousness and leadership success (Kirkpatrick and Locke, 1991; Saucier and Goldberg, 1998);
- the need to focus on task and expectation-setting (Fiedler, 1967);

- use of 'directing and delegating' skills, depending on the follower's maturity level (Hersey and Blanchard, 1969);
- effectiveness of transactional leadership skills such as 'active management by exception', use of rewards, in certain contexts (Bass, 1985);
- role of planning as a possible strategic approach (Mintzberg, 1987);
- importance of goal setting, measuring, monitoring results and corrective action for successful innovative leadership (Bel, 2010; Bossink, 2007);
- need to 'maintain disciplined attention' as part of adaptive leadership (Heifetz and Laurie, 1997);
- making others accountable as a key part of change leadership (Higgs and Rowland, 2005);
- significance of 'professional will' in Level 5 leaders (Collins, 2001);
- need to be able to encourage autonomy, to let go of tasks (Pearce, 2004; Pinnow, 2011);
- leaders need to have discipline regarding hydration, nutrition, sleep, breathing, and exercise to build resilience and enable high performance (Cian, 2000; Connolly, Ruderman and Leslie, 2014).

Archetype 5: The Catalyser

Focusing on discomfort, the Catalyser asks difficult or probing questions, spots poor performance, dysfunction or resistance, and brings any necessary edge which in turn creates the tension for change to happen.

This archetype combines the following theoretical and research elements:

- the links between integrity (or truth-telling) and successful leadership (Kirkpatrick and Locke, 1991; Yukl, 2013);
- the importance for leaders to bring 'presence and impact', eg shifting the direction of conversation (Hawkins and Smith, 2013);
- the need to be aware of the dangers of conflict avoidance and 'the undiscussable' (Argyris, 1990);
- links between 'intellectual stimulation' and 'active management by exception' with leadership success in certain contexts (Bass, 1985);
- challenging the status quo, questioning assumptions, being 'devil's advocate' are all important abilities for strategic leaders (Schoemaker *at al.*, 2013);

- the need for change leaders to identify the adaptive challenges (Heifetz and Laurie, 1997);

- how leaders need to be courageous and have robust discussions (Snowden and Boone, 2007);

- 'ethical leadership' may mean being willing to be unpopular (Seidman, 2010);

- systemic leadership involves seeking feedback, allowing tensions and conflicts to emerge (Pinnow, 2011);

- leadership maturity means staying open to difficult realities of one's own life; allowing crises (eg Paris, 2016).

From clusters to the Five Qualities Framework

As a result of the clustering exercise above, we derived an elegant yet substantial framework, now known as the Five Leadership Qualities, which we then started to experiment with and validate more thoroughly over a period of eight years. This validation process is summarized in Part Five, and set out more fully in the Appendices.

The Five Leadership Qualities are introduced above in summary form. Much work has been done since 2007 to define the qualities more precisely, and provide more help to leaders in learning the skills and 'inhabiting' the archetype. This work is presented in its more up-to-date form in Part Five and includes rich descriptions of each archetype, lists of associated core and advanced skills, self-rating mechanisms for each, suggestions for overcoming development barriers, ways to get started on experimenting with the Qualities, and lots of case studies and examples.

Note: All references cited in the text above can be found in their relevant chapters.

Table II.1 An overall map of leadership territory

Part Two: Chapter title	Leadership Archetype					
	Architect	Motivator	Connector	Implementer	Catalyser
2. Leadership traits and characteristics	Cognitive ability (Kirkpatrick and Locke, 1991)	Extraversion (Saucier and Goldberg, 1998) Self-confidence (Northouse, 2007)	Sociability (Northouse, 2007)	Drive (Kirkpatrick and Locke, 1991) Conscientiousness (Saucier and Goldberg, 1998)	Integrity (Kirkpatrick and Locke, 1991)
3. Contingency theories	Thinking through decisions (Vroom and Yetton, 1973; Vroom and Jago, 1988)	Importance of expectation-setting (Vroom and Jago, 1988)	Focus on relationship (Fiedler, 1967)	Focus on task (Fiedler, 1967)	–
4. Situational leadership	Considering how best to lead (embedded in Hersey and Blanchard, 1969)	Supporting, coaching (Hersey and Blanchard, 1969)	Supporting, coaching (Hersey and Blanchard, 1969)	Directing, delegating (Hersey and Blanchard, 1969)	–

5. Psychodynamics, power and the shadow	Personal power (Yukl, 2013)	Influencing skills: push and pull (Dent, 2009)	Influencing skills: push and pull (Dent, 2009)	Authority (Hawkins and Smith, 2013)	Presence and impact (Hawkins and Smith, 2013) Beware of conflict avoidance and 'the undiscussable' (Argyris, 1990)
6. Transformational and transactional leadership	Intellectual stimulation (Bass 1985)	Idealized influence, inspirational motivation (Bass 1985)	Individualized consideration (Bass 1985)	Active management by exception, use of rewards (Bass 1985)	Intellectual stimulation, active management by exception (Bass 1985)
7. Strategic and innovation leadership	Pattern, Ploy, Position, Perspective (Mintzberg, 1987) Anticipate, Interpret, Decide (Schoemaker et al., 2013) Ideas generation (Bel, 2010) Strategic (Bossink, 2007)	Align (Schoemaker et al., 2013) Ideas generation (Bel, 2010) Charismatic (Bossink, 2007)	Learn (Schoemaker et al., 2013) Leverage human and social capital (Hitt and Ireland ,2002) Interactive (Bossink, 2007) Based on interactions (Lichtenstein et al., 2006)	Planning (Mintzberg, 1987) (Schoemaker et al., 2013) Idea implementation (Bel, 2010) Instrumental (Bossink, 2007)	Challenge (Schoemaker et al., 2013)

(continued)

Table II.1 (continued)

Part Two: Chapter title	Leadership Archetype				
	Architect	Motivator	Connector	Implementer	Catalyser
8. Change leadership	Enable others to act (Kouznes and Posner, 2003) Get on the balcony (Heifetz and Laurie, 1997) Framing, creating capacity (Higgs and Rowland, 2005)	Inspire a shared vision, model the way, and encourage the heart (Kouznes and Posner, 2003) Shaping, framing (Higgs and Rowland, 2005)	Enable others to act (Kouznes and Posner, 2003) Regulate distress, protect the voices of leadership from below (Heifetz and Laurie, 1997) Creating capacity (Higgs and Rowland, 2005)	Maintain disciplined attention, give the work back to the people (Heifetz and Laurie, 1997) Shaping (Higgs and Rowland, 2005)	Challenge the current process (Kouznes and Posner, 2003) Identify the adaptive challenges (Heifetz and Laurie, 1997) Be courageous and have robust discussions (Snowden and Boone, 2007)
9. Leadership responsibility and values	Conceptualization, foresight, stewardship (Spears, 1998)	Motivating others through values (Schwartz, 1994) Persuasion rather than coercion (Spears, 1998)	Integrity (Yukl, 2013) Care about others, trustworthy (Brown and Trevino, 2006) Servant leadership: (Laub, 1999) Personal humility (Collins, 2001)	High-performance culture, robust systems (Kellogg website) Professional will (Collins, 2001)	Integrity (Yukl, 2013) Wiling to be unpopular (Seidman, 2010)

10. Leading Across organizations and networks	Systemic leadership: understanding all parts (Cameron and Green, 2015)	Systemic leadership: conferring meaning, role-modelling	Shared leadership: interdependence (Pearce, 2004) Distributed leadership: working through relationships (Bennett et al., 2003) Collaborative leadership process (Chrislip and Larson, 1994)	Shared leadership, autonomy (Pearce, 2004) Systemic leadership: delegating and letting go of tasks (Pinnow, 2011)	Systemic leadership: seeking feedback, allowing tensions and conflicts to emerge (Pinnow, 2011)
11. Leadership health: mind, body and spirit	Importance of space to ponder and reflect (Swart, Chisholm and Brown, 2015) Creative thinking (Zaleznik, 2004) Sense-making (Mead, 2014) Accessing own inner depths (Schuster and Brunning, 2014)	Managing your emotions, recognizing and understanding other peoples' emotions (Goleman, 1995, 1998) Imaginative story (Mead, 2014)	Importance of trust (Brown, Mayer and Swart, 2009) Managing your emotions, managing relationships (Goleman, 1995, 1998)	Importance of discipline around hydration, nutrition, sleep, breathing, exercise – for resilience and high performance (Cian, 2000; Connolly et al, 2014)	Staying open to difficult realities of own life; allowing crises (eg Paris, 2016)
OVERALL THEMES	Potential to learn and grow (Chapters 4, 5, 11) Importance for leaders to attune to context (Chapters 3,4,6, 7) Leadership at its best is in service of the whole, not the individual (Chapters 6, 8,10,11) Need for leaders to take responsibility (Chapters 9, 10, 11)				

Conclusions from Part Two

Part Two has surveyed the field of leadership research over the last century and described in detail both the seminal theories and the emerging themes.

Leadership continues to be one of the most researched and talked-about areas in business. So, as we draw together the threads of Part Two and move into Part Three, which focuses on learning to lead in practice, what lessons and key points can we make?

The research described has established that there is clearly something about the leader – their personality, characteristics and behaviours – which influences the way work is done in organizations, and the level of performance that is achieved and sustained. However, it is also clear that there is no one right profile for a leader, either as a starting point or ultimate goal.

There are many factors which leaders need to pay attention to when pursuing outcomes, for example, the competence, confidence and motivational levels of followers. Other important elements are the contextual factors: the complexity of the task, the health of the organizational systems, structures and processes to name just a few.

Personality types and interpersonal dynamics are influential too, and less open to being controlled. Leaders also have to pay attention to sources of power and how to influence others, including those who don't report to them. This is complex and requires practice.

So we might conclude that it is the interplay between these factors, and the resulting calibration of the thinking and behaving of the leader, that contributes to leadership effectiveness.

But of course it's not so simple. Strategic and innovative leadership both require continuous attention to the environment and the emerging future, the application of a range of leadership skills, and the development of a culture of learning. Change leadership also requires attention to a multiplicity of factors; and at the same time, in more complex, ambiguous contexts, the leader needs to develop new skills, and to learn how to trust and serve the whole system without trying to control the action or outcomes.

Leading responsibly is also important, and a challenge for some of us to live up to given the potential monetary gains of acting unethically, and the uncomfortable consequences of speaking up against actions or activities that we disagree with.

The notion of leadership residing in just one person or the top team is being challenged by the emergence of ever-flatter organizational structures and the democratizing impact of the Web. In today's complex and changeable environments, other forms of leadership – shared, distributed and collaborative – might be more effective.

A healthy mind, body and spirit support sustained performance at work. Attending to all three takes effort and commitment, but leaders need to take care of themselves and their people, supporting their teams to build their own resilience to stress at work. Too much controlled communication can dull the spirit, and leaders in today's organizations also need to allow themselves to be more creative and reflective.

The Overall Map presented after Chapter 11 and immediately before this conclusion sets out all the theoretical material discussed in Part Two and sorts this into several clusters of skills and qualities. This will be helpful when we introduce an integrated framework in Part Five to support your understanding and continued development which will be the focus in Parts Three and Four.

Although there has been much research in the leadership arena and much advice offered, we are clear that there is no 'one right way' way to lead. The exercise of responsible leadership is dependent on an understanding of the different, interrelated variables and a high level of sensitivity to the context. It's also imperative for the leader to stay open to developing the skills and qualities he or she needs to be able to become ever more competent and mature. The process of expanding and deepening a wide range of leadership skills and capacities is a very worthwhile journey.

We can now turn to how leaders learn to develop the necessary qualities.

PART THREE
Learning to lead in practice

Overview

How do people learn to lead in practice? What are the relative contributions of classroom versus on-the-job approaches? Every enterprise, big or small, requires some sort of leadership for it to be brought into reality and guided towards achieving its intent. The leadership might rest with one person alone, or it might work via a formalized hierarchy, or perhaps it might be more of a collective endeavour. Whichever way it works, this section asks: how do these leaders or groups of leaders learn how to bring good, effective leadership?

The core objectives of this part of the book are to:

- identify what new or different types of leadership leaders in the 21st century need to practise, and examine current progress towards this aspiration (Chapter 12);

- find out which approaches are most successful in enabling leadership development and discover what supports adults to learn (Chapter 13);

- explore the concept of leadership maturity and how this can help leaders to grow their capacity for complexity and adaptability, in tune with 21st-century demands (Chapter 14).

Throughout these chapters, we're keen to explore what works to support leadership learning, what doesn't work, and whether different approaches are required at different stages of a leader's development or for different types of leadership. We ask whether there is such a thing as a fully developed leader, and how much context influences what can be learned. Do training courses or MBA studies support the development of leadership in practice?

Is our understanding of leadership changing, so that new learning strategies are now required?

This section is all about learning to lead *in practice*. We are shifting focus from learning *about* leadership to learning *how to do* leadership. Leadership is a practical, adaptive skill developed in relationship with the world, and although theoretical models and case studies support this, much more is needed before someone can be declared a competent leader!

Anyone who has tried to learn how to drive or ski by reading a book will understand the limitations of this. You quickly realize once you get on the road or on the slopes that the real thing requires something much more. And the trickier the territory, the more live practice you need. Reading theory can offer helpful frameworks, tips and examples, but learning how to do something in practice is likely to be more deeply affecting. That's why half of this book is devoted to shedding light on the question of learning *how* to lead. Our wish is to offer helpful evidence of what works, together with practically oriented frameworks and tools to support this intent in a 21st-century context.

By exploring recent research and theories of learning, we aim to enable you to discover some of the keys to developing and growing yourself as an effective leader in a range of contexts, and thus becoming a more successful and agile deliverer of organizational outcomes.

What does 21st-century leadership require?   12

The leadership challenges ahead

In our view, the big challenges for 21st-century leaders are as follows. Many of these are mentioned in Parts One and Two (Chapters 7–11), and we expand upon them below. These are in no particular order, are not exclusive, and are subject to debate – and are offered here as a way of setting out the increasingly complex territory that leaders need to deal with in responsible ways:

- responding to environmental threats;
- dealing with an increasingly VUCA context;
- embracing the opportunities provided by the Web and its rich networks of expertise and information;
- being aware of the potential for 'viral' PR disasters via 24/7 news;
- being sensitive to the rise of global inequalities;
- being protected against terrorist or cyber attacks;
- including the passions, skills and preferences of a global, multi-generational workforce;
- letting go of old mindsets, rigid ways of working and hierarchical forms of power, ie accepting a flow towards 'democratization' of leadership.

Is leadership development working?

Research since the 1980s and more recent meta-studies have explored the impact of leadership development interventions within organizations. They indicate that the approaches used have a broadly positive impact on behaviour (Hayward and Voller, 2010). We believe it is unwise to deduce much more than this, given that it's difficult to discern, for example, exactly what impact a leadership development programme has had on an individual's performance, because of possible time lag and other situational factors.

A great deal of money and effort is spent on leadership development across the globe, with the United States alone rumoured to spend between $15 and $50 billion. Despite this, recent UK and global research indicates that leadership in today's organizations still needs to get much better, with some urgency. A recent CMI survey (McBain *et al.*, 2012) in the UK indicated that nearly half of those asked thought their leader was ineffective or highly ineffective. In the United States, despite a high degree of focus and spending on leadership development over the years, only 30 per cent of organizations asked in 2003 believed their leaders had the right capabilities to exploit international opportunities (Gurdjian, Halbeisen and Lane, 2014).

Globally, the picture is similar. Research conducted by Ashridge Business School (Peters and Gitsham, 2009) at the height of the global financial crisis indicated that less than 8 per cent of the CEOs asked were satisfied that the knowledge and skills being developed in their leaders would equip them to tackle the complex social and environmental issues being faced at the time. More recently, IBM sought the views of 1,500 CEOs around the world, who indicated that rapid change and increasing complexity were forcing leaders to learn how to be much more open to innovation and novel partnerships, and to consider radically new business models (IBM, 2010, 2015). Thinking strategically and innovatively, dealing with ambiguity, and leading agile change are all becoming much more important skills than they were 10–15 years ago.

The leadership performance gap

The views of employees around the world, tracked in various ways by Gallup, are also significant. Gallup point out on their website (www.gallup.com) that levels of enthusiasm and absorption at work have been consistently low worldwide over the last few years, and that 70 per cent of the problem appears to be poor leadership. Surveys and studies between 2000 and 2016 indicate that engagement figures around the world are pretty much static, with 32 per cent of employees in the United States, and 13 per cent worldwide, feeling engaged in their jobs and workplace. Mann and Harter (2016), writing in Gallup's *Business Journal*, say, 'The world has an employee engagement crisis, with serious and potentially lasting repercussions for the global economy', and suggest that leaders' poor performance management and failure to communicate positive progress over time are likely to be significant contributors to this global problem.

The structure of populations in the United States and Europe is also a key influence: mass retirement of baby-boomers, fewer Generation X leaders due to a dip in birth rate, and the influx of new, Generation Y or Millennial leaders ripe for development (see Part Six, Chapter 26 for a definition of these terms). Japan and India appear to have similar issues, though different in structure. The context therefore demands that organizations get better at 'growing' leaders rather than simply recruiting them and teaching them some skills. This makes leadership development an ever-more-pressing issue.

How social media and the Web are impacting leaders

The social media tools and connectivity provided by the Web are enabling and encouraging new types of interactions between people that are making them question the value of traditional organizations. The ease with which information can be shared is shifting power away from centralized, boundaried organizations towards more fluid networks and individual contributions. This is already forcing a move away from rigid, hierarchical structures towards more emergent, self-organized, collaborative approaches to getting things done, which in turn demand a different type of leadership and a looser, more open structure if organizations are to thrive.

For organizational leaders, this is a challenge. It can mean sharing decision making and opening up to more outside influence and exchange with customers, competitors and other key players in their domain. This work has started already, and can range from continuously involving all employees in strategic decision making and innovative thinking, to devolving decision-making power to more diffuse networks of employees and suppliers, to innovative collaborations between organizations or stakeholders that don't normally work together. For examples, see Turiera and Cros (2013) and Morgan (2013).

A new set of leadership principles

The Bertelsmann Foundation, a non-profit organization based in Germany which produces stimulating socio-economic research, has offered this new set of principles for leadership, given the influence of two decades of the

Web and the complexity this brings (McGonagill and Doerffer, 2010). Drawing on the views of leadership learning experts in the United States, Canada and Europe, they refer to the possible end of 'single paradigm' leadership, and say that new forms of leadership will need to align with the following criteria:

- adaptive (capable of responding to ongoing change through continuous learning);
- supportive of emergence (able to appreciate the capacity of teams and networks to self-organize and create novel solutions);
- cognizant of complexity (aware of the need to attune the leadership response to the complexity level of the context or particular challenge);
- integral (inclusive of a range of perspectives on people, organizations, society);
- outcome-oriented (more focused on results than methods).

These new attitudes will need to be accompanied by new or improved skills such as self-leadership, boundary setting, building organizational capability, dialogue, collaborative leadership, network leadership, facilitating complex meetings, use of symbols and meaning making, systems thinking and action-reflection coaching. See Part Two (Chapter 7–11) and Part Five for more on these types of skills.

Refreshing leadership education

It is apparent that much management and leadership education, often content-heavy, competency-focused and individualistic, is lagging behind this demand for new, more sophisticated capacities. Basics such as planning, delegation, coaching, meeting management and dealing with difficult people are still important as foundations. However, there is a strong sense of a widening gap, with many experienced leadership development professionals pointing to a need for a significant refresh of direction and focus (Petrie, 2014). Key elements of this change are:

- Greater focus on developing leadership 'maturity' (see Chapter 14 for a definition of this) or depth as well as developing key leadership skills.
- Greater ownership by individual leaders of their own development paths and options, rather than HR 'doing learning to' people.

- Increased focus on encouraging collective forms of leadership across networks, rather than only targeting individual development.

- More experimentation and diversity in modes of delivery/development, eg via technology, combined approaches and learning partnerships, rather than sticking to familiar formats.

So the challenge here is for organizations to support leadership development in radically new ways, and for leaders themselves to take more responsibility for their learning. All leaders need to become more agile, more open to innovation, more collaborative, more able to focus and more equipped to handle complexity. This requires a step up in interpersonal skills, emotional intelligence, strategic skills and overall maturity. The question is, how to enable this?

Pause for Learning Points

The challenges of 21st-century leadership are considerable and leaders need to rise to them.

Recent comparisons between money spent on leadership development and the ability of leaders to perform as required indicate a considerable gap between expectations and outcomes – evidenced by CEOs lacking confidence in senior leaders, and employees remaining disengaged from their work.

The development of the Web has had a huge influence on the challenges of leadership. A new definition of leadership is emerging, with new personal qualities and wisdoms required: more adaptive, more supportive of emergence, and more collaborative.

Changing demographics suggest that organizations need to get better at growing new leaders rather than expecting to recruit them 'ready-made', and leaders need to take more responsibility for their own growth and development.

Stop and Reflect!

What are the top five leadership challenges facing your organization, or one you know well, over the next two to three years? Reflect on the readiness of the leadership population to deal with these challenges, using the Bertelsmann Foundation list above to guide your thinking. What are the gaps, and how might they be filled?

Consider your own development as a leader. How could you bring more strategic, innovative or collaborative qualities to your leadership right now? What would be the benefits to the organization? What support might you need to do this?

References and further reading

Gurdjian, P, Halbeisen, T, and Lane (2014) Why leadership development programs fail, *McKinsey Quarterly*, January

Hayward, I and Voller, S (2010) How effective is leadership development? *The Ashridge Journal*, Summer

IBM (2010) Capitalising on complexity: Global CEO Study 2010, IBM Institute for Business Value

IBM (2015) Redefining boundaries: Global C-Suite Study 2015, IBM Institute for Business Value

Mann, A and Harter, J (2016) The worldwide employee engagement crisis, *Gallup Business Journal*, 7 January

McBain, R, Ghobadian, A, Switzer, J, Wilton, P, Woodman, P and Pearson, G (2012) The business benefits of management and leadership development, *Chartered Management Institute* [online] http://www.managers.org.uk/sites/default/files/u28/Business%20Benefits%20MLD%20Exec%20Summary.pdf

McGonagill, G and Doerffer, T (2010) *Leadership and Web 2.0*, Bertelsmann Stiftung Leadership Series

Morgan, J (2013) 12 habits of highly collaborative organizations, *Forbes* [online] http://www.forbes.com/sites/jacobmorgan/2013/07/30/ the-12-habits-of-highly-collaborative-organizations/#6dcc8bd5f129

Peters, K and Gitsham, M (2009) Developing the global leader of tomorrow, *EFMD* (Ashridge) **3** (1)

Petrie, N (2014)*The Future of Leadership Development*, Centre for Creative Leadership

Turiera, T and Cros, S (2013) *50 Examples of Business Collaborations*, infonomia

How do leaders learn? 13

Given the extreme challenges now being faced by leader as set out in Chapter 12, the subject of leadership learning is becoming even more central to organizational effectiveness.

Principles of adult learning

It's no longer true to say 'you can't teach an old dog new tricks'. It's much more possible than people used to believe for adults to change and learn as they grow older. The literature of psychology over the past 20 years indicates that, given the right sort of practice, you can improve your mastery of just about any task, whether it's perceptual, motor, cognitive or a combination of all three. Deep, lasting change is therefore possible at all ages.

It is still true that for adults, learning new mental or physical behaviours can be difficult and may take months or even years of practice. However, neuroscience discoveries confirm that, with focused practice, new responses will become easier over time, and any old habits will eventually fade (see Chapter 11, Leadership Health). Of course, this requires that you have the motivation and willpower to bring enough focused attention to the learning process. Incentives can help, such as good links to the organization's purpose, visible rewards, and good-quality role-modelling by influential people.

Necessary conditions

So what conditions are necessary for successful adult learning to take place? The following principles, gleaned and adapted from the various works of Knowles, Holton and Swanson (2015), Lieb (1991) and Fidishun (2000) provide a useful guide to this territory:

- **Relevance:** learning needs to be relevant to what the person wants to achieve, and tends to have added impetus when this is serving the greater good.

- **Ownership**: results are better when learners are responsible for their learning and able to be self-directed.

- **Problem-centred**: learning is more likely to stick if it is problem-centred rather than content-centred.

- **Refers to existing experience**: it's very helpful if the learning process refers to existing experiences and knowledge, so that the new learning makes sense.

- **Practically-oriented and affecting**: practical experiences which have an emotional effect need to form the basis of adult learning.

- **Learning process is focused and conscious**: adult learners benefit from being supported to develop their focused attention, and being able to reflect on what's been learned/how it's been learned.

- **Respect and feedback**: adult learners thrive when there is respect for the learner, a positive atmosphere, encouragement and honest feedback.

A knowledge of the learning cycle is useful for understanding how learning is embedded. Many people are familiar with Kolb's Learning Cycle (1974), which was further adapted and made popular by Honey and Mumford (1982). This is a useful basic framework that illuminates how the continuous process of learning works and distinguishes four learning styles, illustrated in Figure 13.1: Activist, Reflector, Theorist and Pragmatist. This means, for instance, that to learn most deeply from experience, you need to reflect on it, draw conclusions and create new hypotheses, and then make a plan for your next steps.

Figure 13.1 The Learning Cycle. Adapted from Honey and Mumford (1982)

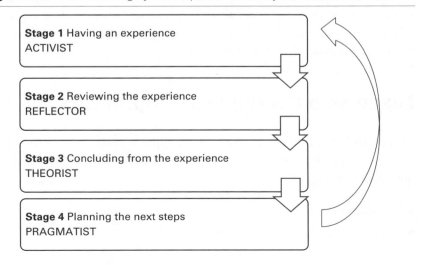

Stage 1 Having an experience
ACTIVIST

Stage 2 Reviewing the experience
REFLECTOR

Stage 3 Concluding from the experience
THEORIST

Stage 4 Planning the next steps
PRAGMATIST

Table 13.1   Cortex regions affected through learning
Adapted from Mauritz Institute (2010)

Sequence	Zull Cycle label	Zull Function	Region of cortex	Kolb Cycle label
Stage 1	Information	Getting information	Sensory	Experience
Stage 2	Meaning	Making meaning	Integrative (near sensory)	Reflection
Stage 3	Ideas	Creating new meaning	Integrative (near front)	Abstraction
Stage 4	Action	Acting on ideas	Motor	Testing

The collective research from Kolb and Honey and Mumford indicates that embedded learning requires all four stages to be included, and that people tend to have a preference for learning in one style. This can be advantageous or disadvantageous, depending on the context.

Involving the senses

Zull (2002) developed this cycle by incorporating new insights regarding the plasticity of the brain and the vital role of emotions in the learning process. He mapped Kolb's original four stages onto the four major functional regions of the cerebral cortex, emphasizing that the more neurons that are being fired in more areas of the brain, the greater the chances for learning (see Table 13.1).

This implies that the more a learning experience can involve the senses, some action or movement, and also a cognitive element, the more successful it is likely to be. Later in the book we will refer to this as the need to engage 'Head, Heart and Belly' or all three 'brains'.

Leadership development approaches

Recent studies of leadership development approaches (Hayward and Voller, 2010; Petrie, 2004) indicate the following as the most frequently used methods for developing leaders:

- training courses;
- executive coaching or mentoring;

- specific job assignments;
- action learning groups;
- 360 appraisal;
- developmental assessment centres;
- shadowing/feedback on performance;
- regular 1:1s/coaching sessions with line manager.

Research mentioned above indicates that these methods, in combination, have been working reasonably well and will remain important. However, the deeper attitude shifts that many organizations are now requiring of leaders, outlined above, need something new and/or more powerful if there's a serious intent to encourage this type of personal development. The traditional approach of identifying leadership competencies and tackling these is clearly limited. The challenge is how to accelerate and open up each leader's capacity to learn, think, adapt and collaborate.

Democratization of leadership

Twenty years ago, we might have assumed that only leaders with the greatest levels of responsibility or seniority needed this sort of development. Yet it seems that the Web is opening society up to a democratization of leadership, which is requiring different skills and capacities from all of us, not just those in the most senior roles in traditional hierarchies. Kegan and Lahey (2009) argue that we are asking more and more of leaders at many levels to lead and contribute to transformative change, which requires us all to take part in reforming structures and changing mindsets again and again, over time.

Our own experience indicates that leaders needing to develop these new skills and capacities, whatever their role or seniority, require good-quality training combined with tailored support and encouragement. The latter is even more important if they are being asked to give up behaviours and attitudes that for some have become hard-wired. This support needs to include skilled coaching, based on robust frameworks. Clear, transparent incentives to change are important too; sometimes, new ways of working such as increased collaboration can be deeply counter-cultural.

Research by Kempster and Stewart (2010) supports this need for more personal support, indicating that the most significant learning opportunities for leaders, in large or small businesses, are most likely to be triggered by real-life incidents or episodes rather than formal courses or pre-arranged interventions. More importantly, he claims that any learning is likely to perish unless the leader develops a habit of high-quality, critical reflection, which enables transformative learning over time. This habit can be nurtured through coaching.

Developing mental complexity

The work of Kegan and Lahey (2009) focuses on the development of human capability, which they say is critical for leaders in the 21st century. They say that the challenge of increasing complexity in our environment is showing up our own lack of mental development or 'mental complexity'. This is not about IQ, or about learning new skills, but about using a more fully-developed system of meaning which allows us to tackle 'adaptive challenges' (Heifetz, 1994). They say developing mental complexity is more than a cognitive pursuit, and needs to be developed in parallel with the emotions and in the midst of real work activity, ie involving *head*, *heart* and *belly*. We refer to this from now on as 'body-mindset', as it involves more than 'head-centred' knowing.

So for leaders to truly develop, they need to be faced with 'optimal conflict' that engages them in a variety of ways:

- they persistently experience some frustration, dilemma or puzzle…
- that causes them to experience the limits of their current ways of knowing…(Head)
- in an area of lives that they deeply care about…(Heart)
- and there is sufficient support that helps them to stay with the difficulty, and work it through, rather than collapsing or walking away (Belly).

(Adapted from Kegan and Lahey, 2009).

Salovaara and Ropo (2013) point to the habit that some businesses have developed of transacting with business schools or other providers to acquire leadership 'knowledge', which is only part of the solution to their more complex leadership challenges. They recommend a move away from this individualized, brain-focused, externally-led learning which is limited in its impact, towards seeing leadership as embodied, happening in practice, within an existing context. This means that more customized approaches to developing skills and knowledge need to be delivered in partnership and in connection with live organizational issues.

Pause for Learning Points

Learning new skills and capacities as an adult can be challenging, particularly where there is 'unlearning' to be done. Motivation, relevance, stimulating experiences and the opportunity to reflect on action are all essential.

Leadership development is becoming much more important for all those responsible for delivering outcomes. It's not simply the reserve of those in senior roles with a large span of control.

New forms of leadership development are likely to require new frameworks, more tailored support based on 'live' challenges and greater attention to organizational incentives.

Stop and Reflect!

Reflect on your own recent learning as an adult. What new, practical skills have you learned recently, and what has supported you and got in the way of your developing these skills and capabilities? Also reflect on the key interventions, supports and experiences that have enabled you to develop so far as a leader, regardless of your seniority. What forms of support might you now want to initiate or request?

What are the implications of the above for your HR Department, or whoever is in charge of talent management or leadership development? What do they need to do to nurture more up-to-date leadership skills?

References and further reading

Fidishun, D (2000) Andragogy and technology: Integrating adult learning theory as we teach with technology. Fifth annual instructional technology conference: extending the frontiers of teaching and learning, Middle Tennessee State University, Proceedings [online] http://frank.mtsu.edu/~itconf/proceed00/fidishun.htm [accessed 18 August 2016]

Hayward, I and Voller, S (2010) How effective is leadership development? *The Ashridge Journal*, Summer

Heifetz, R A (1994) *Leadership Without Easy Answers*, Harvard University Press

Honey, P and Mumford, A (1982) *Manual of Learning Styles*, P Honey, London

Kegan, R and Lahey, L (2009) *Immunity to Change: How to overcome it and unlock the potential in yourself and your organization*, Harvard Business School Publishing, Boston, Mass

Kempster, S and Stewart, J (2010) Becoming a leader: a co-produced autoethnographic exploration of situated learning of leadership practice, *Management Learning Journal*, January

Knowles, M S, Holton, E F and Swanson, R A (2015) *The Adult Learner*, 8th edn, Routledge

Kolb, D A and Fry, R E (1974) *Toward an Applied Theory of Experiential Learning*, MIT Alfred P. Sloan School of Management

Kolb, D A (1981) *Experiential learning: Experience as the source of learning and development*, Prentice-Hall, Upper Saddle River, NJ

Lieb, S (1991) The principles of adult learning [online] http://www.design2learn.ch/downloads/principles_of_adult_learning_lieb.pdf [accessed 18 Aug 2016]

Mauritz Institute (2010) White paper: The neuroscience of learning [online] http://www.themaritzinstitute.com/~/media/Files/MaritzInstitute/White-Papers/The-Neuroscience-of-Learning-The-Maritz-Institute.pdf [accessed 22 October 2016]

Petrie, N (2014) *The Future of Leadership Development*, Centre for Creative Leadership

Salovaara, P and Ropo, A (2013) Embodied learning experience in leadership development, in *The Embodiment of Leadership*, ed R Melina, G J Burgess, L Falkman, and A Maturana, Jossey-Bass, San Francisco

Zull, J (2002) The Art of Changing the Brain, Stylus Publishing, Sterling, VA

Zull, J (2004) Teaching for meaning, *Educational Leadership*, **62** (1)

Levels of leadership maturity

What is leadership 'maturity'?

A very useful and relatively new concept in leadership development is the idea of leadership 'maturity', similar to the previously mentioned 'mental complexity'. In essence, this is the notion that leaders can progress through various developmental milestones during their adult life, which involves more than simply acquiring new knowledge and skills. This maturing requires that they develop a new set of logics mindsets at each significant step along the way.

Over the past 10–15 years, much work has been done to map out how a leader's maturity, or 'mental complexity' develops over time, and what impact this has on their ability to lead. Interestingly, leadership maturity appears to correlate positively with the capacity to innovate and transform teams and organizations (Rooke and Torbert, 2005).

It's helpful to consider these frameworks as you would a map of child development; they are phases that people move through at different paces with the appropriate levels of experience, freedom and support. The difference is that the rate of development for adults tends to be slower and requires more active work. In adults, each phase includes the previous phases, and it takes time for each person to develop through the phases. Some continue to broaden their capacities at a particular level without moving on. Later stages are not better or healthier – just more adapted to ever more complex forms of thinking and being.

Maturity frameworks: Kegan and Torbert

Nick Petrie of the Center for Creative Leadership (2014) has set out an over-arching framework that encapsulates this leadership development journey.

He identifies three clear phases, based on the work of researchers Robert Kegan and Bill Torbert, whose frameworks are described below:

- **Dependent-Conformer**: a leader who is more likely to seek direction and align with others than to bring initiative.
- **Independent-Achiever**: a leader who thinks independently and drives his or her own agenda in a self-directed way.
- **Interdependent-Collaborator**: a leader who thinks longer term, can hold multiple frames and perspectives, sees systems and patterns, spots and works with interdependencies and paradoxes.

Petrie points out that adult development does not happen automatically. Adults have to work at their own growth. He adds that in order to be effective, a leader's thinking needs to be superior to the complexity of the environment and that in a world of order and routine, the Dependent-Conformer leader might do very well. However, many leaders now have to deal with multiple interdependencies and a great deal of ambiguity, which requires Interdependent-Collaborator leadership.

Part Five sets out all the key skills that leaders need to acquire to become rounded, effective leaders of change; they are extremely important for leaders to learn. However, these skills are enacted very differently, depending on the maturity level of the leader. The box below illustrates how familiar leadership competencies are applied differently via the body-mindsets of leaders at different levels of maturity. This shows how each competency is enacted at the different phases of maturity.

How leadership competency develops with maturity (Petrie, 2014)

Dependent-Conformer

Strategic thinking:
Short-term view, high need for certainty.

Leading change:
Expects change to come from above.

Negotiating conflict:
Feels torn by conflict.

Leading across boundaries:
Distrusts outsiders.

Independent-Achiever

Strategic thinking:
Medium-term view, sees some patterns and connections.

Leading change:
Has own views about best change.

Negotiating conflict:
Works out conflict behind closed doors.

Leading across boundaries:
Focused on success of own silo, works in partnership with other functions.

Interdependent-Collaborator

Strategic thinking:
Long-term view, sees many patterns and connections.

Leading change:
Sees change as a collaborative process.

Negotiating conflict:
Encourages conflict as a way of gathering more views.

Leading across boundaries:
Focused on success of own silo, works in partnership with other functions.

Kegan's four levels

We have selected the work of two key researchers to illustrate this maturity journey in more detail. Robert Kegan (1994) names four leadership levels, each with a different meaning-making system as described below. You can see Kegan's framework mapped against Petrie's broader definitions in Table 14.1.

Self-Sovereign Leaders:

- focused on own perspective;
- follows rules and regulations.

Socialized Leaders:

- able to see the world through the eyes of others;
- follows internalized value set which comes from significant others.

Self-Authored Leaders:

- aware of own perspective, and the views of others;
- develops own, personalized set of principles.

Self-Transforming Leaders:

- sees multiple perspectives simultaneously, can use these to continuously self-transform;
- open, curious, able to see and navigate complex patterns across and within.

Kegan points out that this meaning-making system is not immediately obvious to others, and may even be out of awareness for the individual, particularly at the earlier stages of adult development. He adds that this model confirms that there is 'life after adolescence' and illustrates a path for developing more adaptive capabilities beyond the more easily identifiable leadership skills such as planning, delegating, reviewing, appraising etc.

Kegan's framework was taken further by Berger (2012), who mapped out the struggles that leaders may have at each of Kegan's first three stages of development as their role becomes more complex (see box):

Self-Sovereign Leaders:

- likely to struggle to see that short-term losses can lead to long-term gains;
- can find it hard to manage multiple stakeholders;
- may get concerned when cause and effect logic becomes muddied.

Socialized Leaders:

- may need help drawing out implications of increasing time span;
- tend to seek and privilege a 'correct' perspective;
- may revert to cause and effect logic even when not applicable.

Self-Authored Leaders:

- may struggle to hold the complexity of multiple perspectives;
- may get frustrated by the difference between outcome desired and what is actually happening;
- tendency to hold onto a belief in the perfect way of operating.

Leaderhip struggles at three of Kegan's levels.

Adapted from Berger (2012)

Torbert's action logics

Bill Torbert has proposed a different but complementary model of maturity. Torbert and Rooke's *Harvard Business Review* article (2005) brought their 'action-logics' framework to the attention of many organizations. Co-developed with psychologist Susanne Cook-Greuter (2013), this 'action-logics' model, established through research and consulting work, sets out seven leadership types differentiated by the way each type interprets and reacts to events. Here we offer a summary of the characteristics and strengths of each type. See Table 14.1 for how these align with Kegan and Petrie.

Opportunist:

- manipulative, self-oriented, focused on winning;
- good in an emergency; grasps opportunities.

Diplomat:

- focuses on doing what's expected within acceptable norms;
- good teamworker.

Expert:

- focuses on problem solving, improvement and efficiency;
- good as an individual contributor.

Achiever:

- delivers outcomes through teams, to serve the whole system;
- effective, goal-driven manager.

Individualist:

- weaves together different, competing agendas and communicates well with different groups;
- good at consulting roles and new ventures.

Strategist:

- focuses on short and long term, open to deeper inquiry, attentive, present;
- effective transformational leader.

Alchemist:

- integrates personal, material and deeper societal transformation;
- able to lead large system transformations.

Non-linear development path

Although leaders can transform from one stage to the next, progress is not necessarily predictable or linear but bumpy and discontinuous with significant time required at each stage (see Torbert (2004) for a wonderfully complex map of this). The experience of being 'upended' or thrown back to a previous phase can happen any time while moving from Diplomat to Achiever. Beyond Achiever, Individualist is not seen as a destination, but more of a journey that circles back and deepens understanding of the previous stages before reaching the Strategist stage. Then the journey from Strategist to Alchemist is of a different order. The leader moves beyond using traditional frames for understanding the world towards developing a deeper 'reframing spirit' or habit, including 'listening to the chaos below what can normally be perceived'. If the latter feels difficult to understand, that's fine and quite normal! The further you are from a particular level of maturity, the more difficult it is to grasp the body-mindset involved.

Using values or 'needs' as an indicator of maturity

As a fresh way of looking at this life journey, it's illuminating to compare the above two developmental frameworks (Kegan and Torbert) with the work of Schwartz (2005). He mapped out a set of basic human values recognized in all cultures around the world, expanding and deepening the work of Maslow (1943, 1970), who set out a hierarchy of human needs that progressed towards self-actualization. Rather than looking at the 'meaning-making' or 'action-logics', Schwartz's work is focused on understanding people's dominant motivational goals. These can be categorized and summarized as follows, and grouped under a slightly extended version of Maslow's headings, provided by Griffiths (2015):

Sustenance-directed

Conformity – restraint of actions, inclinations, and impulses likely to upset or harm others and violate social expectations or norms.

Tradition – respect, commitment, and acceptance of the customers and ideas that traditional culture or religion provides the self.

Security – safety, harmony and stability of society, relationships and of self.

Outer-directed

Achievement – personal success through demonstrating competence according to social standards.

Power – social status and prestige, control or dominance over people and resources.

Transitional outer-directed

Hedonism – pleasure and sensuous gratification for oneself.

Self-direction – independent thought and action; choosing, creating, exploring.

Stimulation – excitement, novelty and challenge in life.

Inner-directed

Benevolence – preserving and enhancing the welfare of those with whom one is in frequent personal contact.

Universalism – understanding, appreciation, tolerance and protection for the welfare of all people and for nature.

Schwartz says that values develop according to life circumstance. Rather than necessarily a one-way developmental path toward greater human service, the opportunities, demands and constraints in life tend to influence our values in different ways; they are an adaptation to circumstance, with people having the flexibility to upgrade or downgrade values with various degrees of difficulty. These values, he says, are also a significant driver of behaviour, although clearly people make trade-offs between their different values when there is conflict.

It's also possible to see this set of values as a broad developmental progression that involves working through struggles and conflicts, and throughout which people can experience plateaus, stuckness, pain and developmental leaps depending on circumstance and personal focus. For instance, it's common for people to experience a shift in interests and needs after the age of 45–50, with status and achievement starting to seem less attractive than a walk by the sea or an opportunity to do voluntary work.

In the case of leaders, the journey from 'dependence' to 'interdependence' described by Petrie seems to run roughly parallel with Maslow's four headings (see Table 14.1). Therefore, it's possible that insight into one's dominant values can illuminate the type of leadership development support a leader requires to be able to grow their maturity. For those interested to explore more, see the Dominant Needs Analysis questionnaire provided via **http://www.integralchange.co.uk/online-psychometric/** or the Schwartz Values Survey, via for example **www.yourmorals.org**.

The leadership maturity gap – a call to action!

As can be seen from Table 14.2, which illustrates the distribution of the different levels of maturity across various populations, it's clear that around half of the adult population, and an even greater proportion of the manager population are not yet at the Self-Authoring/Achiever stages identified by Kegan and Torbert respectively. Yet most serious leadership roles expect people to be operating at least at this level, ie dealing with some complexity, delivering outcomes for the system, being selective and patient about their interventions. It's important therefore that people who aspire to be successful leaders, and those supporting their development, understand how the development of leadership maturity works and take responsibility for ensuring that this is attended to.

This is a puzzle for HR leaders and learning and development experts. The question is, how can leadership maturity be encouraged and supported in an organizational setting? This requires new strategic thinking, which in turn requires reflection time and space to devise and implement successfully.

For individuals wanting to mature, there are a number of prerequisites:

i) be self-aware regarding their skills;

ii) be realistic about their current maturity level;

iii) have a level of motivation and life ambition;

iv) be prepared to bring some discipline and rigour to the learning process.

For organizations interested in shifting to a more mature leadership culture, it's clear that growing leadership maturity as a whole system is a complex endeavour which requires a multi-layered, networked approach; this is explored in Part Six.

Suggestions for growing leadership maturity

In the case of growing individual leadership maturity, we offer some areas of focus for leaders and the people they coach.

To support Dependent-Conformers to move from 'Diplomats' to 'Experts', help them focus on:

- finding out about the perspectives of others, that they are different and varied;

- experimenting in small ways with different ways of doing things;

- imagining what others might want or feel, and what might help them;

- understanding that any 'behavioural' difficulties are likely to be developmental rather than 'personality' problems;

- tuning in to their own emotions, noticing impulsive explosions or withdrawals.

To support Dependent-Conformers to move towards being Independent-Achievers, help them focus on:

- authoring a plan or way forward, without simply adopting another's framework or standards;

- questioning authorities and accepted wisdoms, assumed or real;

- staying alert to self-generated stress caused by striving to meet imagined/perfectionist standards;

- getting interested in why things are the way they are; why people say the things they do;

- understanding that every encounter and interaction holds new perspectives; staying open to what's really going on.

To support Independent-Achievers move towards being to Interdependent-Collaborators, help them focus on:

- asking for and welcoming all personal feedback rather than needing to make it 'fit' with an existing self-image;
- experimenting with sharing decision making and/or considering different solutions which deliver different levels of satisfaction for the various parties involved;
- starting to track change at multiple levels, from multiple 'angles' – personal, team, departmental, whole business…;
- becoming more aware of one's own reactions to others, including unearthing appreciations and inquiring into irritations;
- practising 'immediacy': checking in, maybe twice a day, on one's mental, emotional and physical state.

The move within Interdependent-Collaborator from Strategist to Alchemist is a more mysterious, less well-charted process. However, examples of developmental 'signs' are:

- developing great humility, and owning own foibles and darker sides;
- stepping back and comparing integrating systems in a fluid, non-attached way;
- realizing the futility of map-mapping and striving for higher states…;
- recognizing the 'central functioning' role of the ego and seeing through own attempts at 'meaning-making';
- surrendering to ambiguity, seeing it as a generator of creativity.

Alchemists, according to Torbert (2004), are open to 'new revelations and new wonderment' on a continuing basis. They continually participate in the work of historical/spiritual transformation and treat time and events as symbolic rather than literal. Whether or not they can make good organizational leaders depends on the context!

Table 14.1 Comparing and aligning i) Adult developmental stages and ii) Schwartz's clusters of values (adapted from McCauley *et al.*, 2006)

Framework/ phases*	Dependent-Conformer		Independent-Achiever	Interdependent-Collaborator
Kegan (1994, 2009)	Self-Sovereign	Socialized	Self-Authoring	Self-Transforming
Perspective	Focused on own perspective	Able to see the world through the eyes of others	Aware of own perspective, and the views of others	Sees multiple perspectives simultaneously, can use these to continuously self-transform
				Open, curious, able to see and navigate complex patterns across and within
Relationship with authority	Follows rules and regulations	Follows internalized value set which comes for significant others	Develops own, personalized set of principles	

(Continued)

Table 14.1 (Continued)

Torbert (2004)	Diplomat	Expert	Achiever	Individualist	Strategist	Alchemist**
Action logic/ dominant strategy	Do what's acceptable	Be seen to be attaining technical merit	Deliver outcomes for whole system	Everything is relative; there are many different ways of seeing and understanding	Change is an iterative developmental process; constraints are transformable	External freshness of life; significance of death; awareness, truth
Focus	Routine tasks, short-term horizon	Problem solving, improvement, efficiency	Listening to feedback, delivering through others	Noticing contradictions between belief and action, communications, developing self	Weaving together agendas/visions that encourage transformation, paying attention at many levels	Noticing interplay of awareness, thought and action, participating in transformation of self and others
Schwartz	Sustenance Directed	Outer-Directed	Transitional Outer-Directed		Inner-Directed	
Dominant Values	Conformity, Tradition, Security	Achievement, Power		Self-Direction, Stimulation, Hedonism	Benevolence, Universalism	

* Petrie's phases

Each phase includes and transcends earlier stages, ie earlier perspectives remain accessible but do not dominate.

Torbert also names a later stage, which is beyond the scope of this book – Ironist – represented in 0.5 per cent of the population.

Table 14.2 How leadership maturity is distributed in the US population – an illustration

Population/Phase	Dependent-Conformer		Independent-Achiever		Interdependent-Collaborator	
	Diplomat	**Expert**	**Achiever**	**Individualist**	**Strategist**	**Alchemist**
Torbert definitions (2004)	Diplomat	Expert	Achiever	Individualist	Strategist	Alchemist
497 Managers (Torbert, 2004)	10% (+3% at earlier stages)	45%	35%	7% (from Individualist upwards)		
Kegan definitions (1994)	Self-Sovereign	Socialized	Self-Authoring		Self-Transforming	
US adults (Kegan 2009)	13%	46%	40%		1%	

Helpful practices for maturing leaders

Based on our experience and the above research, we suggest the following supports that leaders who are motivated to become more mature in their leadership can draw on.

Responsibility taking

Leaders need to take responsibility for their own learning as much as possible. Highly structured talent management plans and programmes of learning may unintentionally encourage 'dependency' habits such as leaders waiting to be told what their next developmental step or project is, or waiting to be chased for assignments or feedback. This means that the leaders themselves need to be doing things like: seeking out good-quality reading; asking someone they respect to mentor them; inviting and exploring feedback on the impact and effects/outcomes of their leadership; requesting and rooting out their own development opportunities; and honestly charting their own progress.

Action-reflection loops

Leaders need to practice continuous, iterative action-reflection loops, as these are vital for the development of maturity (See Figure 14.1). This helps build increased awareness of how leadership actions are working out, and supports the leader to stay open to important feedback. This important adaptive practice can be supported by good-quality executive coaching, and needs ultimately to be embedded in every leader's day-to-day life.

The cycle in Figure 14.1, adapted from the Learning Cycle introduced above, identifies four clear phases for leaders to continuously cycle through – *alone, in 1:1s, and with their teams* – to ensure both delivery and learning/growth.

At an individual level this might mean journaling (see below), and/or good-quality preparation for monthly 1:1s with a line manager. At a team level, this means making space at regular team meetings for reflections on the past week/month's team performance and mutual inquiry about courses of action and outcomes. For more about the importance of this, and of uncovering obstacles to deep change, see Tobert (2004) and Kegan and Lahey (2009).

Regular journaling

As mentioned in Part Two, and reinforced here, reflective practices are extremely helpful to those wishing to develop their leadership capacity and

Figure 14.1 Action-Reflection Loop (adapted from Fig. 12.1)

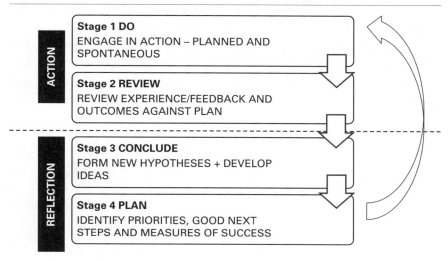

maturity. The act of regular journaling in response to a particular set of questions can help leaders to inquire into their own actions and the impact of these, thus surfacing gaps between plans, actions and outcomes. This requires some support and courage to do well and with integrity, and really starts to bear fruit as a self-reliant practice after the Expert action-logic stage.

Drawing on flexible leadership archetypes

Leadership checklists and four-box models are all around us, and although helpful in understanding concepts and styles, they can be rather restrictive when it comes to expanding and maturing into one's own leadership potential. Many of them are no match for the complexities faced by today's leaders. We encourage our clients to use more flexible definitions of leadership qualities, so that conversations about leadership can range from the focused to the more imaginative.

The realm of depth psychology, which is full of archetypes and myths, offers a relatively unscientific but infinitely flexible way of looking at the world and what goes on in it. Archetypes traditionally include what we see on the surface, what is possible via the imagination, and what is darker and less seen (Jung, 1968). From the Ancient Greeks right through to Star Wars, and in our own political systems, we encounter certain archetypal figures who represent a universally resonant pattern of aspects of human nature, both heroic and demonic.

In Part Five, we introduce our suite of five flexible leadership archetypes or 'qualities', supported by recent research and a synthesis of much of the leadership literature (see Part Two – Overall Map). Experience indicates that this type of adaptive, unifying framework can lead to a deeper appreciation of the range and depth of qualities that are required from any individual or network of leaders to enable a collective purpose to be enacted in any particular context.

Pause for Learning Points

Leadership maturity appears to correlate with the capacity to innovate and transform, and to deal with ever more complex organizational challenges. Core leadership skills are important, yet these are enacted differently by leaders at different levels of maturity.

Adults mature more slowly and unpredictably than children, and need to invest considerable effort and self-discipline in order for this maturing to happen.

Torbert and Kegan have defined and researched the key phases/stages of leadership maturity and the underlying meaning-making systems and logics that underpin each, with Petrie providing a useful, overarching three-stage model.

Research from 2004 indicates that there are too few Independent-Achievers and Interdependent-Collaborators, at least in the United States' leadership population at that time, with 55 per cent at Dependent-Conformer level. This must change if 21st-century challenges are going to be tackled successfully.

Values and dominant needs have a clear relationship with leadership maturity, and these can be influenced by circumstance, particularly when contextual changes are great, such as feeling physically unsafe.

Leaders can draw on various supports if they are keen to develop their leadership maturity: taking responsibility for their own development; practising action-reflection at a personal and team level; journaling regularly about their leadership; and seeking out more flexible, imaginative leadership frameworks.

Stop and Reflect!

Reflect honestly on your own level of leadership maturity, without judging yourself as lacking in any way. Use the Torbert and Kegan frameworks to pinpoint this as accurately as you can, then discuss this with your line manager or a close colleague and see what they think.

How well are your skills and your level of leadership maturity matched to the challenges you face?

What is the gap and how might you work on growing yourself as a leader?

What ambitions do you have as a leader?

What practices might you need to start incorporating into your work/life to help you to grow into these?

References and further reading

Anderson, L, George, M, Kempster, S, Gold, J and Thorpe, R (2006) So what works in SME leadership and management development? The state of the field, Northern Leadership Academy

Berger, J G (2012) *Changing on the Job: Developing leaders for a complex world*, Stanford University Press

Cameron, E and Green, M (2008) *Making Sense of Leadership*, Kogan Page, London

Cook-Greuter, S R (2013) Nine levels of increasing embrace in human development [online] http://www.cook-greuter.com/Cook-Greuter%209%20levels%20 paper%20new%201.1'14%2097p%5B1%5D.pdf [accessed 18 August 2016]

Griffiths, N (2015) Needs and values equivalence in evolution, *Dominant Needs Analysis* [online] http://dominantneedsanalysis.com/images/Placing%20 Personal%20Values%20In%20An%20Evolutionary%20Context%20 (Dec%2015).pdf [accessed 18 August 2016]

Hanson, R and Mendius, R (2009) Buddha's Brain: The practical neuroscience of happiness, love and wisdom, New Harbinger, Oakland, CA

Jung, C G (1968) *The Archetypes and the Collective Unconscious*, 2nd edn (R F Hull, trans.) Princeton University Press, Princeton, NJ

Kegan, R (1994) *In Over Our Heads: The mental demands of modern life*, Harvard University Press, Cambridge, MA

Kegan, R and Lahey, L (2009) *Immunity to Change: How to overcome it and unlock the potential in yourself and your organization*, Harvard Business School Publishing, Boston, MA

Maslow, A H (1943) A Theory of Human Motivation, in *Dominance, Self-esteem, Self-actualization: Germinal papers of A H Maslow*, ed R J Lowry (1973) Wadsworth

Maslow, A H (1970) *Motivation and Personality*, Harper & Row, New York

McCauley, C D, Drath W H, Palus C J, O'Connor, P M G and Baker, B A (2006) The use of constructive-developmental theory to advance the understanding of leadership, *The Leadership Quarterly*, **17** (6) pp. 634–53

Petrie, N (2014 (2)) *Vertical Leadership Development Parts 1 & 2*, Centre for Creative Leadership

Rooke, D and Torbert, W R (2005) Seven transformations of leadership, *Harvard Business Review*, April

Schwartz, S (1996) Value priorities and behavior: applying a theory of integrated value systems, in *The Psychology of Values: The Ontario Symposium, volume 8*, ed C Seligman, J M Olson and M P Zanna, Lawrence Erlbaum, Mahwah, NJ

Schwartz, S (2005) *Basic Human Values: An overview*, The Hebrew University of Jerusalem

Torbert, W R and Associates (2004) *Action Inquiry*, Berrett-Koehler, San Francisco

Conclusions from Part Three

There are many significant 21st-century challenges for leaders to rise to, yet the approach being used to develop leaders in many organizations is not yet delivering what's required. More facility with complexity and much higher levels of adaptability need to be acquired by more leaders. This means developing existing leaders, and nurturing the perhaps better-adapted skills of incoming Millennials (see Part Six).

If leadership development approaches are to become more effective, these need to be targeted at developing both skills and body-mindsets. Leaders at all levels, and their organizations, need to be motivated to take leadership development seriously. This needs to be worked at, individually and collectively, through creative, action-reflection loops that focus on live challenges.

PART FOUR
You and your development

Overview

The purpose of this book is to help enable you become a better leader – more effective in what you do, more able to motivate those around you, and more able to see your leadership role in the context of a wider system.

In Part Two we introduced key leadership theories and frameworks from the last 100 years, and in Part Three we explored how you can learn to lead in practice. In Part Four, as we move towards introducing the Five Qualities in depth – essential qualities needed for any leader wherever you are in your organization or your community – we need to turn our focus onto you.

The first thing to realize is that in order to step further in your leadership, you need to know yourself. It's important to be able to access all your experiences and talents if you want to expand your ability to perform well. It is also crucial to know where you want to go, what you want to achieve. There are many questions that you may care to answer about yourself as you start to develop as a leader:

- Who are you?
- What do you stand for?
- What are your gifts?
- What are your behaviour patterns?
- How do you think and feel?
- Where does your passion lie?

Psychometrics and 360-degree feedback mechanisms will also help, as will simply asking people to tell you what's special or brilliant about you, what they appreciate about you, what irritates them about you and what they'd advise you to do differently.

The aims of Part Four are to get you started with this process by:

- taking you through a process of self-assessment;
- helping you to clarify your leadership development goals (and intended outcomes); and
- offering you some ideas, tools and tips to support you on your leadership journey.

Chapter 15 will help you to take stock of your leadership performance so far, and Chapter 16 encourages you to think through and formulate your goals and development supports.

Writing in the book?

Please note that we have left blank spaces and provided tables in these chapters for you to fill in your answers. This is meant to illustrate the type of process we'd advise you go through, and to stimulate you to join in! However, we realize that many people don't like to write in books. We also realize that this process can be quite difficult if you're reading the book electronically. *So please do get a pen and notebook handy now if this is the case.*

Taking stock and self-rating   15

Introduction

The aim of this chapter is to take you through a process of self-reflection for you to better understand who you are in relation to your leadership. We will discover how you see yourself, how your past experiences and personality structure have shaped you, and how what you stand for and want to make out of your life, and contribute to others (organizationally and in the wider community), also define who you are.

If you're not yet in a formal leadership position or have little experience of the working world, then in this section please consider leadership roles you've had so far – in your family, community, sports, clubs – and how you've handled that. Some questions might be more taxing than others, so do skip them if they don't apply. The important thing is for you to get to know your own leadership skills and patterns, and to get a sense of how they've been developing in you so far.

This chapter is therefore mostly *reflective*, so do notice whether this is something you are familiar with, something you enjoy, or something you shy away from. The process we invite you to participate in does require engagement on your part. In order to develop, you need to be open to thinking differently, interacting differently, behaving differently. As we saw in Part Three, we all have different preferred learning styles; however, we encourage you to work through the whole learning cycle as we take you through different activities to enhance your self-awareness.

The process will take you on a journey, looking at how you see yourself, your formative experiences and your future hopes. We will also look at your shadow side; those things which have the potential to sabotage you and your leadership.

We will also review how you see yourself in relation to the leadership frameworks you read about in Part Two.

Some of the exercises are skewed towards organizational leadership. Please adapt them to your own circumstances ('direct reports' can become friends, volunteers, community co-workers etc).

Self-reflection

So, *who are you?* If you could describe yourself in a hundred words or so, what would you write?

Spend some time jotting down key words – both positive and perhaps less so – and then craft a paragraph or two which you feel aptly describes you, and which you feel would be recognizable by others.

Here's one of the authors:

'Mike is a thoughtful man constantly looking for the meaning behind things. He values family and friendships and believes passionately in truth and justice. He takes time in thinking about things and weighs up the pros and cons before making a decision. He values loyalty and competency in both himself and others and finds it hard when either are missing in a relationship.

'Introverted Mike is both planful and organized, tends to see the bigger picture, patterns and connections between things. He doesn't relish the detail. He finds it hard to enter into conflict with people but will do so when the stakes are high or when it's a matter of values.'

You might be able to see some of my values and personality coming through and how that might relate to my leadership style.

Now it's your turn!

In six to ten words, describe your leadership or influencing style (eg motivational, passionate, coercive, decisive, disciplined, collaborative, thought-leadership, strategic, performance-oriented, relational…)

When you review these words, which ones are there because they are your natural gifts, which ones because of formative experiences in your life which have shaped your personality, and which ones because you've consciously learned to be that sort of manager/leader?

If you've answered because of formative experiences in your life, briefly make a few notes about your thoughts on that. What were those early experiences (eg in your family), and how do they tend to play out in the way you try to influence others?

On a good day, how might people describe your leadership or personal style? That's when you are 'in the zone' and able to relate to both the thing you are doing and the people involved in an effortlessly effective way. Write down the key words and expressions.

On a bad day, how might people describe your leadership or personal style? This could be when, on reflection, you felt somewhat regretful of your behaviour towards others or your lack of attention to the task. This might be due to personality pitfalls or pressured circumstances. Don't beat yourself up, just observe and note it down.

Let's now fast-forward. And let's say that, having read and applied the lessons in this book, and continued to reflect on and develop your leadership through experience, you have built on whoever you are today and really grown as a leader and made a lasting impact in some small or large way. How would you like to be remembered? What would people say at your funeral about how you have served the world? What would your epitaph be?

Stop and Reflect!

Take some time out to review three experiences where you have demonstrated leadership, both effective and ineffective. This could be inside or outside work. Evaluate them in terms of what behaviours you displayed, what you were thinking, how you were feeling. What was it about your leadership that led to the success or otherwise of the intended outcomes? How would others involved in the situation describe their experience and the impact that your leadership had on them? Are there things you would do differently next time?

Now, take three experiences when you were being led by another person. Include both a good and a bad experience. What behaviours and communications by the leader led to you having the experiences that you had? How might the outcomes have been achieved differently?

In reviewing the experiences of leading and being led, what conclusions can you draw, and what links can you make to the leadership frameworks you have read about so far?

Another useful model for thinking about self-awareness is the Johari window (Luft and Ingham, 1955). This helps us understand that what we know about ourselves, and what others know about us, are different. Through inviting feedback from others, we can helpfully expand our self-knowledge, although there will always remain hidden or unknown elements.

This model indicates that there are levels of our behaviour that we are unaware of. Yet, through our actions and non-verbal messages (of which we may be quite unaware), others hold information about us that we do not. There are also levels of our behaviour which we know about but choose to keep hidden from others. This may be because of fear, lack of confidence, poor self-esteem, or a high level of sensitivity or privacy, etc.

The 'unconscious' realm is that level of behaviour about which both the individual and others are unaware. This can be reduced by being open to feedback from others and being more open with others, but it is unlikely to be totally revealed.

The open area is that level of behaviour that is public knowledge and widely known about an individual. It is the arena from which we generally function and communicate. This is the area in which capacity for developing ourselves readily appears. To improve our interpersonal skills, we could show more of our resources, practise our potential skills and more visibly demonstrate our behaviours into this open arena.

In order to become more self-aware you could:

i. Ask your line manager and/or other people who regularly work alongside you for information about how they perceive your leadership or influencing style.

Figure 15.1 Johari Window

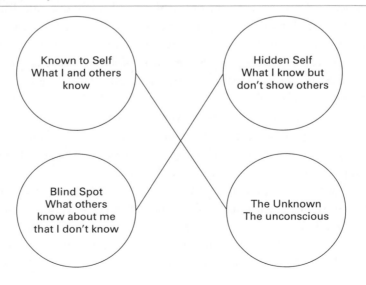

Figure 15.2 Johari Window template

Known Self	Hidden Self
Blind Spot	The Unknown

ii.   Ask your suppliers, clients, customers, or your coach if you have one, for feedback about the ways in which they experience you as an influencer.

iii.   Ask people you work with in other areas of your life to tell you about how they experience you as a leader or influencer.

iv.   Use the four boxes below to make some notes about your own levels of self-awareness, and what was revealed.

The behaviour patterns that result from your personality type can also be useful to explore. This is also an excellent way to find out more about how you behave, and what your natural gifts are. There are several proprietary personality profiles and some are available free online. We use the Myers-Briggs Type Indicator (MBTI™), as it tells you how you prefer to take in information and make decisions compared to other people. It holds up a mirror and sheds light on your learning style, your leadership and communication preferences as well as potential pitfalls. It will also give you a good sense of which activities and ways of working you find easy and enjoyable, and which activities and ways of working are more stressful and draining for you. It can also give you pointers about where you need to focus effort to develop yourself, given your aspirations or ambitions. This sort of questionnaire can now be accessed very easily online, and is a great starting point for increased self-awareness.

Once you have completed such a questionnaire and digested the results, summarize in the box below what you consider the main points that have meaning to you. What does it say about your strengths and weaknesses? What might you find a stretch in terms of leadership, if you confine yourself to operating within your profile?

Knowing what you stand for in the world is important too. Are you in favour of an unregulated free market? Do you welcome the free movement of workers around the world? Would that include refugees and asylum seekers? Is there a role for 'big government', or can society operate with minimal intervention? What's your political stance? What's your position on climate change and care for the planet? How much does your faith or absence of faith (religious or otherwise) influence your world view? What's really important to you? What are you trying to achieve for yourself, your family, your organization, your community? What are your principles of living? The more you know about yourself in this respect, the more self-confident, authentic and convincing you will become.

Here's one of the authors stands in relation to her work, as an example:

'*I want to devote my working life to enabling a healthy flow of leadership and responsibility taking in complex organizations. I will work hard to establish open, honest and collaborative partnerships with clients, which are underpinned by clear agreements. I strive to treat every assignment as an enquiry, while aiming to be generous with my knowledge and expertise when it's needed.*'

And your turn:

Using theory to develop yourself

This section encourages you to review the leadership theory in Part Two and begin to reflect upon how it can inform your leadership. It may be that you'd like to concentrate on just two or three leadership theories for self-assessment. That's fine, but do skim read the whole section to establish the key ones for you.

Traits (Chapter 2)

Look at the list of traits that researchers have suggested contribute to leadership effectiveness.

Score yourself on each trait twice – as you are today [X], and in terms of what you think would be most effective in your current on future leadership role [✓]. Consider any gaps and note down what you can do to develop that trait, or mitigate that deficit.

Leadership Traits

| Leadership Trait | Lo | | | | Hi | Comment |
	1	2	3	4	5	
Ability to influence other people's behaviour						
Adjustment						
Agreeableness						
Alertness						
Capacity to structure social interaction systems to the purpose						
Conscientiousness						
Conservatism						
Desire to lead						
Determination						
Dominance						
Drive						
Drive for responsibility and task completion						
Drive to exercise initiative in social situations						
Extraversion						
Honesty and Integrity						
Initiative						
Insight						
Integrity						
Intelligence, Cognitive ability						
Knowledge of the business						
Masculinity						
Neuroticism (-)						
Openness						
Persistence						
Readiness to absorb interpersonal stress						

(Continued)

(*Continued*)

Leadership Trait	Lo 1	2	3	4	Hi 5	Comment
Responsibility						
Self-confidence						
Sense of personal identity						
Sociability						
Venturesomeness and originality in problem solving						
Vigour and persistence in pursuit of goals						
Willingness to accept consequences of decision and action						
Willingness to tolerate frustration and delay						

Task-Relationships (Chapters 3 and 4)

Many of the leadership theories differentiate between task-related leadership behaviours and relation-focused behaviours. How would you score yourself (0–10) in terms of focus on task and focus on people? Of course, these can be context-specific, but we generally have a default 'balance'. What's your default balance, are you content with it, and do you consider this balance as you exercise your leadership in whatever context, day to day, year to year?

Contingency and Situational Leadership (Chapters 3 and 4)

How often do you take into account the following variables?

Contingency and situational leadership

	Lo 1	2	3	4	Hi 5	Comment
The competence of your team						
The confidence of your team						
The motivation of your team						
How highly structured the task is						
The complexity of the task						
The formal power you have						
The degree of influence you have						
How clearly do you articulate the purpose of the task you wish to be done?						
Do you articulate the benefits to the individual, the team, and to the organization?						
How clear are you about the role, the responsibility and accountability when giving a task to someone?						
To what extent do you consider the organizational setting and circumstances when allocating tasks?						

To what extent do you consider Vroom's (1973) seven questions when managing individuals and the team?

1 Is the technical quality of the decision very important i.e. are the consequences of failure significant?

2 Does a successful outcome depend on your team members' commitment to the decision? Must there be buy-in for the solution to work?

3 Do you have sufficient information to be able to make the decision on your own?

4 Is the problem well-structured so that you can easily understand what needs to be addressed and what defines a good solution?

5 Are you reasonably sure that your team will accept your decision even if you make it yourself?

6 Are the goals of the team consistent with the goals the organization has set to define a successful solution?

7 Will there likely be conflict among the team as to which solution is best?

How easy is it for you to step into each of the four Situational Leadership styles? What might some of your challenges be?

Directing Involves the leader telling the subordinate what to do and perhaps how to do it. This is required as the subordinate doesn't have the knowledge, skills or experience needed to complete the task, and the leader does.

Coaching Can be performed by the leader when there is still the require-ment to direct what needs to be done but there is more supportive behaviour and the subordinate has some confidence and some competence.

Supporting Behaviour from the leader is indicated when the subordinate has the ability to complete the task but perhaps variable levels of commit-ment or confidence.

Delegating Occurs when the subordinate is both competent and committed and thus little or no direction or support is required.

Power (Chapter 5)

This next assessment asks: where do you get your power from and what do you rely upon when you need to influence people? Different groups within the organization may be swayed by different types of power, as will stakeholders outside the organization.

Types of power

Positional power	Description	Comments
Legitimate power	Comes from the position or rank the person holds in an organization, the job role and place in the hierarchy and the status of that role	
Reward power	Comes from the ability to control promotion, salary increases and current and future role activities	
Coercive power	Comes from the ability to penalize, punish, compel someone to do something and withhold rewards	
Information power	Comes from the ability to access and control dissemination of data and information; and to allow or deny access to important others	
Ecological power	Comes from the ability to determine physical, technological and organizational infrastructure matters	
Personal power		
Expert power	Comes from the person possessing more in-depth or broader knowledge, skills, understanding, competence and/or experience of the task, activity or business area	

(Continued)

(Continued)

Positional power	Description	Comments
Referent power	Comes from the fact that direct reports can identify, like and/or respect the leader	

Transactional and transformational leadership (Chapter 6)

Assess yourself across the transactional and transformational leadership spectrum. Do you appraise the situation and the people involved and use whichever leadership style is required, or do you default to just one? Remember, there is a role for both transactional and transformational leadership if exhibited effectively. Note: the laissez-faire style is not true leadership.

Transactional and transformational leadership

Transactional Leadership	Description	Comments
Contingent Reward	Exchanges rewards for effort and achievement	
Management by Exception – Active	Searches for and corrects deviations from rules and standards	
Management by Exception – Passive	Intervenes only if standards are not met	
Idealized Influence	Provides a role model for ethical behaviour, instils pride, gains respect and trust	
Inspirational Motivation	Articulates an appealing vision in an engaging way, challenges with high standards, communicates optimism	
Intellectual Stimulation	Challenges assumptions, invites creativity, encourages people to think independently	

(Continued)

(Continued)

Transactional Leadership	Description	Comments
Individualized Consideration	Attends to each follower in a different way, is empathetic, gives advice, acts as mentor	
Laissez-faire	Abdicates responsibilities and avoids making decisions	

Strategic and innovation leadership and change leadership (Chapters 7 and 8)

Much of the leadership theory in Part Two relates to day-to-day management of the business and the employees within the business. However, whether you are a team leader, a middle manager or part of the senior management team you should have one eye on the horizon. If, typically, it is the senior management who set the direction of the business, it is also the responsibility of team leaders and middle managers to translate that strategic intent to their direct reports and their customers. Likewise, when there are significant changes within the organization, it is important for leaders at all levels to be skilled in the art of change management and leadership. The following questionnaire allows you to assess yourself against key criteria across the strategic, innovation and change leadership dimensions.

Strategic and innovation leadership and change leadership

	Lo 1	2	3	4	Hi 5
Strategic and Innovation Leadership					
Anticipate, scan the environment, pick up trends, project yourself forward					
Challenge, question the status quo, assumptions about reality and about your decision-making process					
Interpret, be able to make sense of data and information, surface assumptions, pick up weak signals, filter out noise					
Decide, have a robust and inclusive problem-solving and decision-making process					

(Continued)

(*Continued*)

	Lo 1	2	3	4	Hi 5
Align, ensure coherence across the strategy and alignment within the organization					
Learn, foster a culture of learning from one's actions, mistakes, failures, successes					
Leadership in more complex and uncertain situations and contexts					
Establish shared agendas and priorities across organizational boundaries					
Develop shared narratives					
Build trust and share risk					
Be courageous and have robust discussions					
Spot talent and enable it to act					
Understand the new skills mix and mindsets required to provide strategic leadership in this context					
Exchange information and resources					
Spot opportunities as they unfold					
Create new knowledge					
Enable, facilitate and coach					
Management and leadership of change					
A clear rationale and compelling reason to change					
A clear direction, end point and motivation for change					
A clear sense of how the process will be managed					
Ongoing visible sponsorship					
Demonstrable engagement with stakeholders; enabling them to go through transition					
A credible effective dedicated change management team					
A well-planned and organized approach					
Ongoing, focused, tailored communication of direction and progress					
Attention to task, process and people					

Leadership responsibility and values (Chapter 9)

The final part of the review and self-assessment centres more on you as a person. How much of a values-based and authentic leader are you?

Leadership responsibility and values

	Lo 1	2	3	4	Hi 5
Leadership responsibility and values					
Self-reflection – knowing what you stand for					
Balance – seeing the situation from 'multiple perspectives and differing viewpoints to gain a much fuller understanding'					
Self-confidence – confidence in your abilities, acknowledging strengths and deficits and recognizing that is who you are					
Humility – to be modest, humble, not vain or proud, accepting that others may have a better solution					
Valuing people through believing, serving, and nonjudgmentally listening to others					
Developing people through providing learning, growth, encouragement and affirmation					
Building community through developing strong collaborative and personal relationships					
Displaying authenticity through being open, accountable, and willing to learn from others					
Providing leadership through foreseeing the future, taking initiative, and establishing goals					
Sharing leadership through facilitating and sharing power					

The Five Leadership Qualities

To complete this exercise, it makes sense if you also reflect upon the Five Leadership Qualities that we briefly introduced as archetypes at the end of Part Two and describe more fully in Part Five. Give yourself an initial 'gut feel' score for each quality via Figure 15.4, using Figure 15.3 for guidance.

You now have a choice. You can either carry on to Chapter 16 to complete the goal-setting process now, or you might prefer to pause this process, and read through the rest of the book first. It's up to you!

(Note: We have used initials rather than the names of the Qualities in these figures.)

Figure 15.3 Five Qualities

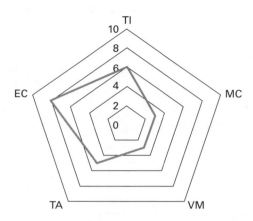

Figure 15.4 Five Qualities template

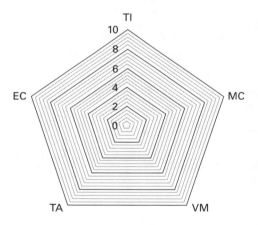

Stop and Reflect!

Reviewing the activities in Chapter 15, what were your key observations and insights?

Of the personal reflections (around your past, present and future self), what stood out as really significant?

How easy was it for you to appraise yourself?

What is affirming, and what is a call to action?

And if you had three emerging leadership development goals, what would they be?

References

Luft, J and Ingham, H (1955) The Johari window: a graphic model of interpersonal awareness, Proceedings of the western training laboratory in group development, UCLA, LA

Vroom, V H and Yetton, P W (1973) *Leadership and Decision Making*, University of Pittsburgh Press, Pittsburgh, PA

Clarifying your goals and intended outcomes

16

Introduction

This chapter builds on the reflective work you have done in the previous chapter and works towards your developing your own Leadership Development Plan (LDP). It will also assist you in gathering the necessary resources and people around you to turn your plans into reality. This builds on the principles of a Personal Development Plan (below), but focuses on how you intend to develop your leadership to deliver the work outcomes required of you.

Personal Development Planning is:

> a structured and supported process undertaken by a learner to reflect upon their own learning, performance and/or achievement and to plan for their personal, educational and career development (Quality Assurance Agency, 2009).

Leadership development planning

As you review your assessments in Chapter 15, what are the key aspects of your leadership which stand out as needing some attention? Write the top three down, for example: 'I need to spend more time understanding the skills of my team so that I can get more out of them'; 'I need to better understand the link between the CEO's new strategy and what we do in our department so I can plan better'; or 'I'm not so good at standing my ground with people in an assertive and non-aggressive way, and that means that people are uncertain about the standards we are working to'.

You may need to think a little more deeply about what you then want to do with these observations. Knowing about your team members' skills and motivation is all well and good, but actually the real question may be, 'How do I know which leadership style to use with my team reports and how can I practise this?'

When you have a good enough statement, then we can begin to work up a specific outcome for this particular leadership development opportunity. One tool which can help is a useful framework for development called the Henley Star (Kruckeberg, Amann and Green, 2011). This can be used at a strategic level, assessing the leadership development you need going into the future – or it can be used operationally for focusing on a specific decision, situation or perhaps a new project that you are about to undertake.

By thinking through the particular outcomes that you require – a motivated employee who grows their skills; a resounding project success that makes life easier for customers; a faultless change programme that allows more streamlined ways of working – you are beginning with the end in mind. Spend some time describing those outcomes in sufficient detail for them to be as SMART (Specific, Measurable, Achievable, Realistic, Time-bound) as possible.

Then you can work backwards to begin to list the effective leadership behaviours that you consider necessary for those outcomes. Your reflections from Parts Two and Three and Chapter 15 will help you get a handle on the necessary behaviours.

Effective leadership behaviours are the product of your levels of knowledge and understanding, and the practical leadership skills that you have; they can be supported or limited by your usual behaviour patterns and values. The next task is to populate the other three areas of the star. You can

Figure 16.1   Adapted Henley Star (Kruckeberg, Amann and Green, 2011)

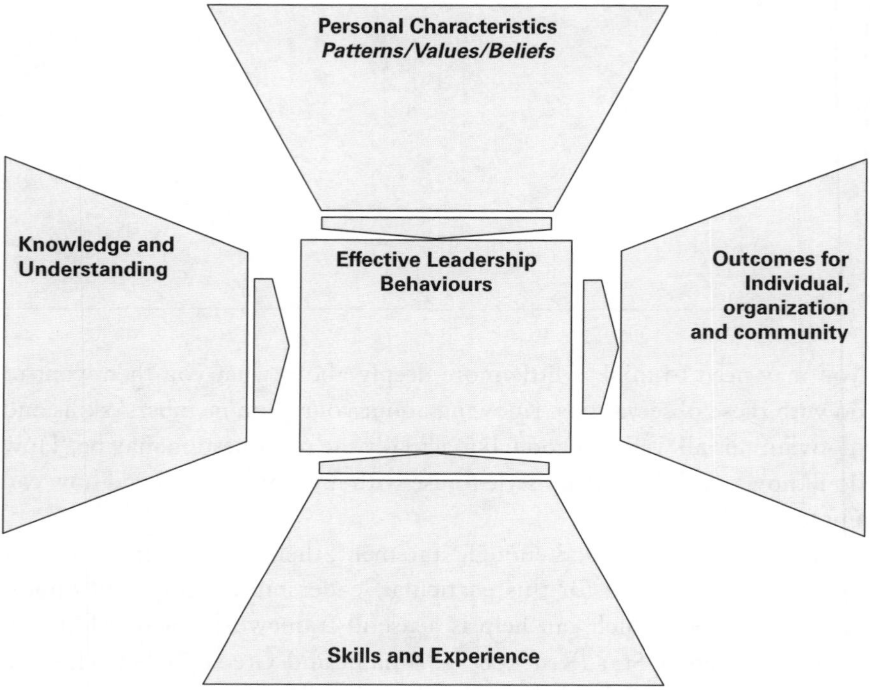

Personal Characteristics
Patterns/Values/Beliefs

Knowledge and
Understanding

Effective Leadership
Behaviours

Outcomes for
Individual,
organization
and community

Skills and Experience

map your current leadership star based on the self-assessments from your reflective activities earlier in this book. This will most likely produce a gap between the current and the ideal.

The next step is to see how you can bridge the gap between your current knowledge and practical skills and this future state. One's personal characteristics can take a bit of shifting; nonetheless you can practise stepping into different, perhaps more unfamiliar and uncomfortable behaviours, and you can also develop enough emotional intelligence to know when to trust that you are capable of achieving the outcomes you have set.

Setting yourself up for your leadership development journey

Let's run you through a couple of examples and then you can have a go yourself. We will use the issue we highlighted above:

How do I know which leadership style to use with my different direct reports and how can I practise them?

Figure 16.2 Adapted Henley Star example 1 (Kruckeberg, Amann and Green, 2011)

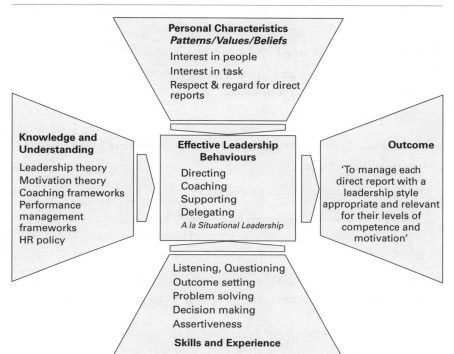

Converted into an outcome, that might look something like:

> To manage each direct report with a leadership style appropriate and relevant for their levels of competence and motivation.

Using Part Two of this book we can see that the Situation Leadership framework would be a useful leadership framework for addressing this issue, and the resulting leadership development 'star' could looks something like this:

And the development plan would start to become populated perhaps like this:

✓ Highlight the issue and discuss with the team, seek their willingness to engage and give feedback (announce at the next team meeting and set a review date in 2nd Quarter).

✓ Start to hold more formal 1:1s with team members (starting next month).

✓ Establish boundary time for 1:1s, and make time to talk about task progress, using good-quality questions.

✓ Choose and practise one of the coaching frameworks (discuss with line manager this week, start next week!).

✓ Gen up on Hersey and Blanchard Situational Leadership theories and begin to practise the different styles where appropriate (read over weekend, start informally and low key next week).

✓ Practise listening, in small bursts (starting in next conversation).

✓ Read up on the concept of powerful questions (web search then read, print off list of powerful questions).

Another example might be:

I need to stand up to my boss more and be more able to have a tough conversation with them.

The desired outcome would be, for instance:

To have an honest, mature conversation with my line manager so that he/she understands my point of view on an aspect of his or her behaviour, and what I would prefer to enable me to be successful in my work.

Effective behaviours would be in the planning and facilitation of the meeting; ability to build rapport; being able to be assertive without being

Figure 16.3   Adapted Henley Star example 2 (Kruckeberg, Amann and Green, 2011)

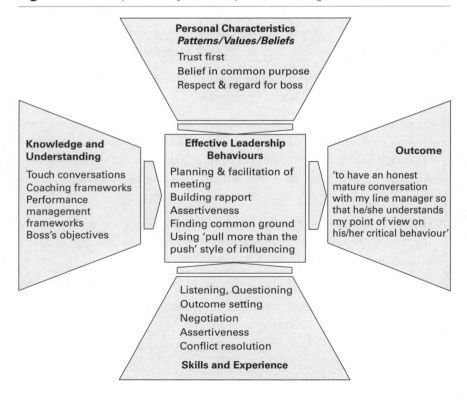

aggressive or submissive; finding common ground; using the 'pull rather than push' style of influencing.

Some of the skills that are needed might include: objective setting; listening and questioning skills, together with negotiating and conflict resolution skills; heightened emotional intelligence (and some of the competencies associated with that); being relaxed, as well as focused.

There might also be a need to shift various patterns, beliefs and values to the extent that, in this example, the aim is to build common ground and establish trust. So recognizing that to engender trust, it's good to trust first, believing there is a common purpose and not prejudging the boss and their intentions.

In order to enact some of these things, there may be a need to learn some of the theory and practice of these skills. There are many books and online videos on coaching (setting outcomes, listening and questioning skills) and on having tough conversations. Learning how to be assertive would also help.

Now it's your turn to think of an outcome within your current role, a wider organizational goal or social or community initiative.

Any development action plan requires three elements – Actions, Support Resources and a Developmental Mindset. The actions you have written down on the Leadership Star above will now need to be developed further by being clear about the actions (are they SMART?), knowing what help and support your need, and checking out what you are saying to yourself.

Remember what we said in Part Three – adults require certain conditions to ensure learning takes place:

- **Relevance**: learning needs to be relevant to what the person wants to achieve, and tend to have added impetus when this is serving the greater good.

- **Ownership**: results are better when learners are responsible for their learning and able to be self-directed.

Practice using the Leadership Star

1 Choose one aspect of your leadership you want to improve.

2 Write down a clear outcome.

3 Populate the leadership star with effective behaviours; skills and experience; patterns, beliefs and values; knowledge and understanding.

4 Use the planning prompts below to generate actions that will address these gaps within a realistic timescale.

Figure 16.4   Adapted Henley Star template (Kruckeberg, Amann and Green, 2011)

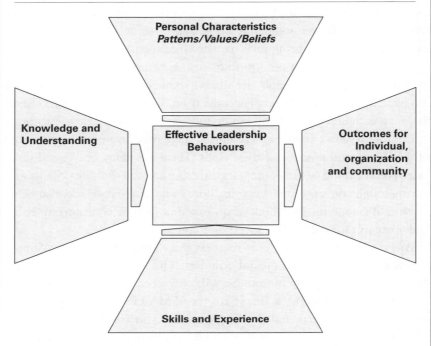

My desired future outcome is:

Which will be achieved by these new effective behaviours:

For which I will need to demonstrate these enhanced skills:

And be aware of these patterns, beliefs and values:

Underpinned by this acquired knowledge and understanding:

- **Problem-centered**: learning is more likely to stick if it is problem-centred rather than content-centred.

- **Refers to existing experience**: it's very helpful if the learning process refers to existing experiences and knowledge, so that new learning makes sense.

- **Practically-oriented and affecting**: practical experiences which have an emotional affect need to form the basis of adult learning.

- **Learning process is focused and conscious**: adult learners benefit from being supported to develop their focused attention, and being able to reflect on what's been learned/how it's been learned.

To support your development, we recommended that you focus on the following:

- **Responsibility taking** – seeking out good-quality reading; asking someone you respect to mentor you; inviting and exploring feedback on the impact and effects/outcomes of your leadership; requesting and rooting out your own development opportunities; honestly charting your own progress.

- **Action-reflection loops** – practise continuous, iterative action-reflection loops, building increased awareness of how your leadership actions are working out; good-quality preparation for monthly 1:1s with a line manager; making space at regular team meetings for reflections on team performance; mutual inquiry about courses of action and outcomes.

- **Regular journalling** – reflective practices are extremely helpful; regular journaling to enable inquiry into your own actions and the impact of these on others and on outcomes.

Many of the developmental approaches mentioned above might require engaging with your line manager or your HR/training and development department. However, there is absolutely nothing stopping you embarking on this journey on your own. Taking responsibility, ensuring you take regular time out for reflection and with the help of a journal (preferably in your own handwriting), you can start the exploration and experimentation right this minute. Being able to reflect on your leadership experiences day to day will be invaluable – whether they were successful or not. When you get lost in the hurly burly of organizational life, don't beat yourself up if you forget to take time out to review and reflect. But do get prompted to 'get back on the development horse' when critical incidents occur. These are times in the day or the week when things happen and just don't go the way you imagined. You've prepared for a one-to-one with a direct report, or perhaps your boss, and you leave the meeting not having achieved your objectives, or wondering what actually happened. There are also times when things go effortlessly well, and it's good to reflect on that too!

When you have a felt sense of being delighted, amazed, joyful – or disappointed, angry, irritated – as a leader, we suggest you train yourself to Stop and Reflect. Review what preparations you had done, what objectives you had set, how you experienced the interaction, your mindset going into the meeting and during it, your interventions, your level of listening, your focus on task, your adaptability, your quality of observation, etc.

If it didn't go so well, how could you have achieved a different outcome through behaving or doing things differently? What would it have taken to have done that? If it did go well, what skills, practices or mindsets did you bring that helped you succeed? How can you use them again or develop them even further?

What you need for the journey

When embarking on your journey you will require resources of one type or another. It can be your time, effort and money, or the organization's. But it can also be the time and energy of others – to give you feedback, to mentor you, to open particular developmental doors for you.

List all the potential stakeholders in your domain – your line manager, your direct reports, your peers in and outside the team, the training and development department, your senior leadership, your customers and your suppliers. They are all impacted by your leadership – motivationally, financially, performance-wise – so why not allow them the opportunity to engage with you on your leadership developmental journey? For each person or group with a stake in your leadership development, write down one thing you can request of them, and one thing you can offer in return, even if it's merely your commitment to be a more effective leader.

You can do this with all those in your work network, or you can focus on those involved in the specific outcome that you are working on. So in the example we drew on above, your stakeholders would be all your direct reports, and perhaps the training department if you needed some coaching training, for instance.

The important thing is to have the conversation so everyone is clear about what is required of them, and to stay open to feedback, no matter how it comes or what the content is.

The other element is what you say to yourself, and perhaps how you might need to challenge your own limiting beliefs. In one sense, it's a good idea to recognize your current limitations, especially those which would take a lot of effort to shift or are in fact impossible to shift. However, it's also important to challenge your own notion of what's possible. Some of our ideas about limitations are entirely false. For instance, the statements below, made by leaders at the start of a leadership development programme, are unnecessarily limiting:

'I can't change the way I am.'

'I am someone who doesn't pay attention to time.'

'I can't just suddenly become inspirational. I have a monotone voice.'

'It's not possible to change your leadership style; it's natural.'

'I only like working with highly motivated people.'

'I don't believe in making things easy for my staff.'

'I am a high-energy manager.'

In *Making Sense of Change Management*, we wrote about the many ways we can shift our limiting beliefs.

Pause for reflection–techniques for change

Reflect upon a time when you didn't achieve one of your results. What did you say to yourself – what was your limiting belief?

What's the opposite belief?

What would it be like to hold the new belief?

How might your behaviour change as a result?

What results would you achieve as a consequence?

List all the positive qualities that you have such as good feelings, good experiences, good results, areas of skills, knowledge and expertise.

Affirmations – make positive statements describing the way that you want to be in a personal, present tense, positive and potent way.

Visualizations – focus on a positive, present mental image of success.

Reframing – reducing feelings and thoughts that impact negatively on performance.

Pattern breaking – physically or symbolically taking attention away from a negative state and focusing on a positive.

Anchoring and resource states – accessing prior positive experiences.

Rational analysis – write down all the reasons why that negative thought in your head is incorrect, set measurable criteria, objectively based, and use your powers of logic.

Seeing the whole picture and expanding your bandwidth

We have just talked you through a process of goal setting and self-resourcing following your self-assessment.

We now want to extend that by getting you to reflect and consciously focus on different aspects and perspectives of your situation. Your leadership will never be in a vacuum. There will always be a bigger picture or a wider context. Depending on your role and current position within the organization, the geo-political external world will have an impact on how you think and exercise your leadership. The more immediate external operating environment will of course be impacted by and be impacting your leadership; more turbulent economic conditions leading to a more hostile trading environment will impact how you manage performance inside the organization. Better or worse conditions for suppliers will also impact your style across organizational boundaries. And always, always, organizational structure and culture will help or hinder the achievement of your objectives.

Be it on an ongoing basis or more time specific, you need to be continually appraising the bigger picture, through conversations with frontline staff; industry and sector experts; local, national and international papers and journals; consultancy reports; etcetera.

Within the organization, you need always to have one eye on 'the ways things are done around here'; to be noting down how the system conspires against you or how there are ways in which things can get done more effectively.

Figure 16.5 Seeing the whole picture

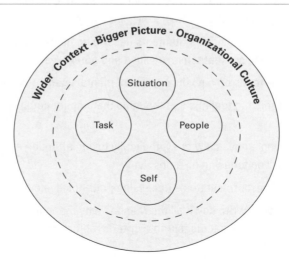

You need to review and reflect upon the dynamic interplay between the situation in which you are making decisions to achieve your objectives, the particular task in hand, and the people and power structures involved. Many of the leadership theories in Part Two demonstrate that you need to be able to understand the nature of the task (for example, its complexity, how structured or unstructured it is); the levels of competence, commitment and confidence of the people who need to be engaged in undertaking the task; and how the organizational structures and circumstances may enable or disable the achievement of the objective.

Being able to understand these variables and their inter-relationships helps you decide how you will think about and intervene with a particular leadership move. And of course this also depends on the levels of authority, power and influence that you have or are perceived to have. We will explore these ideas more fully in Part Six.

Answer the questions in the box below to complete your whole picture reflections.

To develop your leadership bandwidth further, we need to factor in two more dimensions.

What are the bigger forces at play outside your organization that impact your work, positively and negatively?

What aspects of organizational structure and culture support your work, and what gets in the way of it?

What of the above do you need to simply accept, and what might you be able to either influence or align with more intelligently/effectively?

The first dimension is your relationship to time, and the need to be able to operate within short-, medium- and longer-term ranges. Depending on your role you may be drawn towards a daily, weekly, monthly, quarterly, annual, five-year or longer time orientation. The more mature a leader, the greater the ability to move between these timeframes. The leader may need to project him or herself into the future to understand the best- and worst-case scenarios of making a key operational decision today. Or when making a decision as to how to manage a particular direct report – should I just do the work myself as it'll be quicker, or should I tell the direct report exactly how to do it, or shall I engage in the longer process of coaching the person through the task, in the belief that ultimately that will be the optimal solution?

The second dimension is the focus on self – my own objectives in isolation; on the team – our team's objectives at the expense, perhaps, of the organizational goals; on the business – perhaps for short-term profitability; or on the whole system – aiming for developing increased capability and capacity.

Many of us focus on ourselves and our immediate team, and occasionally focus on the short, and maybe the medium term. On a regular, if not overly frequent basis, it is very enlightening to scan across the whole gambit of levels within the system and also across the different time horizons and to put some leadership development goals in place to deepen one's presence in each of these dimensions.

Expanding your bandwidth

Timespan	Perspective	Short term	Medium term	Longer term
Self				
Team				
Business				
Whole system (including suppliers, customers, partners etc)				

Stop and Reflect!

We would now like you to look purposefully ahead and across the various leadership roles and responsibilities that you have. We would like you to spend some time on developing your leadership effectiveness in each of these roles across the different time horizons.

Consider all the discrete leadership roles that you play in your organization, and indeed your community: team leader, project manager on a specific project, expert contributor on a working group, moderator of a knowledge management community of practice, etc. If you are a student or taking time out then include other areas of your life – taking the lead in your family, in a sports situation, in a social or voluntary setting, etc. It's not necessarily important that you have people formally reporting to you, only that you have some sort of possibility to influence.

Pick the two or three more important or valuable roles to reflect on. If you prefer to see your job as one leadership role, that's fine too.

Fill in the blanks in the box below:

As a leader (project manager, team leader, etc.) I'm here to do (your key responsibilities):

In a way that that is characterized by (your own and the organization's underpinning values/principles):

My long-term goals are (1–5 years SMART):

My medium-term goals are (3–12 months SMART):

My more immediate goals are (up to 3 months SMART):

One team goal which I can contribute to (if not included above):

One business goal which I can contribute to (if not included above):

One system-wide (or social/community) goal which I can contribute to (if not included above):

The leadership strengths I can bring to this are:

My weaker leadership areas that may be problematic are:

The opportunities for me to develop are... (these can include particular challenges or new experiences arising from the above, eg leading new projects, adopting new ways of being and doing, connecting across networks, etc., or access to expertise and mentorship, a training course coming up, etc.):

The way I'm going to set myself up for success is ...:

The discipline I want to bring is... (eg regular journaling, asking for feedback, grabbing opportunities...):

The support I will draw on is... (include access to training, coaching, mentoring, etc.):

The resources I will need are... (time, money, advocacy, introductions, etc.):

The mindset that I'd like to embody is... (what you tell yourself, affirmations, etc.):

Where I might just trip up is… (potential barriers/resistances/surprises/
will power):

So my top five leadership development goals are… (eg I want to improve
the way I bring strategic leadership through careful framing of the work
ahead for the next six months to my team. This is so that they get engaged
and bring their best to the delivery target of project completion in July.):

1

2

3

4

5

Commit to sharing with one or two relevant people who you trust (line manager, peers, direct reports, HR, family member, friend) and set up regular dialogues to review progress, get feedback, etc.

References and further reading

Cameron, E and Green, M (2015) *Making Sense of Change Management*, Kogan Page, London

Hersey, P and Blanchard, K (1969) Life cycle theory of leadership, *Training and Development Journal*, **23** (5) pp. 26–34

Kruckeberg, K, Amann, W and Green, M (2011) *Leadership and Personal Development*, IAP, NC

Quality Assurance Agency (2009) Personal development planning: guidance for institutional policy and practice in higher education [online] www.qaa.ac.uk

Vroom, V H and Yetton, P W (1973) *Leadership and Decision Making*, University of Pittsburgh Press, Pittsburgh, PA

Conclusions from Part Four

Part Four has been primarily concerned with you and your development. It has taken you through a relatively structured review and self-assessment against criteria from many of the key leadership theories that are taught today.

It has also provided a process for you to translate your development needs into actual development goals, and for you to recognize the personal discipline, support and resources that you need to bring sufficient attention to these.

Remember also that developing your leadership depth, breadth and bandwidth need not be a particularly formal and structured process, and it is greatly enhanced by your spotting the myriad opportunities every day for learning about how to influence others in support of positive outcomes.

As the quotation from Bennis in Part One indicated, the keys to this are: to take responsibility for your own learning; to see this as part of your self-expression; to be fearless, optimistic and confident; and to make reflection a part of your life.

Whatever you can do, or dream you can, begin it.
Boldness has genius, power, and magic in it.
JOHANN WOLFGANG VON GOETHE

PART FIVE
The Five Leadership Qualities framework

Overview

This part of the book introduces the Five Leadership Qualities framework, which we have developed and researched over a number of years and continue to refine. This framework represents a unique synthesis of much of the leadership literature, as can be seen in the Overall Map section of Part Two. It also combines these historical leadership wisdoms with emerging leadership themes and requirements, as outlined in Part Three. The intention behind this framework is to support 21st-century leaders as they grow and learn.

The following chapters aim to:

- explain how the framework fits together, what its purpose is and how it can be used;
- identify how it has been validated through various strands of research and exploration;
- describe the Five Qualities in an accessible, engaging way;
- provide opportunities for the reader to learn through self-rating, reflection, experiment, exploration and drawing conclusions along the way;
- illustrate how each Quality matures as the leader develops his or her 'mental complexity' or 'body-mindset' (see Part Three for more on this);
- show how the Qualities can be combined in powerful ways once mastered.

A high-level overview of the framework is provided in Chapter 17. This appears together with a summary of our research so far and creative suggestions regarding how the Qualities can be used. Then Chapters 18–22 are devoted to describing the Five Qualities in detail. These chapters each tackle one Quality at a time, and are similarly structured, with sections covering:

- core and advanced skills associated with the Quality;
- examples of the Quality in action;
- a 10-question, self-rating tool for the Quality;
- research headlines connected with the Quality;
- how to 'embody' the Quality more fully, in your heart and your belly;
- what happens when the Quality is overdone in some way;
- how to overcome barriers to learning the Quality;
- 15 ways of experimenting with the Quality;
- examples of the Quality in action;
- 'Stop and Reflect' exercises;
- the chance to draw your own conclusions about your relationship with the Quality.

The topics of learning process, maturity and using combinations of Qualities are covered in Chapter 23, entitled 'Becoming Masterful!'

Introduction to the Five Qualities framework

17

Purpose and approach

The Five Leadership Qualities framework is a flexible, integrated framework which supports leaders at all levels of responsibility and seniority to develop their core skills. It also helps them to develop their own individual, flexible leadership style and grow their maturity. The framework is introduced here and described in more detail in the following chapters. This chapter explains what the framework consists of, how it arose, how it can be used to support leadership development for an individual and for an organization, and what we know about its capacity to support various forms of leadership learning.

This framework was first drafted in 2007 (Cameron and Green, 2008) and was designed to cover the essential skills and qualities required by organizational leaders. It represents a simple yet profound synthesis of much of the leadership literature including the material covered in Part Two of this book (see the Part Two Overall Map), and has been cross-checked against our own experience as well as multiple sets of in-house leadership competences. The framework has also been validated by research across various leadership populations, as summarized below.

Each of the Five Qualities can be considered as both a high-level 'archetype' and as a cluster of interconnected, coherent leadership skills and approaches. Integral in concept, the Qualities can be used by fledgling leaders as a straightforward checklist to get some fundamental skills in place, or worked with in a deeper or more imaginative way to enable leaders to 'fill out' their own, distinctive leadership style. Leaders at any stage of their journey can continue to grow their mastery of these Qualities over a number of years, thus moving towards ever-greater maturity and adaptability.

Each Quality is described separately in the following chapters to enable it to be distinguished and developed as a unique thread. However, as leaders begin to master these Qualities, they start to notice how combinations show up in various situations, with perhaps one Quality in the foreground, another one or two close by and the remainder in quiet support. In every leadership 'move', all the Qualities are present in some proportion, but this shouldn't be an excuse for mushy or deluded thinking about one's own skills. We find that some leaders will say, 'I use all the qualities in a typical working week depending on what comes up, I don't really think about it.' They are unlikely to be particularly self-aware, and unless they progress from this position they will find it difficult to develop themselves as leaders, even when faced with the most stretching experiences.

Most leaders find that they relate more naturally to some Qualities than others, with some showing up more strongly than others in their leadership. But even where a Quality is strong in someone, it can show up in narrow or inelegant ways. In other words, many if not most leaders have some sort of 'blind spot' in relation to several of the Qualities, which can be born out of either strength and over-confidence, or lack of awareness and skill.

Every leader is different and needs to find his or her own, authentic style – ideally, reflecting all of the Five Qualities in their own distinctive way, in order to serve his or her particular context. The descriptions that follow here, and the chapters that follow, will help you to discover and develop your own, flexible 'recipe' of leadership approaches and skills.

The Five Leadership Qualities

Here's a brief introductory overview of the Five Qualities including the key focus of each, its main 'blind spot' or pitfall and a quick snippet from our initial research to get you started.

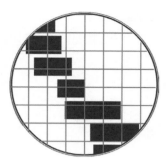

Tenacious Implementer

The Tenacious Implementer Quality is often found in leaders who are good at bringing focus to getting things done. These leaders are likely to be highly proficient in the skills of planning, delegating, monitoring, reviewing and performance management. Contracting well with people and holding them and oneself accountable is key. In more complex settings, the attention is on clarifying priorities and setting firm boundaries.

The focus is delivery, and the blind spot is *micro-management*.

Only 6 per cent of the leaders in our survey named this Quality as their natural leadership role.

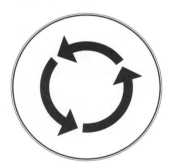

Measured Connector

The Measured Connector Quality is present in those who are good at getting things done through people and by building effective teams. Skills such as teambuilding, coaching, running meetings are key, and attention is paid to the people dimension of work, with the views of others being listened to and factored in. In more complex settings, facilitation skills and building system capability become more important.

The focus is connectivity, and the blind spot is *over-caring*.

Most people in our original research would prefer their line manager to demonstrate this Quality more.

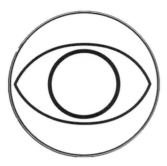

Visionary Motivator

The Visionary Motivator Quality is embodied in leaders who use words, images and stories to engage people in the way forward. They pay attention to the motivations of others and they work to unleash this where possible, while ensuring that they connect closely to their own values and passions. Skills such as inspiring, visioning, engaging others and presenting are all important. In more complex settings, storytelling and meaning-making become more important.

The focus is buy-in, and the blind spot is *superiority*.

Our original survey indicates that those who find the Tenacious Implementer Quality easy to access also tend to find the Visionary Motivator Quality particularly difficult to access.

Edgy Catalyser

The Edgy Catalyser Quality is found in those leaders who are able to bring fresh, probing eyes to any situation in a way that catalyses change. Key skills are questioning, steadiness, a service orientation and the courage to confront. An appetite for tough conversations and an ability to withstand conflict are especially important. In more complex settings, being able to 'wait and see' as well as bringing an outsider mindset in a non-attached way are both helpful capacities.

The focus is discomfort, and the blind-spot is *aggression*.

Leaders in our survey said this Quality was particularly useful during restructuring, in times of crisis or when facing well-defined change.

Thoughtful Architect

The Thoughtful Architect Quality is about thinking and acting strategically, which recent research indicates only about 5 per cent of leaders are able to do well. Those who embody the Thoughtful Architect Quality are continually scanning both the environment and their own inner sense in order to discover how best to design or frame the way forward so that others can join in. In more complex settings, interconnected systems thinking and long-term scenario planning become important skills/capabilities.

The focus is design, and the blind spot is *disappearing*.

Our original research indicates that the Thoughtful Architect Quality is one of the least frequently observed Qualities in organizational life.

Five Qualities research summary

The authors and their associates have carried out various levels of research and validation in relation to the Five Qualities framework, from the time we began to even think about an overarching leadership framework to the time of writing this book, a period of nearly 10 years. The headlines of our key pieces of research appear here, with more in the Appendices for those interested in greater detail together with specific statistics/charts etc.

Original research

In January 2007 we invited experienced organizational managers to complete a questionnaire testing out our Five Qualities framework: 83 people responded, mostly from the UK, and from a mix of sectors. We wanted to find out to what extent these Qualities were being enacted by successful leaders in situations requiring change. We were also interested in how they viewed their own leadership situation in relation to these Qualities.

It was difficult to draw any definitive conclusions from these findings, but the indications were both stimulating and encouraging. Headlines are offered here, with more data and graphs available in the Appendix:

i)   80 per cent of the successful leaders described by participants used all of the five Qualities to some extent.

ii)   Each of the five Qualities was selected in roughly equal measure when averaged out over the whole survey, although it seemed that the Edgy Catalyser, Tenacious Implementer and Thoughtful Architect Qualities were used in slightly smaller doses than the Measured Connector and Visionary Motivator Qualities.

iii)   No strong correlations were identified between the different Qualities, although the Edgy Catalyser and Tenacious Implementer Qualities appear to be slightly, but not significantly correlated.

iv)   The Quality that participants identified most closely with was the Measured Connector, with 42 per cent naming this as 'most like them'. The 'Tenacious Implementer' and 'Edgy Catalyser' Qualities were selected by only 5 per cent and 8 per cent of participants as 'most like them'.

v)   The Quality that most participants would least like to be exclusively led by is the Tenacious Implementer at 43 per cent, with the Edgy Catalyser a close second.

vi)   It appears that the Tenacious Implementer and Visionary Motivator Qualities are 'opposites' in some way, in that those who find one easy to access, tend to find the other difficult to access.

vii)   Overall, the most attractive role model was the Visionary Motivator Quality, with only those whose most familiar Quality was Edgy Catalyser finding this averagely attractive as a role model.

viii)   When asked about the most prevalent leadership Quality in their organizations, 30 per cent said Tenacious Implementer and 20 per cent said Edgy Catalyser.

The least prevalent were the Thoughtful Architect (34 per cent) and the Visionary Motivator (21 per cent).

ix) There appear to be a number of contexts in which the Leadership Qualities are required in uneven proportions, for example:

- when working with partners and stakeholders, organizations need more Measured Connector;

- when growing a new enterprise, organizations need more Visionary Motivator;

- with an unhappy workforce, organizations need more Measured Connector and Visionary Motivator;

- addressing new legislation, tighter compliance, or critical projects, organizations need more Tenacious Implementer and less Visionary Motivator;

- engaging with more complex organizational change or a five-year strategy, organizations need more Thoughtful Architect and Visionary Motivator.

New research data

Since 2007, and the publication of *Making Sense of Leadership* (2008), which featured both the model and the original research, the authors have used the Five Leadership Qualities in a variety of settings. This has enabled us to test the framework's face validity, observe how it can support learning and continue to develop our understanding of the breadth, depth and applicability of these five archetypes. Key projects have been:

- developing an in-house leadership framework and associated skills modules for the senior leadership population of an international financial services company (top 60 leaders – UK);

- building leadership skills and awareness within sector sales teams in a European manufacturing company (50 middle leaders – UK and Netherlands);

- providing a catalysing framework to support a leadership development programme for a utilities company in South Africa (top 70 organizational leaders – South Africa);

- illustrating the role of leadership in change management (150 change leaders – Kuwait, Abu Dhabi, South Africa, Nigeria);

- facilitating leadership development for several hundred local politicians across the UK.

In one of the above cases we facilitated a six-month leadership development programme in a multicultural engineering-oriented setting, featuring the Five Qualities leadership framework. At the end of the programme, as part of the evaluation process, we collected data from 36 middle leaders via a confidential online survey. The findings can be summarized by the following:

- When asked to what extent they found the Five Qualities Framework supportive to their development as a leader, 89 per cent responded, 'very supportive' or 'extremely supportive'.

- The Quality that people felt most confident about at the start of the programme was the Measured Connector (44 per cent), and least confident about Edgy Catalyser (11 per cent).

- On rating their own development through the programme, the area where participants, on average, developed the most was the Measured Connector, with many discovering throughout the programme that they had more room for improvement in this area than they had first thought. (We see this as one of many indications that this Quality is a key stepping stone in the leadership maturity journey from Expert to Achiever.)

- Participants self-assessed their progress on a five-point Likert scale: 1 (a little) to 5 (a lot). Average improvement ratings ranged from 3.3 to 3.8 out of 5. These ratings were checked by programme tutors and broadly agreed with, although tutors tended to score participants' progress 0.5 points lower on average, across all Qualities.

- When asked which of the Five Qualities was making the most impact on their ability to deliver, and which the least, the answers given were as follows. These are indicative of the different functional contexts each leader was working in, and the range of styles and skills being employed. They also show that in this particular environment, the Measured Connector was the Quality where most significant individual progress was being made to good effect.

  - Most:
    - Measured Connector 36 per cent;
    - Thoughtful Architect 22 per cent;
    - Tenacious Implementer 19 per cent;
    - Edgy Catalyser 11 per cent;
    - Visionary Motivator 11 per cent.

- Least:
    - Edgy Catalyser 36 per cent;
    - Thoughtful Architect 22 per cent;
    - Visionary Motivator 22 per cent;
    - Measured Connector 11 per cent;
    - Tenacious Implementer 8 per cent.

- When asked which was the Quality most lacking in the leadership population, 28 per cent said Thoughtful Architect, followed by Tenacious Implementer at 25 per cent. This partly mirrors our original survey data above.

How to use the Five Qualities

The Five Qualities framework can be used in many ways to support leadership development ranging from individual support, to team development, right through to organization-wide initiatives.

At the individual level, it can be used to:

- gauge your own leadership capability;
- find your learning 'edge' and to set some goals and/or experiments for yourself – to reflect on current issues and learn new ways of tackling challenges;
- develop a more embodied approach to leadership, by including head, heart and belly leadership aspects.

At the team level it can be used to:

- compare the different leadership styles that exist within the team;
- discuss to what extent the style(s) of leading being used are working, and what might be done differently;
- discover ways in which team members can learn from each other and/or work in partnership to improve the team's overall performance.

At the organizational level, it can be used to:

- provide an energizing and/or organizing framework for a leadership development programme;
- test the coverage of an in-house leadership competency framework;
- provide a template for individuals to reflect on their own development and progress;

- construct a 360 feedback process for individuals, teams or organizations – to act as a 'language of leadership' that enables good-quality conversations about what leadership is, where there are gaps, what needs to improve, etc.;
- formulate a template for offering feedback when observing leaders in action;
- construct a checklist for building a map of leadership skills for leaders facing different levels of challenge;
- help formulate annual 'leadership development objectives' as part of the appraisal process;
- support leaders to collectively develop more 'advanced' leadership skills and increased capacity to handle complexity/uncertainty.

Pause for Learning Points

The Five Qualities framework offers a flexible, integrated framework for leaders and HR professionals to use in a variety of ways to support the development of leaders' skills at a range of maturity levels.

The research and validation exercises carried out on this framework indicate that it has face validity, consists of five reasonably independent qualities which in combination appear to lead to successful change outcomes, and is helpful to those wishing to develop their leadership capacity.

The structured approach and flexibility offered by this framework can be highly supportive to learning and leadership progress at individual, team and organizational level.

Reference

Cameron, E and Green, M (2008) *Making Sense of Leadership*, Kogan Page, London

TENACIOUS
IMPLEMENTER
MEASURED CONNECTOR
VISIONARY MOTIVATOR
THOUGHTFUL ARCHITECT
EDGY CATALYSER

'Sometimes when I consider what tremendous consequences come from little things… I am tempted to think… there are no little things.'
BRUCE BARTON

Leaders who demonstrate the Tenacious Implementer Quality focus on pursuing the plan through to completion by driving the delivery of specific outcomes to the standard expected and to schedule. They bring clarity, determination, rigorous follow-up and a commitment to hold others to account and be accountable themselves.

IN A NUTSHELL
'Just follow the plan and we'll get this done!'

CORE FOCUS:
Delivery

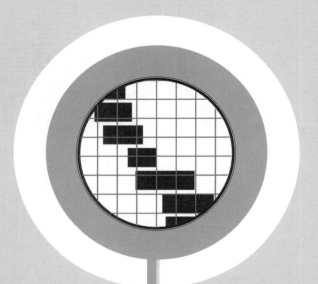

CORE SKILLS

Project management

Planning and reviewing

Contracting and delegating

Holding people to account

Performance discussions

Disciplined delivery

ADVANCED SKILLS

Governance

Hard rules/boundary setting

Timely, well-communicated
decision-making

Priority-setting

THE TENACIOUS IMPLEMENTER AT BEST:

focused
organized
committed
decisive
resilient
mobilised

THE TENACIOUS IMPLEMENTER AT WORST:

blinkered
rigid
slavish
controlling
self-punishing
destructive

Mastering the Tenacious Implementer Quality – core

The Tenacious Implementer Quality is a fundamental Quality for any leader to master, which builds on the 'transactional leadership' model presented in Chapter 6. Our experience is that when demonstrated well, this Quality is right at the centre of any organizational endeavour, in that there is always the need to deliver something in line with an agreed expectation. Whether that expectation is loose or tight depends on the endeavour, and it's important to note that the degree to which the Tenacious Implementer Quality is present needs to be in tune with this.

Those leaders who demonstrate this Quality well are deeply interested in the task and help others to bring the necessary focus to the 'what' and the 'how' of this, such that things get done (see Chapters 3 and 4 for the benefits of focusing on task). Accountability is a core principle, with those demonstrating this Quality remaining just as focused on their own delivery of outcomes as that of their people. They are also good at ensuring that the customers of and suppliers to the team have clear contracts and know what they need to do to ensure that everything runs smoothly.

The skills of project management are part of this Quality, together with patience and a clear-eyed view that enables a good-quality plan to be put together. This plan should demonstrate that the work can be done in the required time with the existing resources, and points to the critical elements that need to be in place to enable this to happen.

The ability to track progress, and keep a good record of plans, decisions and any variations is also a key part of this Quality. Often there are systems in place to enable this, which these leaders adopt, but if not, they tend to bring or create their own and encourage others to follow suit so that everyone is aware of what has not yet been achieved. More generally, leaders demonstrating this Quality take care to set standards and agree working principles. They expect people to stick to this and will hold them to account if not.

Leaders who demonstrate this Quality are good at chairing meetings to review progress, ie organizing everyone to meet and efficiently discuss how progress is going, with good-quality facts and figures to hand. Celebrations of progress are not top of the bill (unless the Visionary Motivator Quality is present!), but everyone will go away very clear about what has been delivered, what hasn't and why, and what they need to do next. Accountability is taken extremely seriously.

Leaders who demonstrate the Tenacious Implementer Quality make a point of sitting down with their people on a regular basis, either to align them with the outcomes expected and support them to think through the plan to get there, or to follow up on agreements. If things are stuck or delayed, this contact enables them to find out what's getting in the way of progress. Their delegation skills are well-honed, such that the work is set out clearly and the amount of special help and follow-up required is agreed. Back briefing, meaning asking the other person to repeat back what they've heard, is often used to check that the other person has understood what has been asked of them.

'Micromanagement' is something to look out for when embracing the Tenacious Implementer Quality. This is a narrow, contorted version of the Quality, and tends to be a sign of a leader's anxiety and their wish to over-control the work of others. Leaders who find it difficult to manage without insisting on having access to a high level of detail from the team usually need to learn what it takes to be 'in charge' as a leader without needing to be in control of everything. As part of this, they might also need to learn how to avoid leaking their anxiety when outcomes don't appear as expected. This can sometimes be experienced by others as aggression or hostility, which is rarely conducive to longer-term productivity.

Another pitfall of the struggling leader is to put a high degree of emphasis on the delivery and accountability of others without placing such stringent conditions on their own performance, even in small things such as keeping to meeting times and responding to emails within an agreed period. Developing the ability to face up to one's own 'disciplined delivery' failure, to apologize and do better next time is key to a leader increasing their Tenacious Implementer maturity.

Goal setting is important to leaders who demonstrate the Tenacious Implementer Quality. The use of SMART goals is particularly attractive to them (Specific, Measurable, Achievable or Ambitious, Realistic, Time-bound), which can support high-quality delegation, as well as breakthroughs in skill development. However, immature leaders who use this as a replacement rather than a support for dialogue find themselves dragging their people through a disengaged, repetitive goal-setting process that can deaden the work in hand, rather than offer illumination or excite ambition.

Mastering the Tenacious Implementer Quality – advanced

Senior leaders need to bring the Tenacious Implementer Quality in various ways to ensure continued clarity about direction and progress, to demonstrate their commitment to agreed goals, systems and rules and to be transparently responsive should their active support be required. Sometimes, mistakenly, senior leaders believe that the Tenacious Implementer Quality is just for operational leaders; that once they are promoted to executive level, they can focus purely on the big ticket strategic items and let go of detail, discipline and attention to outcomes in their day-to-day work – as in, 'That's why I have Departmental Managers!'. However, it has a hugely positive impact on performance if senior leaders are able to demonstrate high levels of discipline in their 'delivery' of leadership to the rest of the organization in a way that's responsive to operational progress and struggles and encourages others to hold them accountable for this (see Chapter 14 for more on developing leadership maturity).

The four advanced skills likely to be required are described here.

The ability to put in place and lead good-quality *Governance processes* is an important element of the Tenacious Implementer Quality at senior leader level. Garland (2009) notes that (project) governance in organizations is still a haphazard affair with few established principles. Cross-departmental initiatives require sponsors and clear governance to be successful, but the burden is often placed on project managers, project support offices and administrative assistants to gather data that proves all is well rather than senior leaders getting clear about how best to unblock any stuckness and support good progress.

Senior leaders who demonstrate the Tenacious Implementer Quality well ensure that a set of supportive *hard rules* or *boundaries* is in place, that people know about these and respect them. Elements such as clear goals and standards, well-managed information gathering and flow, well-defined responsibilities and authority levels, common working principles, agreed process guidelines, etc., all need to be included. This does not imply the creation of a great big bureaucracy, but rather the establishment of 'just enough' boundary setting to allow work to be well-contained and to flow with relative ease.

Timely, well-communicated decision making is another key, advanced element of the Tenacious Implementer Quality. Often it's hard for senior leaders to see how critical it is to performance and outcomes that they prioritize making the big decisions that need to be made. If there are hold-ups, they need to let people know why there is a delay, when the decision will be made and how to progress (or not) in the meantime.

Priority setting is closely related to decision making (above). Senior leaders can get caught up in their own complex worlds, juggling all the pressures and demands that come their way and failing to see how helpful a short priority-setting session can be to their mid-level leaders. Even if the big decisions cannot be made for all sorts of good reasons, the clarification of short-range priorities can be very helpful, particularly in complex or volatile contexts where stress caused by overwork and re-work is a big risk, particularly at middle leadership levels.

Self-rater

Score each of the following statements according to how true it is for you as a leader on the following scale:

1 ...never true

2 ...seldom true

3 ...sometimes true

4 ...often true

5 ...almost always true

1 When something is my responsibility I take ownership of it and expect others to hold me accountable

2 I make decisions in a timely way and communicate these clearly

3 I identify long-range goals and break these down into a clear sequence of manageable, trackable smaller deliverables

4 I clarify the processes and standards that I expect my team to use, and commit to these myself rather than doing my own thing

5 I am good at clarifying responsibilities, goals and expectations and I delegate effectively

6 I follow up with rigour, ensuring that I hold others to account for any non-delivery and resisting taking over or micromanaging

7 I am skilled at facilitating team reviews of progress, where I insist that any failure is named and understood, without needing to punish or blame

8 I work hard to align with stakeholders, keeping them up to date with progress and ensuring they know what I need from them to deliver

9 I deal well with stress and support others to do so too through organized, well-prioritized, non-anxious approaches to work

10 Even when work is complex or multi-threaded, I am able to nudge things along in an insistent yet respectful way or to help remove roadblocks

Scoring analysis

Add your scores for the 10 statements. Your result will be between 10 and 50.

The following guidelines may help you to clarify to what extent you have mastered this quality, and how to progress.

10–15 This quality is almost completely missing from your repertoire and it's important to start to build the associated core skills

16–25 This quality is somewhat lacking in your repertoire and you need to start to grow your skills and capacities in a more concerted way

26–40 You have started to demonstrate this quality quite well at times, and now need to assess whether you've developed it enough given the context you're in

41–50 Your mastery of this quality is good and you can start to consider how you might bring a matured version of the quality to more complex, large-scale or otherwise challenging change contexts.

Tenacious Implementer research insights

This Quality is positively correlated with the Edgy Catalyser Quality and can be effective even in small doses.

Only 6 per cent of the leaders in our survey named this Quality as their natural leadership role.

This Quality is very often evident and observable in organizational life.

Thirty per cent of respondents named this Quality as the hardest to adopt.

The hardest Quality to adopt for someone who can access the Tenacious Implementer Quality with ease is the Visionary Motivator Quality, and vice versa

This Quality is the least attractive in terms of a role model, and 42 per cent of respondents named it as the Quality they would least appreciate in their boss.

Those leaders who naturally exhibit the Tenacious Implementer Quality tend to admire those with the Visionary Motivator Quality and the Thoughtful Architect Quality.

This Quality is seen as useful in many situations, but particularly when the change is well-defined, eg technology-led change, a critical project, tighter compliance, new legislation or specific improvement initiatives.

Embodying the Quality

This section helps you to involve your head, heart and belly as you exercise this Quality (see Chapter 13 for more on the significance of this).

To embody this Quality, we suggest you stand with your feet slightly apart, in line with your shoulders. Sink into your hips a little and breathe into your belly. Notice any judgemental thoughts you've having about doing this and just allow them to be there without paying much attention to them.

Make a very direct and confident 'chopping' action with your right arm, as if you are repeatedly slicing through a large block of wood, karate-style. It's helpful if you imagine this as chopping through all the activities that you need to complete or decisions you need to make, in a way that releases or enables others to deliver the outcomes required. Notice the routine directness of the action. It's predictable, rigorous, repetitive, committed. Just see if you can allow that rigorous repetition to happen, and feel the strength within this. You might find yourself getting hot, and feeling your heart opening. This could be your natural strength and will arriving! Or you might feel a little cold, which could indicate that your actions have become somewhat impersonal. In this case, breathe into the heart area and imagine your team in front of you, ready to do their work. Continue chopping. Are you a little warmer now?

You might find yourself getting bored or feeling weakened by this gesture. Notice this and just test how committed you are to all the activity that you're currently leading, and to what extent it's all making sense to you. Perhaps you are holding back on some ideas or innovations that could help progress, or some things that could be stopped?

On the other hand, you might start to feel a bit irritated or aggressive as you chop. In this case, it might help to reflect on what else you need to do to set people up for success beyond clarifying expectations and providing the drive.

Too much Tenacious Implementer?

The Tenacious Implementer Quality in excess ends up being destructive to relationships and to making progress. A leader who demonstrates the Tenacious Implementer has the propensity to be very persistent in the pursuit of outcomes. In extremis, this can present as blinkered behaviour such as taking a fixed view of who needs to do what by when and in what manner, and ignoring all other views, particularly where there might be unforeseen obstacles that need attention.

In the worst case, the Tenacious Implementer Quality turns into tunnel vision, overshadowing completely the perceptiveness of the Measured Connector Quality. The leader excludes other possibilities and attempts to railroad their plan through, come what may. Obstacles – including other people's agendas, insights, ideas, dilemmas, loyalties and sensitivities – are bulldozed away. Even when under extreme pressure to shift timescales or change tack due to unexpected problems, the leader may refuse to readjust, preferring that followers swallow their objections and comply, which in turn leads to more stress, high levels of resentment, erosion of goodwill and in extreme cases despair – and of course more delivery problems.

The Tenacious Implementer Quality brings with it a love of structure, systems and schedules, and perhaps a slight preference for planning things in advance over improvisation or spontaneity. These preferences, taken to extremes, can become part of the cause of delivery failure. The leader may not stop to look at the bigger picture to clarify where things or people need to be better joined up. They may fail to see that the work they are managing is inextricably connected to the way change is developing within the organization and is just one part of the jigsaw. The jigsaw itself needs to be recognized by the Tenacious Implementer and he or she needs to develop an understanding of how the pieces fit together (the Thoughtful Architect helps here).

In summary, the Tenacious Implementer in shadow mode involves railroading other people towards an unworkable solution or timescale without adapting to changing circumstances. The antidote is to practise the art of remaining true to their own sense of focus and ability to deliver, while holding the possibility that requirements might shift, that the organizational context may change and that people and technology don't act in totally predictable ways.

Typical barriers

Developing the Tenacious Implementer Quality has its obstacles. Some of us are not so decisive or clear in our thinking, and find it difficult to settle down to repetitive or disciplined ways of working.

Here are some typical barriers to developing this Quality and suggestions for overcoming them.

1 *'I just don't have the will power to be this tenacious!'*

If the work you're leading requires you to be tenacious, and you're committed to leading it, you need to think again. What is it that you're resisting taking on, and what in your history is telling you that you don't have what it takes? Maybe it's not true! Consider what might support you to commit to bring the required level of rigour and discipline.

2 *'I'm a big picture person, the details bore me.'*

It's good to notice your preference! However, next time you're in a meeting, see what it's like to focus on the details as well as the big picture. What details would it help to get your head around? What details would it not help to find out about? How might a bit more focus on details enable you to you serve the work in the best way possible?

3 *'If people don't deliver I get rid of them. Why should I chase them to do the work they are paid to do?!'*

This is a pretty uncompromising stance, and if it represents the culture of leadership in your organization it is likely to be difficult for you to break the mould. However, if this just represents your own perspective, it might be worth your experimenting. Try to see whether, through the use of the Tenacious Implementer Quality as described above, you can enable delivery through role-modelling a high level of commitment and follow-through yourself. You may be losing out on some high-potential individuals who still need to learn this!

4 *'Surely if you lead like this, you make people's lives a misery!'*

Using the Tenacious Implementer Quality on its own, with no Measured Connector to enable connection and no Visionary Motivator to envisage a better future, could feel a bit harsh and unrelenting. It's important to remember that the Qualities need to be used in combination, rather than in an isolated way.

5 *'I have other people to do this for me.'*

Reflect on the advanced Tenacious Implementer skills discussed above and see whether you've missed something. Maybe you need to take a bit more responsibility for ensuring other people's success, but at the right level.

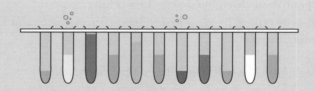

15 quick experiments

Here are a few experiments which will get you practising aspects of the Tenacious Implementer Quality:

1 Complete a task you have been meaning to do for a long time and reward yourself well.

2 Be on time for every meeting for the next week.

3 Next time someone disagrees with you, see what it's like to stick with your initial point a bit longer.

4 In your next PowerPoint presentation, or your next report, use a graph or some statistics to back up your point.

5   Set goals every day, and review how you did at the end of the day. A week later, stretch yourself a little more.

6   Find out exactly what someone in your organization needs, write it down, and deliver it to them on an agreed date.

7   Take a big project that you've been meaning to complete at home and map out all the activities you need to do to deliver this, estimating the time needed for each, and then plot out exactly when you want to carry all these activities out. What else needs to be in place for this plan to become a reality?

8   Notice how reliable you are. Do you do what you say you will do? Try to improve this at home and at work.

9   Next time you meet with a friend, ask about the progress of a task or project they are involved in, rather than asking about how they are.

10 Think of a situation at work or at home in which you are deeply involved and try to write a completely objective description of what has happened so far, who is involved, and what everyone wants and needs.

11 Be firmer with your team about performance levels and goals, and clear about when you are going to follow up.

12 Say no to unproductive activities and prune your network of contacts, extracting those to whom you are unquestionably loyal even though it doesn't do you or your project any good.

13 Give up any joking around for the next three days. See what it's like to take things more seriously.

14 Use simple, uncomplicated language in your next e-mail.

15 Next time you initiate a piece of work, agree standards with your team before you begin and stick to them.

Example 1: Growing the Tenacious Implementer Quality

David had been a technologist for two years within the operations department of a manufacturing business and was highly regarded technically, with many people seeking his advice on a daily basis.

He was promoted to team leader with three people working for him, and things started to go wrong almost immediately. Although he was keen to train up his young, inexperienced team, he found he was so preoccupied by all the things he was responsible for, and so disappointed by the team's lack of speed and agility in dealing with requests, that he started to become quite anxious and aggressive. His team complained about his leadership style to HR, calling him a 'bully' and asking to work for a different team leader.

The HR manager, on hearing this, decided to sit down with David to hear his views and to offer him some regular coaching support, using the Tenacious Implementer Quality as her starting point. Her first step was to ask him to complete the self-rating questionnaire above. She also asked his team to complete the questionnaire anonymously from their perspective. The results were a shock for David, but provided the impetus he needed. It appeared that although the team understood that David was technically gifted, he was tripping up in three key areas:

- not taking the time to set out expectations and check that these had been understood;
- not establishing any sort of work plan or staged deliverables, and sometimes taking work back from people without any explanation;
- not sticking to his promises as regards regular performance discussions, including pushing away or ignoring requests for information or clarification.

David found himself doing quite a bit of uncomfortable reflection over a long weekend, and returned to work feeling motivated to try out some of the new practices the HR manager had been talking about. He realized that he wasn't setting his team up for success well enough, but couldn't remember any manager ever doing this for him in the past!

He started by preparing his alignment conversations with each person much more carefully, and he used a delegation checklist to make sure that everything had been covered. Then he committed to following up and making himself available to support progress, although he was very wary of creating too much dependence on him.

After four weeks of the new style of leading, David's team was performing much better and feeling more confident. David was more relaxed too, and had more time to do his own technical work, and to start planning out some of the strategic projects that he needed to initiate and get the team involved in.

Example 2: Refining the Tenacious Implementer Quality

Yasmin was a talented manager in a property management company who knew how to get project work done through people. With a flair for understanding systems and a knack for seeing how processes could be designed more efficiently, she had worked tirelessly for nine months with a team of eight people to build and rollout a new software system that allowed more sophisticated tracking of assets. This was much applauded and appreciated by everyone!

Her management skills were noted by the board, and pretty soon she was promoted from head of property management with a team of eight to director of operations with a department of 35, which was a big jump in authority and span of control for her.

In her new job she needed to lead a team of six team leaders and had less contact with those carrying out the work at the 'front line'. As someone who was used to demonstrating the Tenacious Implementer Quality every day through delegating and tracking, it required some adjustment for her to find good ways of supporting her team leaders to be successful. At first she found this almost impossible, as she really wanted to dive into the details and give them advice about how to solve problems and what to do next, even if they didn't really seem to need it. She could sense that some of her team were not happy about this and one even asked her outright whether she had doubts about his capability!

Yasmin sought the help of an internal coach, and asked to be observed running a 1:1 performance conversation with one of her team. She received some helpful suggestions about how she could still bring her Tenacious Implementer sensibilities in a way that supported good progress rather than cutting across the authority and competence of her team leaders. This included:

- asking progress questions at a different level, ie regarding achievement against plan and progress towards outcomes, rather than getting onto day-to-day activities;

- inviting the team leader to talk about any obstacles that they were seeing, and how they were planning to tackle them;

- making a space for the team leader to rate him/herself against the self-rate above and set a leadership development objective if necessary, which Yasmeen could explicitly support.

Stop and Reflect!

Managing an improvement project

Think of an improvement idea that you would love to implement in your organization and believe would benefit from being approached in a rigorous way. Choose something that is reasonably well-defined in terms of outcomes and needs to be done to a tight deadline. The introduction of a new process or the improvement of an existing process would be a good choice, or the creation of a new product or service for your customers.

Appoint yourself as project manager and plan it all out in detail, starting by chunking the activities up with milestones in between and giving each milestone a fixed date, followed by listing out all the different activities required to complete the work at each stage and estimating the effort required from those involved. This should include engagement sessions and progress follow-ups.

Clarify roles and responsibilities, including your own and those of key stakeholders and suppliers. Identify a set of three to five high-level outcomes, and do this with care for all the 'parts', so that you are not just describing the finished technical product, but the way others are interfacing with it and the value that's being created.

Ask a colleague, who you know demonstrates the Tenacious Implementer Quality well, to review your plan and help you to identify what you've missed!

Culture of non-delivery

You have just been recruited as the training manager in a highly successful, fast-growing vehicle leasing company. The five-strong training department, however, has a reputation for being a bit out of touch and old-fashioned, lacking in understanding of the training that's really required and possibly rather over-staffed. You've been brought in to bring things up to date and establish a new culture of service orientation and efficient, effective delivery. This will cover growing technical training and management development needs internally.

You've discovered that the department has remained relatively unchanged for the last five years, delivering a package of 20 different short courses via one, faithful supplier. Some of these courses can now be accessed quite cheaply online. A training needs survey was completed two years ago which identified internal training gaps, and quite some dissatisfaction with the provision, but was never followed up with a proposal or any recorded actions.

The chief operations officer has asked you to develop a plan that sets out how you will transform the department and its performance, and has suggested that you need to demonstrate your own Tenacious Implementer skills as well as develop this skill throughout the department. She has also hinted that she believes that you may need to reduce the staff numbers.

Imagine you are going into a one-to-one meeting with your COO next week. What five SMART objectives will you propose for yourself to guide your work over the next three to six months? What will be your next steps over the next two to four weeks, given that this is your key focus? What questions do you need to ask to clarify details?

Where to go to find out more

Useful books to develop the skills of Tenacious Implementer include:

Core skills

Project Management for the Unofficial Project Manager by Kogon, Blakemore and Wood.
Managing Successful Projects with PRINCE 2 by Office of Government Commerce.
Traction: Get a grip on your business by Gino Wickman.
The One Minute Manager Meets the Monkey by Ken Blanchard.
Execution: The discipline of getting things done by Larry Bossidy.
Project Management Step by Step: How to manage a highly successful project by Richard Newton.

Advanced skills

The Art of Action: How leaders close the gap between plans, actions and results by Stephen Bungay.
Project Governance by Ross Garland.
Governance, Risk Management and Compliance by Richard Steinberg.
Successful Project Sponsorship by Michiel van der Molen.

Ten real-life examples of the Tenacious Implementer Quality in action*

Margaret Thatcher, Nelson Mandela, Hilary Clinton, Martin Sorrell, Michael Dell, Angela Merkel, Beyoncé, Jeff Bezos, Mother Teresa, Queen Elizabeth II.

*We have chosen these people as they are relatively well-known, come from around the world and have shown some mastery of this Quality

Reference

Garland, R (2009) *Project Governance*, Kogan Page, London

TENACIOUS IMPLEMENTER

MEASURED
CONNECTOR

VISIONARY MOTIVATOR
THOUGHTFUL ARCHITECT
EDGY CATALYSER

'Only connect!'
E M FORSTER, *HOWARDS END*

Leaders who demonstrate the
Measured Connector Quality
build well-connected, settled
working environments in which
people come together to share
perspectives, collaborate and
learn, and are thus empowered
to bring their best to the work
ahead. They focus on the people
dimension of work and ensure
that there is a sufficiently safe,
enjoyable atmosphere to work in.

IN A NUTSHELL
'Let's get together
and take time to
focus on this.'

CORE FOCUS:
Connectivity

CORE SKILLS

Running effective meetings

One-to-one dialogue skills

Effective cascades/briefings

Performance coaching

Teambuilding

Self-management

ADVANCED SKILLS

Bringing presence

Facilitating complex dialogue

Building organizational
capability

Process sensitivity

MEASURED CONNECTOR AT BEST:

non-anxious

communicative

inquiring

respectful

empathetic

guiding

MEASURED CONNECTOR AT WORST:

lacks urgency

needy for contact

indecisive

tentative

scattered

controlling

Mastering the Measured Connector Quality – core

The Measured Connector Quality is about connecting followers to each other, to the issues at play, to purpose and values, and to work priorities. This focus on relationships is a core thread that runs through all the Part Two chapters. It is an absolutely fundamental part of leadership, as without the presence of this Quality it's very difficult for others to get connected to the leader's intent and to join in!

The importance and centrality of this Quality grows as a leader matures and as his/her leadership challenges become more complex, difficult to predict and multi-layered. In this latter scenario, he or she needs to become even more of a wise guide (see Chapters 12–14 for more about developing leadership for complexity).

The convening of gatherings is a particular focus and is seen as an opportunity for two-way communication. Leaders who demonstrate this Quality take particular care whatever the context. This applies to one-to-one, team or mixed-group meetings and to regular weekly meetings or one-off workshops or conferences. The leader considers what's required in advance: who needs to come, how and where best to meet, how to frame the meeting with sufficient context, which issues will require the most focus and/or time, how much discussion time will be required, what preparation is required by themselves/others and what outcomes to aim for.

Less formal forms of contact with others are also encouraged through ensuring people have access to structure charts and all the necessary introductions and/or contact details, as well as decent quality methods for being in touch – either the physical space to meet, or virtual space that goes beyond the limits of e-mail.

Cascading information to others is important too. Leaders displaying the Measured Connector Quality have often developed an ability to 'cascade' key information to the team and other stakeholders in a form that's consumable and relevant and invites the sharing of perspectives. This requires a certain clarity of thinking from the leader about how the work in hand is connected to higher-level 'business' drivers, and what recent decisions or trends are likely to have an impact. In this aspect, the Measured Connector Quality is supported by access to the Thoughtful Architect Quality.

Leaders demonstrating this Quality insist on making time for regular, productive one-to-one exchanges with any direct reports. Typically these are more inquiring and opening than directive, and focus on building capability as well as tracking progress. In this, the leader takes an interest in the individual's perspectives, capacities and potential, and attunes their leadership and coaching approach according to the other's motivation and skill level.

One to ones with stakeholders are important too. These leaders make a point of meeting regularly with key stakeholders outside set meetings, and when they do, they don't just skirt over the surface, but head into difficult territory if necessary, making time to inquire and listen.

More broadly, leaders who demonstrate this Quality get to know their colleagues by making time to understand what's important to them and what help they need to deliver on their work priorities (see the definition of 'Individualized Consideration' in Chapter 6). This applies as much upwards with their line manager and across with peers and other stakeholders as it does downwards with their own direct reports or team members.

Good meeting management and teambuilding skills are used to ensure that regular team meetings are designed to grow the team's maturity as an interdependent group as well as to discuss progress and hatch future plans. These leaders also develop the capacity to facilitate productive discussions between disparate people and groups, while still providing the right level of guidance and authority where appropriate.

Pressure and worry is dealt with well by building trust and providing good containment for difficult discussions. Those who master this Quality manage stress and any accompanying mood changes or reactivity well by, for example, taking good care of their own health and knowing when and how to get space to think. They are able to stay calm and open, even when under pressure or when others are anxious or angry, and are able to gently, but persistently inquire into and address difficult issues (see Chapter 11 for the importance of paying attention to building trust). They can be compassionate and empathetic to those who are struggling, and are willing to spend time in dialogue if that's what is required – offering guidance on priorities and the various forces at play if required. They will also connect you to useful people and resources if that's what's required.

Those who demonstrate the Measured Connector Quality capably are often very well respected within the organization. They tend to be viewed as authentic and tend to have an ability to remove obstacles quietly through subtle influencing of key players, creating high-quality feedback loops and encouraging people to find out things for themselves.

Mastering the Measured Connector Quality – advanced

For senior leaders facing significant change within a complex organization and/or a highly unpredictable context, the Measured Connector Quality becomes even more central to any leadership role (see Chapter 14 for more on developing leadership maturity). The four advanced skills likely to be required are described here.

Bringing presence while experiencing pressure to deliver in a volatile context is not easy, but is an essential part of leading through complexity and uncertainty. This means remaining grounded and in touch with your own sense of purpose, while staying open to and curious about everything that's currently happening, as it happens. Many of us get caught up in our own distracting inner dialogue or 'reactions' to the way the organization is performing and start to want to control things, instead of understanding them by listening deeply and then being able to provide strong guidance or support. The ability to bring presence depends on a capacity to let go of this inner dialogue and focus on the present moment.

The ability to *facilitate complex dialogue* is another advanced Measured Connector skill. This goes beyond chairing and/or meeting management and means bringing a strong process orientation to any discussion. For instance, this might mean being able to convene discussions that clarify intentions and priorities across different loyalty groups and interests – and valuing all the values that show up! The leader needs to understand how dialogue is different from debate, know how to design the session and then track all the different discussion threads and perspectives. S/he needs also to be skilled at surfacing and addressing hidden agendas or anxieties in a non-anxious, non-defensive way and think clearly on his or her feet when drawing the discussion together towards some sort of conclusion and 'good enough' next steps. This often means being able to hold contradictions and polarities, and understand what's required to manage these rather than solve them.

Advanced Measured Connector skills also include an interest in and a capacity to *build sustainable individual and team capability*. This requires an understanding of how sustainable change arises, ie it needs to be based on a deep common purpose supported by appropriate structure and process and worked towards over time in iterative loops. It also requires a leadership ability to stimulate and support others to discover things for themselves, which in turn requires faith in the process of learning and discovery, faith in your people, patience and highly honed questioning skills.

It's reasonably rare for senior leaders to demonstrate the kind of *process sensitivity* that's required for leading change in complex or uncertain contexts, though we have observed a few leaders who do this extremely well. This requires a high level of attention to all forms of communication, high-quality day-to-day contracting with colleagues and well-thought-through stakeholder involvement. Signs of lack of process sensitivity include: poor quality e-mails written while rushing; failure to involve key stakeholders in the right way at the right time; poor calendar management which results in unfair demands being made of others; lack of clear commitment to a process; and lack of follow-through.

Self-rater

Score each of the following statements according to how true it is for you as a leader on the following scale:

1 …never true

2 …seldom true

3 …sometimes true

4 …often true

5 …almost always true

1   I bring focus and attention to all forms of work communication, including e-mails, phone calls, and face to face.

2   I ensure that I keep my team and stakeholders up to date with any bigger picture/context developments that I believe could impact their work.

3   I am able to keep calm and steadfast, even if I'm feeling anxious under the surface.

4   I encourage and enable those around me to access relevant information and to stay in good-quality contact with each other.

5   I am good at getting the best out of people through the use of good questions.

6   I look after my own health and well-being and encourage others to do the same.

7   I take good care when bringing people together for meetings, from set-up right through to follow-up.

8   I understand how teams develop and grow, and am skilled in adjusting my leadership approach according to the stage the team is at.

9   I ensure I have regular, structured one-to-one sessions with each team member to talk about how they are doing on key tasks, and what they are learning.

10 I am skilled at facilitating dialogue which enables constructive exchange and agreement of next steps, even amongst groups with very different perspectives.

Scoring analysis

Add your scores for the 10 statements. Your result will be between 10 and 50. The following guidelines may help you to clarify to what extent you have mastered this Quality, and how to progress.
The following guidelines may help you to clarify to what extent you have mastered this quality, and how to progress.

0–15 This Quality is almost completely missing from your repertoire and it's important to start to build the associated core skills.
16–25 This Quality is somewhat lacking in your repertoire and you need to start to grow your skills and capacities in a more concerted way.
26–40 You have started to demonstrate this Quality quite well at times, and now need to assess whether you've developed it enough given the context you're in.
41–50 Your mastery of this Quality is good and you can start to consider how you might bring a matured version of the Quality to more complex, large-scale or otherwise challenging change contexts.

Measured Connector research insights

This Quality is very widely used by effective leaders.

Eighteen per cent of the leaders in our survey named this role as the most attractive Leadership Quality.

Most people would prefer their line manager to demonstrate this Quality more.

Nearly half of the leaders in our survey said this was the easiest Quality for them to access.

Only 6 per cent of the leaders in our survey named this Quality as the hardest to access.

Leaders who find the Measured Connector Quality the easiest to access tend find the Edgy Catalyser and Visionary Motivator Qualities the most difficult to access.

This appears to be a very useful Quality in many situations, and particularly so when there are multiple partners and stakeholders involved, when cultural change is required or when morale is low. In high-pressure organizational turnarounds the Quality is not thought to be quite so necessary, at least for short-term success.

Embodying the Quality

This section helps you to involve your head, heart and belly as you exercise this Quality (see Chapter 13 for more on the significance of this).

The gesture that we recommend you try if you would like to sense what it's like to embody the Measured Connector Quality is a 'signal to gather'. Reach out as if to gently pull a group of people towards you, as if to embrace them. Try doing this a number of times. Do it slowly, and feel into the effect this has on you as you open your arms, and consider all the work relationships that you are involved in. Do you feel warm and energized about these relationships, or a bit exposed and uncertain? Or maybe you feel excited, or maybe even a little needy? Perhaps your sensations are different as you imagine gathering different groups or individuals. If you do feel any anxiety, try breathing into your belly while sensing the solid ground beneath your feet. Remember that you don't need to bring people too close. You can set boundaries that help the contact to stay warm, yet businesslike.

The Measured Connector Quality comes alive in relationships, and the act of opening your arms and pulling people towards you can affect your emotional state in a way that can help you to find out more about the way you're feeling about other people's perspectives and attitudes. If this gesture causes some discomfort or animosity in you, that's something to investigate. This might be true about your current situation, or maybe it's an old pattern of yours from your childhood. Explore!

Breathing into the belly and sensing the ground beneath your feet is a good way of supporting yourself in relationships, particularly if the Measured Connector quality doesn't come so easily to you. This sequence tends to have a calming and strengthening effect, and allows a good quality of leadership presence to arise, which is so central to the Measured Connector Quality. We suggest you experiment.

Too much Measured Connector?

If the Measured Connector Quality starts to dominate a leader's thinking or acting, then this can become a problem. Often, this can be a sign of the Measured Connector Quality becoming dominant, and the Tenacious Implementer Quality being squeezed out. Typical indications of this are the team becoming quite cosy, indecisive, slow to act and conflict averse, and the leader spending a good deal of effort making sure everyone has bonded, often to meet his or her own needs for reassurance and company, rather than because it's particularly required to achieve outcomes. The cost of all this is usually low performance and poor delivery.

Another possibility is that the leader becomes lost in the complexity of the issues at play or the range of perspectives in the team. They appear fuzzy or erratic, neglecting to bring focus to the delivery imperatives that exist. The Thoughtful Architect Quality goes missing. If this is coupled with a lack of Tenacious Implementer Quality, the leader's descriptions of purpose or goals may not be concrete enough for some followers, and in extreme situations, their lack of attention to guiding the team towards specific outputs or next steps can be seen as irresponsible or incompetent. People start to work around leaders like this, either ignoring them or going above their heads for more direction or support.

A leader demonstrating the Measured Connector Quality is likely to be appreciative of people's contributions and affirming and respectful of their different agendas, but in extremis, this quality in its shadow form can be seen as indulgent, tentative or non-committal, ie not wanting to upset the apple cart, or not being willing to ruffle people's feathers. The leader might fail to take a stand on an important issue or to provide strong guidance about key drivers when required, because they don't want to risk getting into conflict or experiencing personal rejection, discomfort or failure.

Typical barriers

Maybe as you have been reading this chapter, you have started to experience some of the following typical barriers to embracing the Measured Connector Quality. If so, here are a few simple suggestions/responses to support you.

1 *'I don't believe that this Quality is particularly required in my current role.'*

This is a common misconception. It's more likely that this quality is a little counter-cultural for you, or for your organization. See what it's like to spend 40 minutes with each of your team, once a month, asking them about progress and next month's plans. You'll find it flushes out lots of issues and builds a good level of trust.

2 *'I find it very difficult to relax into the level of dialogue that may be required to connect people with issues or tasks in this way. It just takes too long! I prefer e-mail!'*

There's nothing wrong with using e-mail to record your agreements, or to help communicate the details. However, it's likely that you need to experiment with improving your level of questioning and listening when meeting face to face. This can be very powerful for aligning other with your goals. Note: you may also need to improve the quality of your questions.

3 *'I'm not really a "people person", and my team members don't appear to need this kind of soft approach. They are technicians!'*

See what it's like to stay with the hypothesis that 'being a people person' is an important part of leadership. What might happen, for instance, if you improved the quality of your regular team meetings by making them more enjoyable, or making them safer for people to speak up?

4 *'I am used to giving technical advice, and people will see me as incompetent – or even lazy – if I start asking them for the answer…'*

Experiment! Notice if this happens and see what it's like to carry on anyway, perhaps using the research results above to explain why you're taking a new approach. Maybe they will begin to experience some benefits! And... how else are they going to learn?

5 *'I have trouble setting boundaries around discussions in meetings as people can really talk a lot! What is enough Measured Connector Quality, and what is too much?'*

Experiment with setting discussion boundaries, eg the timing of each discussion, what's in scope and what's not, etc. You might also ask a work 'buddy' to help you to get better at this by observing you running a meeting and watching for where you fail to set boundaries.

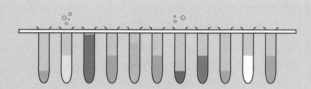

15 quick experiments

Here are a few experiments which will get you practising aspects of the Measured Connector Quality:

1   Read through your sent e-mails from the last two weeks, reflecting on the amount of focused attention you brought to each communication. If disappointing, make a commitment to yourself to improve!

2   If you sense a conflict brewing, try to raise it to the surface calmly and help people to confront the issue in a contained way. Provide some ground rules to enable a sensible conversation.

3   Ask people how things are going for them – begin to make a habit of this, especially in organizational life, and continue to probe if you can, so you can understand even more about what drives them and what makes them tick.

4   Pick three people in your organization who you wouldn't normally have contact with – and make contact. Find out what they do and how that helps the organization meet its purpose. Ask them what they think about your area of the business and what you and your colleagues need to be doing better.

5   Work on enabling people to trust you by revealing things about your own thought processes – what's on your mind, what you're trying to achieve, what's getting in the way, what you care about…

6   Use the following structure of questioning to conduct a one-to-one review every month with each of your team members and restrict yourself to asking good questions rather than offering advice or direction: what were your objectives this month, what did you do/ achieve, what got in the way and what did you learn, what's coming up, what are your next steps, what help do you need from me to succeed?

7   If you normally over-plan meetings, then try letting others speak first and practise building their ideas into an agenda instead of initiating everything.

8   If you normally under-plan meetings, spend 10 minutes beforehand drawing up an outline agenda, purpose and context update and talk people through this at the start.

9   Bring three people together who wouldn't normally talk to each other and convene a conversation. This could be at home or at work.

10 Reflect on the state of maturity of any team you're part of, noticing to what extent the team is dependent on the leader to direct work, hold people to account, initiate ideas, manage stakeholders, etc. If the team is quite mature, see if you can notice what has enabled this over the last few months or years.

11 List what your 'hot buttons' are, ie what behaviour of others or situations tend to trigger your irritation and see if you can tolerate this feeling when it arises, rather than suppress it.

12 When you make a mistake, or fail to deliver, see what it's like to apologize fully. This might make it safer for others to own up to mistakes.

13 Start becoming more mindful by doing yoga or meditation (or long walks) to get good at letting go of self-criticisms or hanging onto and replaying past encounters/actions.

14 Practise bringing presence. This means giving the current situation your undivided attention – switch your phone off, make eye contact, breathe, listen well, put your feet flat on the ground, ensure that you can see everyone…

15 During your next meeting, try practising offering guidance and asking questions rather than initiating or opposing.

Example 1: Growing the Measured Connector Quality

Victoria is the leader of the environmental test team in a busy processing plant:

> I have a technical background with a degree in chemistry. Not long after I joined the company I was promoted to team leader, which felt like a bit of a burden to start with. At first I would just tell people what to do, by e-mail mostly, and then get angry and irritated by the lack of progress. I had quite a technical load myself to get through so I just wanted people to be independent and efficient. But this didn't work out. Sometimes people didn't even tell me when they hadn't finished something I'd asked them to do by the end of the day. They just went home! I couldn't believe it!
>
> Then after attending a leadership programme and receiving some very specific 360 feedback from my team and my line manager I started to experiment with having a bit more face-to-face contact with the team to find out what their skills were and what was important to them. Some were more interested and open to this than others, so I began to get more of a feel for who was motivated to learn and who wasn't really enjoying the job at all. This then opened the door for me to arrange one-to-one sessions with everyone on a regular basis where I could chase up progress, and start to close the gaps in their knowledge about our processes.
>
> Six months on I feel much more confident about the way I'm dealing with my team, and I'm enjoying the relationships more. There are still one or two people who I'd like to be a bit more motivated to learn and do well, but I'm working on this!

Example 2: Refining the Measured Connector Quality

Vincent is the owner of a small but growing business that is part of a 'hub' of similar businesses working on a range of projects:

> I have always seen myself as a 'people person', able to talk with others and get to know people easily. People tend to find me very approachable and enjoy my company. My business took off sort of by accident two years ago when I was made redundant and managed to pick up a contract from a friend to do quite

a big piece of work, and then a few others came on board to help me out. Lots of this was done by word of mouth, with quick e-mail agreements to back things up.

Then more and more clients started asking me to do work for them, because people trusted me and liked me, but I began to realize that I needed to start to take a bit more care with how I spent my time and who I talked to about what.

I was introduced to the Five Qualities framework after about six months, and I realized that the Measured Connector Quality was as easy as breathing for me, in one way – I mean it seems entirely obvious to me that you would look people in the eye and get interested in their perspective – but I hadn't ever properly developed this as a *leader*. I was a bit casual and wasn't really thinking things through or following things up, which was resulting in quite a bit of frustration in the team, which I sensed but I just wanted it to go away and for them to be a bit more independent! I would promise team meetings and then I'd have to cancel at short notice to go and meet a prospective client to discuss other work instead. They just weren't getting any guidance at all.

So I started to pay more attention to the way I organized my time, ensuring that team meetings and one-to-ones were booked in months in advance. I also began taking more care with the way I e-mailed people – reading their e-mails to me more carefully and answering all the questions that I was being asked. I also paid more attention to the way I brought people together to discuss issues, or plans. Then, although I felt enormous awkwardness round this at first, I started to meet with my team one to one on a regular basis. This was to see how I could help them, and to check in on progress in a more structured way. So I gave myself more guidelines and frameworks for how to do all these things as a leader, rather than relying on my natural, kind of unstructured friendliness and openness.

This resulted in my team being much more settled and productive – and our working relationships have become smoother, more enjoyable and actually more creative. Without this realization about the importance of this connecting Quality, I'm not sure whether my business would have lasted as long as it has! My team are certainly pleased and I feel I'm getting more out of them too.

Stop and Reflect!

Restructuring in response to cuts in funding

Sarah is the director of social care and runs a unit that provides a range of services to the local community. The unit's record of meeting its performance targets has been very good over the past two years, but there are big cuts in funding ahead that Sarah has to now respond to. She has to come up with a plan in six weeks' time to present to her peers in the executive team. This plan will need to illustrate how the cuts are to be made over the coming six months.

She leads a team of eight area managers spread out over a fairly wide territory, who meet every two months. Because of the challenging geography and the apparent difficulty of finding good times to meet regularly, this team isn't very well-connected or coherent, and three distinct 'cliques' have formed of those who have worked together in the past, those who play squash together and a remaining two who often travel to team meetings together.

As staff costs are Sarah's biggest expense, it's possible that some of the areas will have to amalgamate to form five or six areas, which will mean some job losses at area manager level, as well as the next level below.

Sarah has called you in to advise her on how to use the Measured Connector Quality to support her through this change. What steps would you suggest she takes to plan, agree and implement the necessary cuts in a way that maintains good relationships, engagement, motivation etc.? Should she do much of her thinking alone, or in one-to-one meetings with her area managers, or with her line manager the CEO? Who else might she need to connect or consult with? Map out a suggested process for her to use over the next six months and list the benefits of the approach suggested. Also identify any disadvantages and put forward some ways of mitigating these.

Raising awareness about information security

Faisal is the head of IT in a complex financial services organization of 800 people with a team of six people supporting him alongside various contractors. He has been brought in to ensure – in particular – that information security gets immediate attention after a recent scare and the subsequent retirement of the previous, very popular, head of IT.

Faisal believes he has a clear idea of his priorities for the next one to two years, as he has worked in a similar business before, but he needs to clarify the state of other people's awareness, as his approach will be to ensure that everyone is strictly following procedure and is equipped to react well to possible threats. He also needs to make sure people know what work is being done behind the scenes to upgrade security so that people are reassured at this level.

One difficulty is that his boss, the chief operations officer, is not very up to date with the scale of the threat and how to tackle the various issues at play, and he needs to ensure that she understands and has bought into the plan.

The board is very preoccupied with the topic of security because of possible reputation damage to the organization, and the executive team of 10, including the COO, also needs to be on board with the plan and playing their parts. Then there's the extended leadership team of 60 section heads – Faisal's peers – who meet face to face every quarter to discuss key issues, although the last meeting was cancelled when it transpired that a number of people weren't going to be able to make it due to work/client commitments.

There are also all-staff Town Hall meetings every six months where staff gather at four different locations to hear updates, plans, and to talk. In addition, there's a bi-weekly blog from the chief executive that is read by many but needs to be very concise.

How would you advise Faisal to approach this period in his career, and in the organization's life, to maximize success using the Measured Connector Quality in particular? Who does he need to get together to discuss what in what order? How might he set up these gatherings? What regular meetings does he need to set up? How can he use existing structures and connecting mechanisms to help him to get his message across? Who else might he need to connect to – head of financial services, head of admin, head of HR, head of legal/compliance? What skills will he need to demonstrate?

Where to go to find out more

Useful books to develop the skills of Measured Connector include:

Core skills

Facilitator's Guide to Participatory Decision-making by Sam Kaner.
Leading Great Meetings by Richard M Lent.
Dialogue and the Art of Thinking Together by William Isaacs.
Coaching for Performance by John Whitmore.
The Five Dysfunctions of a Team by Patrick Lencioni.
Primal Leadership: Unleashing the power of emotional intelligence by Daniel Goleman

Advanced skills

Presence by Peter Senge *et al.*
Organizational Culture and Leadership by Edgar Schein
On Dialogue by David Bohm
Connective Leadership: Managing in a changing world by Jean Lipman-Blumen

Ten real-life examples of the Measured Connector Quality in action*

Nelson Mandela, Alexis Tsipras, Desmond Tutu, Richard Branson, Deepak Chopra, Mark Zuckerberg, Clement Attlee, Angela Merkel, Christiana Figueres, Thomas Paine.

*We have chosen these people as they are relatively well-known, come from around the world and have shown some mastery of this Quality.

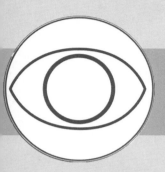

TENACIOUS IMPLEMENTER
MEASURED CONNECTOR

VISIONARY
MOTIVATOR

THOUGHTFUL ARCHITECT
EDGY CATALYSER

'In dreams begin responsibilities.'
W B YEATS, 'RESPONSIBILITIES'

Leaders who demonstrate the Visionary Motivator Quality use words and images to describe ways forward, or pictures of the future that inspire and motivate others to engage. Through their ability to relate to others, and to embody their own values and intent, they are able to bring people on board, who then help shape and deliver the next stage.

IN A NUTSHELL
'Let's all move towards a brighter future.'

CORE FOCUS:
Buy-in

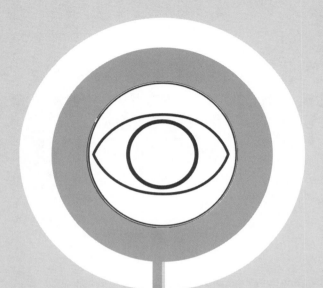

CORE SKILLS

Visioning through
words and images

Inspiring others

Engaging presentations

Motivational skills

Experimentation

Reframing

ADVANCED SKILLS

Imagining or opening
to the future

Behaving as an 'attractor'

Narrative leadership
and storytelling

Use of symbols and
meaning-making

VISIONARY MOTIVATOR
AT BEST:

expressive
imaginative
articulate
open-hearted
appreciative
authentic

VISIONARY MOTIVATOR
AT WORST:

impulsive
dreamy
verbose
fake
gushy
superior

Mastering the Visionary Motivator Quality – core

The Visionary Motivator Quality is concerned with engaging others in a journey, whether that journey is very clear, or more uncertain and emergent. This Quality builds on research into transformational leadership (Chapter 6), values-based leadership (Chapter 9) and systemic and symbolic leadership (Chapter 10). We know that once there is a strong sense of purpose and direction that a team or group can buy into and contribute to, this can be very motivating and inspiring for people, particularly when it connects with their own interests and values. Leaders who access the Visionary Motivator Quality understand this well, and instinctively seek ways of working towards it. They also have high-quality interpersonal skills, and are able to motivate and inspire people with their vitality and passion for responding to what's required in service of a wider intent. Giving individualized forms of encouragement, stimulation and challenge, perhaps via 1:1 coaching, is often central to their capacity to ensure that everyone feels motivated to make their unique contribution to the journey.

Leaders who demonstrate this Quality are able to articulate a sense of where the team needs to be heading without being too narrow or prescriptive, and are able to issue a strong invitation to others to contribute and play their parts. Their own passion and commitment for the work ahead is rooted in a set of values that inspires others. They develop the skill to communicate the way ahead through words and images that transcend cultural barriers and help to connect people into ideas and possibilities whatever their starting point. This, coupled with a high level of competence in delivering engaging presentations when required, is likely to help create a culture of possibility and enthusiasm in teams, even when there are difficult challenges to face up to.

It's important to add that these 'engaging presentations' don't need to be particularly polished or 'neat' (unless the local culture particularly demands this) but they do need to be thought through, heartfelt and connecting. Often a well-chosen story, backed by a few simple frameworks and followed by some work at the flipchart, can be much more compelling and inviting than an overly-comprehensive slide pack.

When delivering presentations or motivating 'inputs', those leaders who combine the Visionary Motivator Quality with the Measured Connector Quality are likely to be most successful. They will take care both with framing their propositions or direction-setting moves within the wider context and with opening up to others' contributions and alternative perspectives.

Another key element of the Visionary Motivator Quality is a commitment to role-modelling espoused principles or ways of working. If this is done with integrity and without obvious strain, it will draw people along in its wake, even if done in a relatively humble way. Leaders who demonstrate this Quality have clarity of purpose and a dynamism to go with it. The respect and trust of followers is won through the leader inviting people to believe that with a clear sense of direction, and sufficient commitment, they can achieve more than they thought possible in a way that will be satisfying to all.

Creative experimentation is a key feature of the Visionary Motivator Quality. This might appear in small ways – such as innovative coaching suggestions or 'in at the deep end' developmental tasks – or in bigger ways, such as setting up pilots to test out radically new ideas or ways of working in a ring-fenced way. Imaginative reframing of problems and making space for exploring and trying out innovative approaches are also features of Visionary Motivator leadership. These can be very stimulating and enriching for people, particularly when the work demands it.

The skill of reframing is worth describing here, as it can be a transforming process once leaders master it, and especially if combined with the dialogue skills that come with the Measured Connector Quality. It requires a lightness of touch and an agility of mind. The key is to help others to see a problem or issue in a new way, such that they feel more empowered to act. This might involve turning an issue you have with internal customers on its head, eg, 'Let's step into their shoes and look at it this way…'; or it might be useful in a one-to-one setting where the other person has become bogged down with some high-pressure work, eg, 'If you could take one very small but significant step forward, what might it be?'.

In the fast pace of organizational life, leaders who demonstrate the Visionary Motivator Quality are also able, when challenged, to quickly marshal the facts to produce an on-the-spot compelling business case for change in a way that's attuned to the individual and the context. In this, they are often supported by regular investment in Thoughtful Architect leadership. This means that they continually do the groundwork of reflecting on the context, looking at trends and patterns, making sense of the issues at play, clarifying key priorities and devising supporting structures.

Mastering the Visionary Motivator Quality – advanced

For senior leaders needing to inspire significant change within a complex organization, access to the Visionary Motivator Quality can be a very powerful tool. If brought in an authentic and value-driven way and used in close conjunction with the other four Qualities, it can be a transforming element and a key enabler to success. Otherwise, leaders can end up asking for loyalty in a way that's coercive and diminishing rather than empowering.

The four advanced skills likely to be required are described here.

Imagining or opening to the future, also known as 'futuring', opens the door to a valuable set of practices for senior leaders to develop and experiment with when considering the way forward, and needing to co-create an inspiring vision. Eight are suggested here, some of which overlap with advanced Thoughtful Architect Qualities:

- scanning news bulletins to keep tabs on competitors, threats and more widely on politics, economics;
- staying abreast of new research by reading up on recent research papers;
- watching trends by examining various data sources to understand the nature of change, and the rate of change in your sector or areas of interest;
- surveys or polls which test views and probe into perspectives;
- scenario planning by imagining future scenarios based on various possibilities;
- road-testing your high-level vision or 'story' and inviting others to engage and contribute their own stories and perspectives;
- co-creative exercises which encourage multiple stakeholders to envisage their ideal future state, often supported by acknowledging the story so far;
- reading up about the bigger trends and understanding what recognized futurologists are saying.

The phrase *'behaving as an attractor'* offers a way to think about Visionary Motivator leadership within complex organizational contexts. In these contexts, multiple visions and values may be present; top-down approaches are unlikely to be particularly productive. This involves a leader bringing two opposite but complementary qualities which enable the organization to be highly flexible without fragmenting: enough 'form' to keep an organizational system sufficiently stable and coherent, together with an immense creativity and capacity for flexibility that enables significant change to happen quickly. An example of this is an entrepreneur who has a bold vision and a sense of next steps, yet creatively facilitates others to bring their best in a collaborative and inspiring way.

Narrative leadership or storytelling provides a way for leaders to work with their organizations in more subtle ways, to make sense of the past and shape the future of their work together. It has to be said that everyone loves a good story! It's a powerful way to build relationships and bring different loyalty groups together – or indeed, to divide people into factions! It's also a fundamental way in which we as humans can create change, through the imaginative stories we tell about what we think is possible, how things might be in the future and what it's going to take from everyone to get there.

Symbols and meaning-making have been used by leaders throughout history to either persuade or enable their followers to understand the reality of what's happening and find a constructive way through. Words, gestures and images are used to ascribe particular meaning and value to particular individuals, events and ideas. This is designed to – or sometimes happens accidentally – evoke particular emotions and actions. It is also prone to manipulation for reasons of self-interest. Sometimes more than one interpretation of events and form of language exists, which results in a sense of fragmentation and disruption in a system until the two meaning-making systems are integrated in some way, usually via dialogue.

Self-rater

Score each of the following statements according to how true it is for you as a leader on the following scale:

1 ...not at all true

2 ...seldom true

3 ...somewhat true

4 ...generally true

5 ...very true

1 I am clear and open about my own intent and values. ☐

2 I am able to talk in a compelling, attractive way about where I and the team need to be heading. ☐

3 I demonstrate confidence and commitment that enables people to come along with me, even when the end state is not so well-defined. ☐

4 I genuinely believe that given the right conditions, people can achieve almost anything. ☐

5 I am skilled at helping people to turn sticky problems into solutions. ☐

6 I'm able to deliver a punchy rationale in support of my sense of the way forward. ☐

7 I enjoy finding out what motivates people and helping them to get more of this. ☐

8 I see coaching as a key way to stimulate and motivate people. ☐

9 I enjoy setting up experiments that allow people to take calculated risks. ☐

10 I am able to inspire people through bringing my authentic self to any interaction. ☐

Scoring analysis

Add your scores for the 10 statements. Your result will be between 10 and 50. The following guidelines may help you to clarify to what extent you have mastered this Quality, and how to progress.

10–15 This Quality is almost completely missing from your repertoire and it may mean that you are actually not leading at all.

16–25 This Quality is lacking in your repertoire and you need to start building your capacity to bring it. It's possible you have developed an allergy to this Quality which you need to inquire into as this could be getting in the way of your leadership capability developing.

26–40 You have started to grow this Quality but now need to develop the underpinning skills, or perhaps inquire into any limitations you perceive round your development or the applicability of the Quality.

41–50 Your mastery of this Quality is good and you now need to focus on how you bring a matured version of the Quality to more complex, large-scale or otherwise challenging change contexts.

Visionary Motivator research insights

This is the Quality most widely used by effective leaders.

Selected by the leaders in our survey as the one they would most like to master (47 per cent).

A popular choice as a boss.

Most people want more of this Quality in organizational life.

Twenty-six per cent of the leaders in our survey said this was the easiest Quality for them to access.

Seventeen per cent of the leaders in our survey named this Quality as the hardest to adopt.

Those who find the Tenacious Implementer Quality easy to access tend to find this Quality particularly difficult to access.

This is a very useful Quality to bring during situations that require significant growth, or to combat low morale, or when change is complex and far-reaching.

Embodying the Quality

This section helps you to involve your head, heart and belly as you exercise this Quality (see Chapter 13 for more on the significance of this).

To sense what it's like to embody the Visionary Motivator, try standing up and reaching up and out with your arms, as if you are about to conduct an orchestra. Look slowly around from left to right as if there is a group of people standing in front of you, about three metres away. First, just notice what that's like. Then imagine the crowd growing. You probably feel quite exposed, which you might or might not enjoy! If you feel a little wobbly or over-excited at first, check that your feet are firmly planted on the ground, bend your knees just a little, breathe into your belly, and try again.

The next step is to smile while you are raising your arms and say, 'Join me in this new future!' Try it! Again, reach with both arms upwards and outwards and look ahead as if to a crowd of potential followers. Try doing this a number of times, really feeling how your heart opens (or not), and perhaps noticing how this leaves you feeling energized and present, or maybe a little anxious. See how your knees and legs are feeling – grounded, or shaky? Note that the strength of this quality depends on the depth of the leader's understanding of the content and context and his or her ability to truly relate to the audience, as well as the quality of his/her own thinking and reflections as a leader in this context.

There's a temptation for leaders to try to 'fake' the Visionary Motivator Quality by being extra 'upbeat' and 'positive', which only works in a limited way. However, the risk is that this is experienced by others as shallow and unconvincing at best, or at worst a sign of your own lack of real buy-in and therefore some sort of cover-up. This can set up all sorts of unintended responses in followers, such as cynicism and disinterest, or even distrust and fear.

Too much Visionary Motivator?

When a leader brings the Visionary Motivator Quality, s/he is often grounded in a fundamental belief in the benefits of the direction or destination described. However, if this becomes more of a missionary zeal than a vision, it can become alienating or counter-productive to others who believe that something important has been missed, or that it's just not possible or desirable for some reason. This is one of the ways that cynicism can take hold, and people who might otherwise be followers start to disengage and become disruptive or switch out altogether.

In more complex contexts, the Visionary Motivator Quality needs to be used in conjunction with the Measured Connector Quality to ensure that various agendas are somehow brought together, or at least respected. Over-promoting a particular vision is unlikely to be helpful.

Another possible context is when the leader is required to lead with a vision that has been constructed by others without any contribution from him or her at all, and is struggling to find any true, heartfelt connection with it. This will be quickly picked up by followers who are very sensitive to such gaps in truth and authenticity. In this case, use of the Visionary Motivator Quality in high doses is not recommended, and more pragmatic qualities such as Tenacious Implementer and Measured Connector are more appropriate. Of course, the other possibility is for the leader to make a strong case to his line manager that the vision needs adapting, using the Edgy Catalyser Quality and maybe the Thoughtful Architect Quality to support this move.

In the worst case, a leader demonstrating an excess of Visionary Motivator Quality can get trapped in a high-energy, high-enthusiasm 'persona'. S/he can become addicted to positivity and appear slightly unhinged from reality. In this, the leader might appear superhuman; bouncing back from any setback, unable to properly acknowledge difficulties or fears, becoming totally unstoppable. They may become someone that others over-rely on, make fun of, or hide from. This can also, rather dangerously, lead to burnout if not spotted. This could be pointed out by a line manager or trusted colleague, ideally through a high-challenge, high-support coaching process.

Typical barriers

Maybe as you have been reading this chapter, you have started to experience some of the following typical barriers to embracing the Visionary Motivator Quality. If so, here are a few simple suggestions/responses to support you.

1 *'I'm not a particularly jolly or upbeat person, and believe that others should find ways to motivate themselves.'*

   It's true that people need to take responsibility for bringing their best to their work, but if you could learn how to help them to be even more motivated, would that interest you? You could start by asking your direct reports which parts of their work they find most stimulating and absorbing.

2 *'I have a reputation for being difficult and "edgy", and being positive about something would sound odd and inauthentic.'*

   It sounds like you need to expand your range as a leader, without letting go of your capacity for the Edgy Catalyser Quality. Maybe you could start with something you'd like to change about your working context, and see if you can try instead to tell an imaginative, inspiring story of how this could change.

3 *'I am quite happy to give a factual or technical presentation but find myself a bit lost for words when I'm asked to inspire others or deliver a "vision".'*

   It's very useful to know that you've mastered the rational side of influencing. Now you need to work on the 'emotional' side, which means taking a small risk next time you present, by letting the audience know what you're feeling excited about, or where you're feeling anxious and want to bring attention.

4 *'I would rather work things through slowly and carefully, and don't really believe in getting ahead of ourselves with big ideas.'*

There is certainly a place for slow, careful work for any leader. However, when things are complex or significant change is required, it can really help people to get their heads out of the details and get a sense of the 'big idea' and their own role in this.

5 *'Our work is very uncertain and volatile at the moment, and it feels almost impossible to look more than three months ahead.'*

That might well be true. A three-month horizon may be all that's required. However, if you get the sense that a longer-term view could help, then it might be a good idea to ask your line manager to come to your next team meeting and offer his or her take.

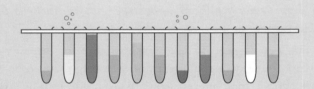

15 quick experiments

Here are a few experiments which will get you practising aspects of the Visionary Motivator Quality:

1 Experiment with doing a job in a novel way. It may not work, but you will learn something.

2 Think of something important to you now. Imagine how this might develop in the future. Try to think of a number of different scenarios, and to what extent you might be attracted to or want to move towards each in some way.

3 If you have a hunch, take some notice of it and follow it up.

4 Make an effort to think about a plan you have in a conceptual or abstract manner. Use descriptive or unusual words, use a metaphor or draw a picture to represent the journey to get there, or the destination you have in mind.

5 Run a workshop session to explore the possible solutions to a problem that you and the team face at work; help people to build on their own and each other's ideas.

6   Ask a couple of people to give you some feedback on your five-year vision for your work life/personal life/social or family life; see if you can bring some passion or authentic truth when you describe the principles and values that underpin this vision, and the outcomes or benefits you would like.

7   Invite a friend or colleague to listen to you for 10 minutes, talking about whatever you are passionate about. This could be anything from baking cakes to watching films to sailing boats. Use colourful language. Don't worry if people switch off. Instead, notice what switches them on.

8   Try to describe your job or role in life in an unusual way, maybe using an odd metaphor or referring to a character or story in a film or a book.

9   Take a risk and share your ideas for the future at your next team meeting. You could try telling an imaginative story and inviting feedback.

10 Keep in touch with what is going on in the outside world and try to use other people's ideas to inform your own.

11 Offer to lead on the next change initiative.

12 Think about a change you dread happening to your team at work. Now list all the possible advantages of that change, and make some notes on how you would persuade the team that this is a good idea.

13 Observe how others stimulate engagement in group sessions. What can you learn from this?

14 Think about a group of colleagues or friends or your family. If you were moved to persuade them of a particular course of action, think about what aspect of the outcomes or process would appeal to each person.

15 Bring community or family members together to talk about a key event that's coming up and how best to mark it.

Example 1: Growing the Visionary Motivator Quality

Jay is the HR Manager for a financial services company:

When I was promoted to HR Manager I was fairly new to leadership and still learning when it came to inspiring my team or hatching any 'big ideas' about the future. I was more interested in planning and implementation.

The business context changed dramatically after six months, with the advent of two major acquisitions, and I had to find a way to recast the HR team's role and agenda in line with a fresh direction for the business. This was not easy, as some had been working in set ways for over 15 years, but the executive team was hungry to hear from us, given the reputation the department had for doing things a bit too much 'by the book'.

After being introduced to the Visionary Motivator Quality, and beginning to see how I would need to draw on this, my first step was to talk 1:1 to everyone about their aspirations for their working lives, and to get them thinking about their hopes and dreams beyond work. Behind the scenes, I talked to as many people as possible in my network about how best to lead this type of change. Quite quickly, I also began to open up a bounded conversation at our regular team meetings with my direct reports about the challenges ahead, and where I thought we needed to be heading as a team, describing how we would be perceived, what sort of things we'd be focusing on, what kinds of values we'd be role-modelling and inviting their responses.

This eventually led to a whole department workshop where I and the team presented our 'HR Story' and invited people to contribute and share their own imaginative stories. I learned to my surprise that there was quite a bit of untapped potential lurking in the team, and very little resistance to growth and development. Over the following weeks, each team worked on their plans, and it seems the whole process has opened up new levels of ambitions and insight...

Example 2: Refining the Visionary Motivator Quality

Marieke is series producer for a TV production company:

I have always been good at coming up with innovative ideas and inventive solutions to difficult problems. Over time, in various production roles I'd acquired the reputation of being highly creative, and even inspiring, but perhaps a bit demanding and 'perfectionist', and not particularly tolerant of other people's ideas and instincts.

I began working on a new series for an existing programme. Due to stiff competition and declining ratings during the previous series, the first task was to work on 'refreshing' and maybe even 're-inventing' aspects of the show to make it more attractive to audiences, and keep them interested once they had started to watch. Luckily I'd just been on a short leadership programme involving the

Five Qualities and had received some feedback about my 'pushy' influencing style, as my new team had some pretty talented and experienced people on it and I needed to learn how to get the best out of them.

After quite some soul searching about this, my sense was that I had to slow the process down and bring some sort of framework to help the team to think through and form a collective view of what was working and what wasn't. After that I hoped we could work together in a structured but creative way to re-imagine our future as a team: what the show would be like, how it would be received, and how we would be working together. This enabled me to set the scene, facilitate and listen, rather than feel pressured to come up with all the ideas. As predicted, the team was pretty creative, and many of the ideas they came up with were in line with my own. The result was a solid way forward, with much more buy-in and engagement than I would otherwise have had. And to my surprise, I enjoyed the process and felt relaxed and confident about the result.

Stop and Reflect!

Engaging people in a big idea!

Nigel is the CEO of a small charity that has a big agenda. The idea is that this charity, funded partly by central government, partly by donations, will bring all sorts of volunteers and small groups together to do support work for the elderly that had previously been done (or not done) by government departments.

Nigel needs to work with others to create a vision for this charity, which others can buy into. Existing groups are keen to carry on the work they've been doing over the past few years, but are wary of increased competition for funding. Volunteers want to be sure that the charity is using any money wisely. The government department wants a business model that will work, but hasn't got the capacity to work on this with much motivation or skill. Potential sponsors and benefactors have lots of other charities that they might give to, and may well believe that the government should be doing this work itself!

Nigel has asked you to support him to build a vision that will be engaging and that others can shape – and to map out a process for launching the charity. What would you advise in terms of process, content, and how he might need to prepare for this as a leader?

Merging two cultures

Susanna is a senior partner in a legal service firm that has just merged with a competitor. Business X, that Susanna belonged to originally, has been doing well over a number of years in a range of areas and has an established, global client base. Competitor Y is a newer, smaller, more dynamic business with a growing reputation, and has developed some innovative ways of working based in new technologies that appear to be attracting new forms of business.

The starting point is challenging. Both firms say they have a unique culture that they believe is fundamental to their success. Susanna has noticed already that charge rate structures and level of 'professionalism' seem to differ between the two firms too. There is no existing plan for integration as the deal was done rather quickly, based on 'gut instinct'. There are also concerns about the new firm, and the risk of some staff leaving and taking their clients with them.

Susanna has been tasked with bringing the key stakeholders together to map out the way forward, in terms of developing a common culture and proposed ways of working together.

You've been asked to help her to do this through developing her use of the Visionary Motivator Quality. How would you suggest she starts, who might she involve, and what would a good change process look like which takes the new, merged organization from where it is now to where it needs to be? Do you have any warnings for her, and any other wisdom to share about the limits and possibilities for this venture?

Where to go to find out more

Core skills

Leaders Strategies for Taking Charge by Warren Bennis and Burt Nanus.
The Inspirational Leader by John Adair.
Visual Meetings by David Sibbet.

Creative Confidence by David and Tom Kelly.
How Great Leaders Think: The art of reframing by Lee Bolman and Terrence Deal.

Advanced skills

Telling the story: The heart and soul of successful leadership by Geoff Mead.
Theory U: Learning from the future as it emerges by Otto Scharmer.
Transformational Leadership by Bernard Bass.
The Dark Side of Leadership by Bernard Tourish.

Ten real-life examples of the Visionary Motivator in action*

Malala Yousafzai, Jeff Bezos, Elon Musk, Martha Lane-Fox, Narendra Modi, Steve Jobs, Pope Francis, Martin Luther King, Jack Ma, Pablo Iglesias.

*We have chosen these people as they are relatively well-known, come from around the world and have shown some mastery of this Quality.

TENACIOUS IMPLEMENTER
MEASURED CONNECTOR
VISIONARY MOTIVATOR

THOUGHTFUL ARCHITECT

EDGY CATALYSER

'If we do not learn from history, we shall be compelled to relive it. True.'
ALVIN TOFFLER, *THE FUTURISTS*

Leaders who demonstrate the Thoughtful Architect Quality scan the internal and external environments to identify the key drivers for change, and to assess the possible impact and the organization's current capability and design strategies for addressing these drivers. Resulting strategies are interdependent and coherent with due regard to the context and the wider system.

IN A NUTSHELL
'Let me explain how it all fits together.'

CORE FOCUS:
Design

CORE SKILLS

Strategic thinking and planning

Diagnosing situations and generating options

Stakeholder analysis

Framing (contexts, processes, issues)

Organization design (including working intelligently via authority)

Creativity/reframing situations and problems

ADVANCED SKILLS

Systemic thinking

Scenario planning

Thought leadership

Challenging the system, thinking the unthinkable

THOUGHTFUL ARCHITECT AT BEST:

observant
reflective
analytical
discerning
clear thinking
strategic

THOUGHTFUL ARCHITECT AT WORST:

hypervigilant
distant/preoccupied
obsessive
picky/pedantic
disconnected
impersonal/academic

Mastering the Thoughtful Architect Quality – core

The Thoughtful Architect Quality is required when you really want to focus on what's been happening and to consider what needs to come next. The ability to step back from the day-to-day and begin to create a strategy to help people get there, building in today's data and tomorrow's possible scenarios, is of great value. Because of this Quality's capacity for deep reflection, in its mature form, the analyses and the designs are likely to be well thought out and grounded in reality.

This Quality builds on the work of, for example, Mintzberg and Schoemaker, who pointed to the need for leaders to bring strategic leadership and high-quality thinking (Chapter 7). It also follows the insights of Heifetz and Higgs and Rowland into the importance of being able to think through and frame the work ahead so that others can step into it (Chapter 8).

The Thoughtful Architect Quality is concerned with scanning the environment, understanding the forces and dynamics at play and assessing whether the organization has the capability and capacity to address those challenges. It is concerned with devising and developing strategies which will work.

In order to achieve this, the leader needs to be able to psychologically 'get up on the balcony' or take a 'helicopter view' of the situation. This involves scanning both the internal and external environments, picking up on patterns and making connections. With this overview, the leader can see current and future situations and scenarios. They then need to analyse, appraise and synthesize.

Because of the thoughtful and reflective nature of this Quality, proposed changes, ideas and issues can be placed within their particular context with different variables factored in. These variables can include the leader themselves, followers, other stakeholder groups, the organization's priorities, processes and deliverables, and the importance of any specific issues in the grander scheme of things. Stakeholder analysis is an important part of the Thoughtful Architect's understanding of the forces at play. As a result of cognitive empathy, that is to step into the other's mind, there is an understanding of other stakeholders' perspectives, which can then be factored in to any strategy. By identifying and understanding stakeholders' views on the issue, the Thoughtful Architect can map interest groups' current position and also where they need to be.

A key part of framing is to help others understand the current context in a way that feels both illuminating and inviting. Leaders need to be on top of the relevant external patterns and trends, understand where key stakeholders are positioned, find a way of making sense of all that's going on and offer it in a way which gets attention. Framing is more about guiding than controlling – asking powerful questions; including people in discussions; getting people to think and grapple with the ideas and challenges. Framing doesn't mean that leaders stop leading; they need to ask the questions with the right people, and orchestrate the discussions. And they need to be doing this continuously, not just at the beginning of a large project.

Once any issue is framed, the Thoughtful Architect has access to a range of problem-solving and decision-making methodologies that not only assist in reaching decisions but also in convincing others. The Thoughtful Architect values competence, knowledge and proven experience and this is the primary route for their constructing the argument in their influencing style. The Thoughtful Architect will be able to describe the problem or issue, seek to identify any underlying patterns or triggers, and by looking into the future, develop ideas or solutions which will begin to address the problem.

Having developed the solution or framework/design, then the leader needs to find ways of communicating this to others. This requires being 'planful' and also having the ability to weigh up different options and make decisions based on sometimes conflicting priorities. The purpose is to create frameworks and designs that others can step into and then act more strategically and coherently.

Both rational and creative problem solving are used – rationality doesn't exclude creativity. The Thoughtful Architect can see issues from multiple perspectives and thinks long and hard about the nature of the issue. Considering the issue within the continuum of past, present and future, together within a wider context, allows for more options to be generated. Spotting patterns and offering useful, approximating frameworks and then reframing the issue or generating ideas around possible solutions comes naturally. Both the early framing activity and reframing, at their best, are done with other key groups and require challenge through questions, pointing out inconsistencies and facilitating the creation of new ideas and scenarios.

The purpose of much of this thinking is to come up with intelligent design, be that as a strategy or in terms of redesigning the organization so it is more likely to be 'fit for purpose', so that the organization has the capability and capacity to achieve its objectives and people can find their place in order to make their contributions.

The Thoughtful Architect Quality can manifest in a number of ways – it can be conventional or radical, mechanistic or innovative – but whichever it is, there is a striving to map out a strategy in a way that is coherent and fits together well. This is true for both the process of mapping out and the generation of the strategy and final outcome. The key elements are the abilities to: scan the terrain external and internal to the organization; scan the past, present and future; see the system dynamics at play; and craft a strategy which frames and accommodates these.

Mastering the Thoughtful Architect Quality – advanced

The Thoughtful Architect quality is particularly important to master for those taking on more responsible and complex roles within the organization or society. Leaders need to apply *systemic thinking* (see Chapter 10 for a definition), and are required to have the capability to manage cognitive complexity and to see across various time spans (see Chapter 14 on how this capacity can open up as leaders mature). The art of strategic analysis is a key factor. Some leaders, notably entrepreneurs, can naturally fulfil this; for most of us, some help is required. Strategy analysis, formulation and implementation is a profession in itself, but the Thoughtful Architect might well learn from observation or from books (Mintzberg *et al.*'s *Strategy Safari*; Johnson and Scholes' *Exploring Corporate Strategy*) or from studying for an MBA. Building on the core skills of scanning the environment and seeing if the internal organization is fit for purpose, the Thoughtful Architect thinks longer and harder than most and is able to use relevant frameworks to undertake their analysis. They are able both to deconstruct issues and contexts and to reformulate in different ways, connecting the current situation with the ideal future scenario.

Part of this strategic thinking is the *development of future scenarios* in order to generate a number of options that will best fit the different possible futures. It isn't merely developing best and worst case scenarios, but developing a range of scenarios which factor in any number and combination of variables. This 'what if' questioning plays out in most situations – whether thinking through a corporate strategy, sitting down with a direct report looking at his or her future career, or solving a pressing problem.

Coherence across the system is desired, with disparate plans and strategies needing to 'stack up'. The Thoughtful Architect values depth and rigour of thought and won't abide sloppy or inconsistent thinking or illogical plans from others.

It is natural that the Thoughtful Architect will be able to develop new ways of thinking about things because of the multiple perspectives that are experienced. This can manifest as *thought leadership*, the person displaying this Quality being recognized as an expert, a specialist with something new to say about their chosen subject. Their authority comes from this expertise and the recognition of their depth and breadth of thinking.

The Thoughtful Architect is interested in developing expertise and competence, valuing reflection and learning as a continual process, and will typically be open to new ideas. It manifests as leading through creating a clear strategy based on original thinking, crafting seemingly disconnected ideas into a viable way forward, and indeed inventing radical new ways of working. Enabling this Quality to emerge allows a leader to step into the role of principal strategist and designer of grand plans – holding the bigger picture in their heads throughout the process.

With an overarching perspective, this Quality will *challenge the system* when there is misalignment and also suggest radical ways to change the organization. *Thinking the unthinkable*, applying deep problem-solving methodologies and using a combination of systemic thinking, organizational knowledge and core purpose can result in very different ways of achieving the organization's goals. Although open to possibility, someone displaying the Thoughtful Architect Quality cannot not point out elements of a plan or initiative which do not fit with the agreed strategy. Even seemingly disparate projects may be the focus of attention if there are dependencies, one to another, or consequences, from one to another. The Thoughtful Architect is resolute in challenging things which don't 'stack up' or lack coherence when seen from a strategic perspective.

Self-rater

Score each of the following statements according to how true it is for you as a leader on the following scale:

1 ...never true

2 ...seldom true

3 ...sometimes true

4 ...often true

5 ...almost always true

1 I spend time scanning the environment and understand what's on the horizon. ☐

2 I make sense of the internal organization and see how roles need to be realigned to fit with future challenges. ☐

3 I am good at seeing the big picture and how the different parts of a complex problem fit together. ☐

4 I will not be hurried into making reactive decisions. ☐

5 I will always take time out to think things through in depth. ☐

6 I am always open to new ideas about the future as long as they resonate with my sense of what I believe is happening. ☐

7 I think a lot about the present and the future and work hard to align any vision with my sense of the overall journey. ☐

8 I am able to set out a framework for the work ahead that enables others to step in intelligently. ☐

9 I am able to identify stakeholder groups and map where they are in relation to the issue. ☐

10 I am good at asking the kind of challenging questions that make people think differently. ☐

Scoring analysis

Add your scores for the 10 statements. Your result will be between 10 and 50. The following guidelines may help you to clarify to what extent you have mastered this quality, and how to progress.

10–15 This quality is almost completely missing from your repertoire and it's important to start to build the associated core skills.
16–25 This quality is somewhat lacking in your repertoire and you need to start to grow your skills and capacities in a more concerted way.
26–40 You have started to demonstrate this quality quite well at times, and now need to assess whether you've developed it enough given the context you're in.
41–50 Your mastery of this quality is good and you can start to consider how you might bring a matured version of the quality to more complex, large-scale or otherwise challenging change contexts.

Thoughtful Architect research insights

This Quality is best used in smaller doses.

Eighteen per cent of the leaders in our survey named this Quality as their natural leadership quality.

Twelve per cent of respondents named this Quality as the hardest to adopt.

Natural Thoughtful Architects tend to find the Edgy Catalyser Quality the hardest Quality to access.

Twenty-six per cent of respondents named this Quality as the most attractive role model.

Those leaders who exhibit the Thoughtful Architect Quality tend to find the Visionary Motivator to be their most attractive role model.

The Thoughtful Architect Quality is one of the least frequently observed Qualities in organizational life.

This Quality is particularly useful in complex organizational change, or when working on a long-range strategy. It is seen as least useful when morale is low, or there is a critical project to deliver urgently.

Embodying the Quality

This section helps you to involve your head, heart and belly as you exercise this Quality (see Chapter 13 for more on the significance of this).

There are a number of gestures which help embody this Quality, and to a degree it depends on what fits with you and your reflective process. Raising the hand to the face and either tucking your thumb under your chin and placing the rest of your hand between your chin and your mouth; holding your head with one hand half-cupped, under your chin and up one side of your head; or your hand in front of you, fingers curled towards you, head resting on your knuckles. Rodin's Thinker is a useful pose to experiment with.

You can be standing with one of these gestures or you can be sitting back in a comfy chair holding your hands to your front in a relaxed way or behind your head.

To practise this Quality, try looking outward and towards the horizon, imagining what might be coming your way. Begin to notice all the things that are moving and stationary. Also practise going within yourself, connecting with the ground and your belly, and start to reflect upon and make sense of what you have been observing. Note that all things are inter-connected; try to 'join the dots' between the different things.

This Quality is about observation and reflection; analysis, and framework building. It requires a lot of sensing and thinking. This is the primary mode of being. It is an internal process of making sense of the world, and trying to find a model, a plan or a framework in which to order it. It requires spending time reviewing the current situation and scanning the horizon; making connections and seeing the bigger picture by putting the current situation into the wider context.

Thoughtful Architect can be a slow-moving and pensive Quality, with occasional and sudden moments of clarity. For some this might require a degree of detachment – sometimes just observing the world, at other times seemingly lost in thought. For others, it's a quietly private process that is barely observable.

Too much Thoughtful Architect?

There can be a tendency for Thoughtful Architect to take too much time over things – always looking into the future, thinking it through, ensuring there is an inner consistency and developing a strategy. This Quality in excess doesn't allow much time or energy for reactive or responsive leadership. Reflection must precede action and that reflection can end up looking at too many 'root causes' or patterns and not getting to the nub of the issue – 'paralysis by analysis'; and it can mean there are too many options generated, leading to 'multiple choice neurosis'.

Leaders who bring an excess of Thoughtful Architect Quality may lack spontaneity and tend to let opportunities slip by. They require time and space, and these are often in short supply. The purity of the strategy can be favoured over the impact on people; sometimes the needs, wishes and feelings of others are not factored in. Leaders who over-value this Quality may be intolerant of others who don't spend the same amount of time and effort thinking things through.

The Thoughtful Architect Quality brings coherence but this can cause frustration in others when there is a need for every plan and decision to fit neatly into the bigger picture. Most managers accept compromise and work with the art of the possible; the Thoughtful Architect sometimes fails to see the pragmatic need to get something working operationally now, rather than the perfect design.

When you link the helicopter thinking with the desire to work things out on their own or with like-minded people, you can begin to see how the Thoughtful Architect – on a bad day – might appear to be quite arrogant. Having spent considerable time thinking through the myriad possibilities, a leader can sometimes descend triumphantly from the mountain with their grand strategy, and then be shocked when people dare to disagree or criticize. The Thoughtful Architect can also come across as the principal critic of other people's ideas and proposals.

Because of this focus on the grand design, there isn't always enough time spent investing in relationships and partnerships that are explicitly committed to the common endeavour. The ability to come up with conceptually watertight strategies must be balanced with the need to meet others in their domain, rather than always doing things on the Thoughtful Architect's terms.

Typical barriers

Developing the Thoughtful Architect Quality has its obstacles – some of us are not naturally reflective or able to be future-focused, preferring to act in the moment on more operational issues.

Here are some typical barriers in developing this quality and suggestions for overcoming them.

1 *'I haven't got time for reflection, there's too much to do right now.'*

Remember the phrase 'failing to plan is planning to fail'. Some moments drawing breath and taking just a few minutes time out will repay dividends.

2 *'I'm a detail person, I don't see the big picture.'*

Next time you're in a meeting, don't focus on the individual agenda items as things to be done today. Reflect upon the purpose of the meeting, and how it might be used to achieve the organization's Vision.

3 *'A problem is a problem not an opportunity to be reframed.'*

Often if you think about a problem in a different way it becomes less of a problem, or the solution can present itself.

4 *'I leave the thinking to others.'*

Okay, so you like to just get on and do things? Whatever experience or know-how you have, you can be sure that it could add value to the conversation. Thinking is a discipline, so you might need to apply yourself some more!

5 *'I can't think strategically.'*

What if you could? Sometimes it's easier to start from here, then think through all the steps of what you want to do, out into the future, then divide it into phases – medium and longer term for sure. And that's one to five years at least.

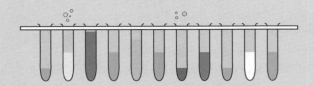

15 quick experiments

Here are a few experiments which will get you practising aspects of the Thoughtful Architect Quality:

1   Try to keep an open mind about those around you rather than making hasty judgements.

2   Seek out some technical/expert books and journals that cover your current work area. Read these and inwardly digest.

3   Work with someone who is an accomplished strategist to devise lots of different ways of seeing the future for your organization, community or neighbourhood.

4   Look at trends and predictions for your industry; find these on the internet.

5   Devote more time to considering things more deeply and with more concentration.

6   Build up your one-to-one relationships and get to learn about others' ideas and perspectives at greater depth.

7   Ask questions of others and listen carefully to the answers. Make notes and try to pull all the ideas together into a bigger picture.

8   Think carefully before acting and then act.

9   Think of the way a process at work is designed, or the way a department is structured. Completely redesign that process or structure in two different ways, then compare the three designs, using a set of success criteria.

10 See if you can think ahead and plan something creative for the future.

11 Find out about the history of your organization or department. How have things changed in the last 10 years, and what prompted these shifts?

12 Set some key principles that underpin the work of your division or unit.

13 Offer yourself as an objective, dispassionate sounding board for someone else's ideas.

14 Refuse to get bogged down in details.

15 Only contribute to discussions if you feel it is really worthwhile.

Example 1: Growing the Thoughtful Architect Quality

Ian works for a financial services organization and has been newly promoted into his position as a first-time team leader in charge of a sales force of 20 people.

He was promoted partly because of his outstanding individual performance, but also because of his interpersonal skills and his ability to 'toe the company line'. He was tremendously proactive, though only with his own personal business objectives; he was also able to exert influence, but he only ever used these skills with customers. He was also very short term in his thinking, which fitted with the monthly sales targets that individual sales people were given.

Ian recognized the need to shift his focus across a number of dimensions and took up the offer of a series of coaching sessions over a nine-month period. It soon became clear that he needed to develop his Thoughtful Architect.

He started to explore his situation from different perspectives – his time horizon; the different stakeholder groups; how his and his team's objectives fitted into the company strategy; where he needed to shift his focus from the things he had been doing to the things which were now becoming important.

His new challenges were: how to motivate his sales team; how to meet the yearly team targets; how to push for change within his department to get the resources that his sales team were calling for (for example newer technology and more effective admin processes); and how to enhance the reputation of both his team and the larger organization, the company having received criticism from customers about their advice.

By taking time out to reflect on these issues, Ian was able to shift his focus from the short term to the medium/longer term. He could see how by being better aligned to corporate strategy, the team would be able to create win-win situations, and he was able to start pointing out inconsistencies in the strategy and resource allocation to demonstrate the need for some (albeit minor) organizational change.

Example 2: Refining the Thoughtful Architect Quality

One head teacher that we worked with is a successful Thoughtful Architect. She was appointed as the new head of a primary school that was suffering from falling morale and a rather controlling culture. The previous head and the chair of governors had become in the habit of giving direction and others had become in the habit of following. The new head was very clear about how she saw things changing, but her challenge was to get others to take responsibility for helping her get there. She had a well-thought-through plan for how to do this, and she was completely aware of the different and sometimes competing interests amongst the stakeholders.

Her appointment coincided with tremendous change in the education sector with various government initiatives, some of which would present opportunities, some requiring more defensive strategies. She was very conscious of budgetary constraints and a potential shortfall in the short term, though with careful management the finances looked more stable in the medium to longer term, given the influx of new children down the line.

How did she approach these various challenges? Initially she constructed a mental roadmap of the process of organizational change. She populated a stakeholder map, ensuring that the wider educational system was included (this included the local education authority as well as central government). She identified and assessed the various drivers for change. Her next step was to create a leadership team, and to start to shift each senior staff member's mindset from simply managing the school to thinking about contributing to the vision and culture of this living community.

The initial visioning process was purposefully led by the head. She began by explicitly seeking the ideas of senior staff, and over time others became involved. Central control was gradually relinquished. Staff began to have a greater say, as did the parents who, through a revitalized Parents Forum, were also included. The pupils themselves were encouraged to set up a School's Council and become 'Associate Governors'. This had all been part of her grand design, but she worked slowly and thoughtfully at enabling others to make it come alive.

Traditionally her school was linked into a geographic cluster, but recognizing the need to build capacity and connections across the system she purposefully made contact with similarly minded heads who were then able to form a coalition to press for more autonomy to shape their own futures, albeit in a collegiate way, mindful of the core values operating within the sector.

Stop and Reflect!

Taking up a new position in financial services

You work in a financial services company and have been recently promoted and appointed team leader, following a corporate restructure.

The corporate structure followed a strategic review of its core business, having weathered a period of downturn, and with a need to become more customer-responsive whilst at the same time ensuring ethical values were demonstrated.

The role is looking after a team of about 20 people, not all currently in post, and the team's role is to offer a back-office administrative support to the three service areas (savings, mortgages and investments). Traditionally the team had been organized along geographic lines, servicing the company's four main regions.

At the time of your appointment, your boss suggested to you that the company was keen for you not only to restructure into a team better fitted to purpose but also to streamline some of the operational processes.

Although overall the company has a 'traditional banking' culture, there are pockets of more entrepreneurial thinking and acting, most notably in the investments division, though that only accounts for 15 per cent of costs and profit, the rest being shared equally between the other two areas.

Your task is to respond to your boss's suggestion for restructure. Can you deliver a proposal to her which sets out your initial ideas? You might also like to develop an action plan of some of the key activities you will need to be doing.

The future of our university

You have been asked by the vice chancellor of the university for which you work to attend and present at a strategy conference he has organized for the top 20 leaders across the university.

He has expressed concern at the various internal and external drivers for change, many of which appear to be threats rather than opportunities. In a rather speedy fashion he listed, in no particular order, some of his key concerns:

- The current business model didn't appear sustainable, involving ever-increasing student numbers, many drawn from overseas, resulting in too big a student-lecturer ratio.

- Lecturers were rewarded for research achievements, not teaching ability.

- The rise and rise of Massive Open Online Courses (MOOC), which seem to be taking over.

- The increase in tuition fees faced by students, resulting in huge debts as they enter a world where house prices continue to rocket.

His parting remark was that there are probably other issues you need to include. The VC would like you to present to his top team on:

- the internal and external drivers for change which the university is facing;
- some future scenarios which they may need to take decisions around; and
- some possible solutions to meet these challenges.

Where to go to find out more

Useful books to develop the skills of Thoughtful Architect include:

Core skills
Strategy Safari by Henry Mintzberg *et al.*
Exploring Corporate Strategy by Gerry Johnson and Kevan Scholes.
The Strategic Mind (Trilogy) by Bob Gorzynski.
Making Sense of Change Management by Esther Cameron and Mike Green.
Dance of Change by Peter Senge.
Leading at a Higher Level by Ken Blanchard.
Steal Like an Artist by Austin Kleon.
The Creative Habit by Twyla Tharp.

Advanced skills
Systems Thinking: Managing chaos and complexity by Jamshid Gharajedaghi.
Wings for Change: Systemic organizational development by Jan Jacob Stam and Dymphie Kies.
100+ Management Models by Fons Trompenaars and Piet Hein Coebergh.
Integral Life Practice by Ken Wilber *et al.*
The Artist's Way by Julia Cameron

Ten real-life examples of the Thoughtful Architect Quality in action*
Angela Merkel, Christine Lagarde, Jimmy Wales, Larry Page, Elon Musk, Ayaan Hirsi Ali, Bill Gates, Mohammed bin Rashid Al Maktoum, Lee Kuan Yew, Barack Obama.

*We have chosen these people as they are relatively well-known, come from around the world and have shown some mastery of this Quality.

TENACIOUS IMPLEMENTER
MEASURED CONNECTOR
VISIONARY MOTIVATOR
THOUGHTFUL ARCHITECT

EDGY CATALYSER

'*Obstacles cannot crush me. Every obstacle yields to stern resolve. He who is fixed to a star does not change his mind.*'
LEONARDO DA VINCI

Leaders who demonstrate the Edgy Catalyser Quality ask the difficult, penetrating questions about the organization and performance, spot dysfunction and resistance, and create sufficient discomfort and unease when things aren't improving to ensure movement. The Quality in action focuses on creating constructive tension between what is and what could or should be, and sees the process of facing uncomfortable truths as a precursor to healthy change.

IN A NUTSHELL
'This is a serious problem. Let's bring some energy and focus to this.'

CORE FOCUS:
Discomfort

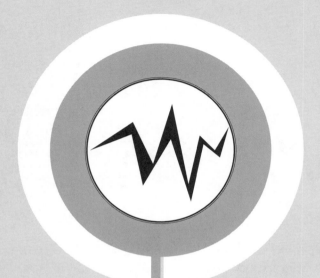

CORE SKILLS

Ability to step back and spot
what's causing stuckness

Tough conversations

Questioning skills/probing

Courage to withstand discomfort

In service of organizational
or team outcomes

Confronting organizational/
cultural dysfunction

ADVANCED SKILLS

Negative capability

Boundary negotiation

Shifting limiting mindsets

Providing perspective on
what is happening
(Bystanding)

EDGY CATALYSER AT BEST:

EDGY CATALYSER AT WORST:

AT BEST	AT WORST
incisive	hypervigilant
probing	distant/preoccupied
catalysing	obsessive
courageous	picky/pedantic
steady	disconnected
observant	impersonal/academic

Mastering the Edgy Catalyser Quality – core

The Edgy Catalyser Quality builds on the theory and research suggesting that a leader needs, at times, to be a truth-teller (Chapter 2), a 'Devil's advocate' (Chapter 7) and possibly unpopular (Chapter 9). This Quality enables a leader to 'smell the rat' and point it out. It allows the person to be an intelligent agitator who spots real problems, especially if they are hard to face, and brings the right amount of tension and pressure to ensure that the difficulty is addressed. This process is likely to feel quite uncomfortable for those involved, but remaining steady during conflict helps.

Leaders who demonstrate the Edgy Catalyser Quality have the ability to ask the right penetrating or probing question, draw attention to one part of the organization, or question the accepted wisdom in order to get people to see that things might need to change. It illuminates tensions and conflicts that, if focused on and worked through, will lead to renewal. Leaders who display this Quality are happy to be seen as the troubleshooters, maybe occasionally even 'troublemakers', and definitely catalysts for change. However, at its best, the Quality brings a humility and an inquiring rather than accusatory gesture – supporting this with observed data, even if painful for the other to hear.

The ability to step back and spot what's causing stuckness is a key skill. This manifests in two ways: through knowing what 'right' looks or feels like and seeing when that isn't happening; and by looking at a situation, a process, a behaviour and recognizing that it can be changed for the better. The ability to step back is really about being able to review and reflect upon things in the moment.

Having spotted what is wrong, the Edgy Catalyser leader becomes determined to have the tough conversations that will address the problem. This isn't about arguing for argument's sake. It is a conversation with a purpose, the outcome of which is a disturbance of the status quo. Using this Quality skillfully means having a dialogue with the other person, or with the team, which can separate what needs to be changed from the person themselves. The objective is not to blame, but to engage the other in a conversation inquiring into what is happening at the moment, and what now needs to change. The skill is being focused on what needs to change, and to communicate that in a way which increases the likelihood of it changing.

For many of us, having tough conversations, confronting people with what they are doing and how it's impacting, evokes a certain trepidation. The leader who demonstrates the Edgy Catalyser Quality has the courage to withstand this discomfort, yet doesn't become aggressive. They might have to court the anger of others by having a potent mix of courage and good judgement, a touch of compassion and a high degree of steadiness. They might confront people or teams with their unhelpful behaviours if people-focused, or with their disappointing results or ailing processes if task-focused. This courage to withstand discomfort, in oneself and in others, is best achieved when one is very much aligned with one's own sense of purpose, and 'on message' with the organizational goals. The higher purpose trumps any sense of discomfort you may have, or you may be causing.

The Edgy Catalyser Quality is focused on serving outcomes. Indeed, the skill is to hold the strategic direction and organizational purpose in mind, and see clearly where the structure, the systems, the infrastructure or the people are failing. It is this commitment to organizational purpose that is the powerhouse of this Quality, letting people know where there is some lack of alignment with intent and outcomes. This Quality also allows a leader to amplify a productive pattern as well as disrupt an unhelpful one.

The Edgy Catalyser is sometimes a role model for doing things differently, especially when there needs to be a shift towards a more performance-oriented culture. A typical example would be a new leader arriving in an organization and seeing everything with a fresh pair of eyes, drawing everyone's attention to what's not working as it should be, what's surprising, or how things look compared to other organizations.

People with cross-organizational leadership roles such as performance directors, quality managers, corporate social responsibility managers and health and safety managers often need to bring this Edgy Catalyser Quality, alerting people to issues and being a thorn in people's sides until they take action. These leaders are not intimidated by politics, but are clever enough to respect and work with its power. They can assimilate and respect the prevailing vision and values, and point out for example where executives are failing to role-model agreed values, or where systems (eg IT) are falling short of expectations.

Edgy Catalysers tend to see things from a systemic point of view, having an awareness of what's going on beneath the surface. They can highlight the log jams, and with minimal intervention alter the flow of things by enabling or diverting attention, energy or resources. This capability of review, reflection then action operates on both local and global issues.

Mastering the Edgy Catalyser Quality – advanced

The more advanced skills associated with the Edgy Catalyser Quality are concerned with creating an environment where deep change can occur. This requires framing the extent of the changes, and having the ability to hold the tensions of the situation within oneself long enough to enable others to begin to see things in a different way.

The poet Keats (1817) coined the term *negative capability*. It can be described as:

> the ability to receptively support teams and individuals to continue to think and struggle in challenging situations, by holding or 'containing' a situation or context. Positive capability is the more familiar face of leadership, which features decisive, active interventions based on knowing (Cameron and Green, 2015).

Or to put it another way, the ability to withstand the impetus to act on one's inner urges because of the discomfort, anxiety or uncertainty that the current situation is engendering. Some leaders feel the compulsion to act, whereas what might be required is the ability to resist the urge to act or to drive self or others to come up with a quick solution, instead holding the creative tension.

Boundary negotiation is a term we use for testing out the specific ways of being and doing in play. A boundary in this context can be a physical, social, ideological, psychological or behavioural representation of a limit or constraint or dividing line between what is allowed or not allowed, acceptable or not acceptable. The Edgy Catalyser leader will view the ways things are, the ways things are done around here, and actively and purposefully test out those boundaries in order to enable the organizational purpose to be progressed. Examples include the behaviours and attitudes that people need to stop doing – and those that they need to start doing. They tend to be cross-functional ones – who delivers what to whom, who has what authority, who gets to make decisions. On an individual basis, it might mean sitting down with an employee to agree the extent of their autonomy, authority and mandate, for them to be able to do their job effectively.

One of the more advanced skills of the Edgy Catalyser Quality is to be able to *shift limiting mindsets*, of themselves and of others.

Typical tools for shifting mindsets include: powerful coaching-type questions; self-reflection; giving and receiving feedback; stepping into others' shoes and seeing things from multiple perspectives; sharing 'edgy' feedback and data across boundaries. Any technique which allows or forces others to compare their own thinking with how others conceive the world will enable them to start seeing things from different perspectives and to broaden or deepen their worldview.

Being able to hold both one's own inner tensions and those of others, having sought to establish and negotiate the extent of the boundaries in play and begun to shift others' mindsets, the fourth advanced skill of the Edgy Catalyser is to act as the 'Bystander' (Kantor, 2012). That is, to provide the perspective on what is happening by watching the situation or events as they happen – be it the dynamics of a team meeting or power politics playing out as a result of an organizational change initiative.

The role of the *Bystander* is to act as witness, absorbing and making sense of the dynamics, synthesizing and relating what is happening to organizational purpose in a non-attached way. The bystander – not a casual passer-by – is an active presence in the situation, and is thus acting as a container to ensure others are held in such a way as to allow meaning and resolution to emerge. A mirror is thus held up to an individual, to a team or to the organization at large.

Self-rater

Score each of the following statements according to how true it is for you as a leader on the following scale:

1 ...never true

2 ...seldom true

3 ...sometimes true

4 ...often true

5 ...almost always true

1 I am clear and precise with the facts when I need to argue a point.

2 I don't tend to just let things go if I think they are important in achieving agreed outcomes.

3 I am recognized for my ability to deal with conflict bravely and well.

4 I am courageous when speaking up about a problem or performance issue that others don't see.

5 I enjoy a robust conversation and transparently welcome honest feedback.

6 I am good at spotting problems and can quickly see which are important and which are trivial – and what might help.

7 I am comfortable with the notion that some people don't like me, but I can still work with these people without that getting in the way.

8 I can show my disappointment or my sense of urgency in a way that impacts people without getting angry or aggressive.

9 I can tolerate conflict and difficulty in a steady way while staying open to others' upset or difficult reactions.

10 I am able to demonstrate how a specific process or behaviour is sub-optimal, or hindering the organizational purpose.

Scoring analysis

Add your scores for the 10 statements. Your result will be between 10 and 50. The following guidelines may help you to clarify to what extent you have mastered this quality, and how to progress.

10–15 This quality is almost completely missing from your repertoire and it's important to start to build the associated core skills.

16–25 This quality is somewhat lacking in your repertoire and you need to start to grow your skills and capacities in a more concerted way.

26–40 You have started to demonstrate this quality quite well at times, and now need to assess whether you've developed it enough given the context you're in.

41–50 Your mastery of this quality is good and you can start to consider how you might bring a matured version of the quality to more complex, large-scale or otherwise challenging change contexts.

Edgy Catalyser research insights

Best used in small doses.

Selected by the leaders in our survey as the least attractive role model.

Not a popular choice as a boss.

Positively correlated with the Tenacious Implementer Quality.

Eight per cent of the leaders in our survey said this was their natural Leadership Quality.

Thirty per cent of the leaders in our survey named this Quality as the hardest to adopt.

Leaders who naturally bring the Thoughtful Architect Quality tend to find the Edgy Catalyser Quality particularly difficult to access.

Useful Quality during restructuring processes, in times of crisis or when facing well-defined change.

Embodying the Quality

This section helps you to involve your head, heart and belly as you exercise this quality (see Chapter 13 for more on the significance of this).

Natural Edgy Catalysers very often have a straight back, and tend to move around quite a bit, and look around – to test out multiple-perspectives; always scanning the area for people or things, very often sitting forward in their seats.

To be able to access this Quality, you can place your body in two positions. The first is where you are grounded and on the front foot. You have spotted something wrong and you are pointing at it – not aggressively, but very definitely. You are invoking a sense of dissatisfaction and maybe irritation on behalf of stakeholders, and summoning up the energy from within to say or do something about this. You are breathing into your belly – like an athlete preparing for the big moment – filling yourself up for action.

The second pose is one that will allow you some moments of reflection before action. Feet firmly on the ground, shoulder-width apart, pointing slightly outwards, arms akimbo, eyes looking intently at what is happening, taking it all in. Once again breathe into the abdomen and sense what now needs to happen.

Too much Edgy Catalyser?

The Edgy Catalyser Quality demands quite a bit of attention and focus, which can tip into obsession. The leader can end up putting too much pressure on him or herself, and on others. Taken to extremes, there can be an inability to rest on their laurels, even for a moment, to enjoy some success and completion; or to appreciate others before moving on to the next situation to 'put right'.

Possibly haunted by the possibility that things are not good enough, and imperfection, stupidity and failure are only a step away, those with too much Edgy Catalyser Quality exhaust themselves and everyone else involved. In this way it's easy to start to destroy goodwill and motivation.

Natural Edgy Catalysers often find it difficult to calibrate their leadership approach in terms of directness and level of open criticism. Some organizational contexts need a lot of edge and tension, while others need more appreciation and support. Edgy Catalysers may not be good at noticing when the context has changed, and they can be slow to back off or turn the volume down.

In the worst case, the Edgy Catalyser Quality might appear harsh rather than incisive; more interrogating than probing; seen to be troublemaking rather than catalysing; foolhardy not courageous; inflexible rather than steady; and detached rather than observant. Although the Edgy Catalyser can be questioned and challenged, other, less forceful people may shy away from this, particularly when they are lower down the organization or where there is a power differential.

Their focus on righting all wrongs can come across as being indiscriminately critical, and as being provocative for the sake of merely stirring things up. Their questioning and probing attitude can be more like an interrogation or inquisition. Sometimes they can take on too many battles, lacking sensitivity to the politics of the situation, and come across as foolhardy. The need for those with this Quality to have emotional resilience can be usurped by a closedness of mind, and the resulting inflexibility lead to being seen as thick-skinned.

Often someone with an Edgy Catalyser Quality is recruited for that very Quality, but doesn't fit well with the existing culture, and either leaves or is forced out.

Typical barriers

Developing the Edgy Catalyser quality has its obstacles. It can take a certain personality type to have the energy and focus and seeming lack of concern for stable relationships.

Here are some typical barriers in developing this quality and suggestions for overcoming them.

1 *'I want people to like me.'*

That's probably a normal human condition. However, becoming an employee, and indeed a manager, requires you to take responsibility for organizational performance. Sometimes focus on the outcomes can mean risking the ire of some of your co-workers.

2 *'Being aggressive with people is not my style.'*

Don't mistake assertiveness for aggression. You can be clear and unequivocal without being aggressive, bullying or threatening. Try becoming an elegant Edgy Catalyser with style and sensitivity!

3 *'Telling people they're wrong doesn't get engagement.'*

Sometimes it's a tough call – do we motivate people towards the vision, or do we need to create a sense of unease and urgency to get things moving? There's a place for both, and research suggests that pointing out what's not working in a trusting context can create the impetus for change.

4 *'I don't feel I'm resilient enough for this.'*

It is true, the Edgy Catalyser doesn't win too many friends, and it can feel like an unrelenting responsibility. Looking after yourself, having back-up or a confidante is useful, and developing stress management techniques is critical.

5 *'I like to think positively not negatively.'*

Remember every Yin needs a Yang. Spotting the obstacles along the way and reducing them produces positive movement – addressing the pros and cons, accentuating the positive and reducing the restraining forces is a balanced approach.

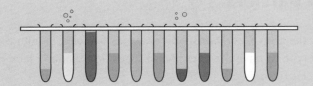

15 quick experiments

Here are a few experiments which will get you practising aspects of the Edgy Catalyser Quality:

1. Find something in your neighbourhood that you care about and make a fuss of them.

2. Invite other people to talk openly about their discomforts.

3. Describe your emotions about an issue to someone you wouldn't normally say this to.

4. Commit openly to resolving an irritating issue and pursue it doggedly with the help of others.

5. Complain about something that you have bought. Take it back to the shop. Be specific and say exactly what you want instead of this.

6. Ask someone who isn't getting around to something what's stopping them from doing it.

7. Ask a colleague what you think they are hoping you won't ask them.

8. Don't talk about people, talk to them (this is challenging!).

9. Stop making trivial and insensitive remarks when you are talking to people who matter to you.

10. When someone else whines about a colleague, ask them when they are going to confront that person about their behaviour, and if not, why not.

11. Name a problem that no one else is brave enough to name.

12. Speak only of things that seem to matter; speak only from the heart.

13. Apologize to people to whom you have behaved badly.

14. Praise people who you meant to praise months ago, and apologize for not getting around to it. Commit to doing better next time.

15. Use silence when emotion runs high. This will slow down the conversation and give everyone time to say what they really think or feel.

Example 1: Growing the Edgy Catalyser Quality

Jenny was newly promoted team leader in a public sector organization dealing with disadvantaged elderly adults. She was one of three internal candidates for the job. A key reason for appointing her was that the interview panel were impressed with some of her ideas for making positive changes to the section.

She had been forced to take a step back from her day-to-day business to prepare for the interview. What was somewhat startling for her was how she was able to list all her gripes and groans about the way the section was being run and then recognize that it was now down to her to make some progress on them. She began to see that previously she and her co-workers had moaned a lot but hadn't really done anything. Indeed, in some ways it suited the team to let these things remain – it meant they always had something or someone to blame.

Jenny scheduled in an extra 'special' team meeting for a section and team working review. She let people know that there were things, which they had endlessly discussed, that needed to change, and now she had been given the authority to recommend and implement ideas.

She kicked off the meeting stating what she thought the organization required of them, and her in particular. She continued by starting to write up on a flip chart some of the things she knew were wrong with the way they worked. She then prompted her co-workers to brainstorm even more.

Using some of the facilitation and coaching techniques she'd learned in her profession, she started to get people to look at some of the root causes of these issues. When some people starting pointing to factors outside of the room (other departments, other people, processes, etc.) she didn't let it go, as she would have done previously, but pushed back and suggested that at least 70 per cent of the issues lay with them and those were the ones she, and they, were going to address.

There were periods of intense discomfort, some defensiveness, some irritation. It seemed that there was an iterative process at play – issues identified, issues blamed on others, Jenny questioning and pushing back and having tough conversations, issues owned, ideas for resolution.

Although Jenny felt exhausted, and somewhat relieved, at the end of the day, she left the building with a sense that she and they could really make a difference to the organization and more importantly to their clients.

Example 2: Refining the Edgy Catalyser Quality

Jenny continued with her improvements in the section and, though uncomfortable at times, her relationship with her co-workers moved from suspicion about her motives to one where working for her was, as one mentioned, 'tough but fair'.

Due to continuing national austerity and government budget cuts, Jenny was under continued pressure to find ways of reducing costs at the same time as improving services. The biggest budget line was personnel, so it came as no surprise when Jenny was asked to merge her section with a sister section, whose head had recently retired.

Emotions were running high, employees from both sections feared for their jobs, and the pressure was on to restructure, lose headcount and get on with performance improvements. Jenny resisted this call to immediate action. What some might have seen as dithering was actually Jenny going out and having conversations with employees, other organizational players and indeed client advocates.

Jenny continually pressed people to engage in looking at what was going right, what could be improved, and very provocatively, if they were starting from scratch, what would a new service look like.

At staff meetings she brought in clients and their advocates to act as witness to how poor the service was in some respects. She also brought in managers and staff from similar organizations who had a story to tell of their transformation process.

Many of the staff, who had served loyally in the one organization for many years, were shocked to see how poorly the clients were treated, and that the way they were providing the service wasn't the only way, and indeed certainly not the best way.

Jenny rarely went home without holding some 'negative' feelings. The staff continued to experience emotional disquiet concerning their jobs; their minds were full of feeling blamed, but also confused by all the choices that were there to perform better. Jenny contained these feelings within herself, recognizing that if they leaked out it would impact staff. Indeed, she acted as a lightning rod for their emotions. Always tough, always questioning, she could continually hold up to her staff the organization purpose of providing a safe and secure environment to disadvantaged people, and also hold up a mirror of how well they were doing. She managed to negotiate a good degree of autonomy with senior managers and was thus able to demonstrate to her staff that if their ideas were viable and cost effective, they could be implemented.

Jenny recognized that she needed to manage her staff's discomfort and not overwhelm them – their roles were stressful roles anyway. She ensured there were 'islands of stability'; certain processes, meetings, rituals that she made sacrosanct, and which would not change. Psychological boundaries were drawn around these to inspire some feelings of safety and surety. And as soon as enough people had left through natural wastage (early retirement, voluntary redundancy, etc.), she clearly stated that there would be no more redundancies.

The root and branch review of the service, coupled with synergies from the merger, left the new department battle-weary, but performing at a higher level than before, and with a sense of relief that the worst was over.

Stop and Reflect!

The not-for-profit without ambition

You have just been appointed as a non-executive chair of a small not-for-profit organization, helping young people in difficult family situations, through counselling and advice, to find their way into adult life.

There is a sense that the organization has been 'coasting' (the current CEO has been in post for 20 years). There is nothing particularly wrong with the organization, it just doesn't seem to be performing as well as it could, although there isn't any benchmarking data with similar not-for-profits.

In addition to the CEO, the number of salaried staff is five: two advisors (financial, state benefits, education guidance), two counsellors and one fundraiser.

There are 20 volunteer advisors and counsellors with varying levels of commitment, competence and motivations.

You have suggested to the board of trustees that you will review and report back to them with recommendations at the next meeting, in six weeks' time. What will be your focus, and how will you go about conducting your review?

Crisis in an expanding SME

After two years in this small but rapidly expanding logistics company, you have made a reputation for yourself, particularly for creating highly motivated and performing teams.

However, the company seems to have lost its way a bit, dependent on just two major clients, and with its infrastructure (systems, policies and practices, HR, structure, etc.) not keeping pace with the company's growth in sales and employees.

The senior partners seem to be locked in an internal battle regarding the future direction of the company – some seeking diversification, others commitment to their current clients.

Lack of communication with both middle managers and employees has resulted in a dip in motivation and engagement, with a few key staff leaving and others looking for jobs, often with the two major clients.

Although under-resourced, Sales and Business Development have been asked to submit a tender bid (to one of the existing clients) which would guarantee ongoing work for a number of years... if they are successful.

At the same time, two of the partners, who favour diversification, have asked you to suggest ways in which the company can move forward. The other partners have reluctantly agreed to allow you to do this, but have said they may not have much time to discuss things with you.

What are your initial thoughts about how you might tackle this assignment, using advanced Edgy Catalyser skills?

Where to go to find out more

Useful books to develop the skills of the Edgy Catalyser include:

Core skills

Change Your Questions, Change Your Life: 10 powerful tools for life and work by Marilee Adams.
The Fifth Discipline: The art and practice of the learning organization by Peter Senge

Making Sense of Change Management by Esther Cameron and Mike Green
Mindset: The new psychology of success by Carol Dweck

Advanced skills

The Skilled Facilitator: A comprehensive resource for consultants, facilitators, managers, trainers, and coaches by Roger Schwarz
Fierce Conversations by Susan Scott
Dialogue: The art of thinking together by William Isaacs
Leading with Questions: How leaders find the right solutions by knowing what to ask by Michael Marquardt

Ten real-life examples of the Edgy Catalyser Quality in action*

Desmond Tutu, Steve Jobs, Bill Gates, Charles Kennedy, Ngozi Okonjo-Iweala, Vladimir Putin, Lady Gaga, Jose Mourinho, Aung San Suu Kyi, Yanis Varoufakis.

*We have chosen these people as they are relatively well-known, come from around the world and have shown some mastery of this Quality.

References

Cameron, E and Green, M (2015) *Making Sense of Change Management*, Kogan Page, London
Kantor, D (2012) *Reading the Room*, John Wiley and Sons
Keats, J (1817) cited in Li, Ou (2009) *Keats and Negative Capability*, Continuum International Publishing Group

Becoming masterful!

23

Developing your mastery of the Five Qualities involves developing each Quality both horizontally and vertically. This means building fundamental skills as well as growing in leadership maturity or 'mental complexity'. The latter includes learning how to use the qualities flexibly and in various combinations. In this chapter we explore the process of learning how to master the full set of Qualities, how this mastery develops as a leader matures, and some of the possibilities that exist for combining qualities.

The Five Qualities learning process

Many new leaders start leading by using their easiest to access Quality. This tends to happen quite naturally, often without their being particularly conscious of this process or knowing anything about the Five Qualities. In our experience this initial leadership movement is likely to be based, somewhat imprecisely, on the Tenacious Implementer, the Measured Connector and the Visionary Motivator Qualities, individually or in some combination. Some may start their leadership career by leading via the Thoughtful Architect or the Edgy Catalyser. However, these latter two starting points can be fraught with problems, as often the leader is missing basic task and relationship capabilities. It usually makes more sense for leaders to get the basics of the other three Qualities embedded first.

It's useful to notice that the Five Qualities can be ordered in a way that mirrors an individual or organizational change process (see Figure 23.1). The Visionary Motivator, Measured Connector and Tenacious Implementer Qualities are sufficient for implementing single-loop change such as moving office or implementing a new, simple IT system, as this is a change in which core processes or mindsets don't need to shift. However, the full cycle of all Five Qualities that appear here is required for double-loop change, which requires a step back from the day to day (see more about single- and

Figure 23.1 How the Five Qualities combine to create individual or organizational change

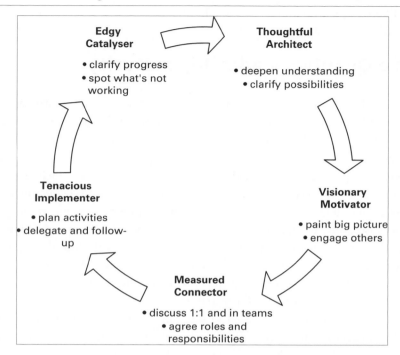

double-loop change in Part Six). This is why it's natural for new leaders to begin by learning the Visionary Motivator, Measured Connector and Tenacious Implementer.

Figure 23.1 is also useful for supporting individual learning. It can help diagnose where a leader is struggling either in their day-to-day work, or in their overall process of learning how to lead. This works at the basic skills level of pinpointing where the struggle is in the above leadership cycle and how that's impacting their work. It also works in a more integrated way by looking at how each Quality 'serves' the next one in the cycle. For example, if a leader is struggling to engage the team, he or she may need to simply develop the Visionary Motivator Quality using the relevant chapter in this section of the book to provide support. However, it may also be that the Quality that comes before Visionary Motivator in the above cycle – ie the Thoughtful Architect – is also lacking, which can weaken the strength of the Visionary Motivator Quality. An example of this is a leader who is very passionate and engaging, but doesn't take the time to sit back and reflect on the current status, and map out the way forward at a strategic level. This means that no matter how heartfelt and inspiring his presentations are, the thinking that's gone into them is somehow flimsy or flawed, and the team are likely to pick up on this at some level.

Five Qualities leadership maturity

In Part Three, we introduced the concept of leadership maturity and explained how this is a challenging and unpredictable journey for leaders, through a number of levels. Each level is associated with an ever more mature 'body-mindset' or level of 'mental complexity' and allows a new set of leadership capacities to emerge. The maturing process, which requires focused practice, feedback and deeper reflection from the leader, increasingly enables a greater ability to work with complexity and uncertainty.

We also pointed out in Part 3 how the majority of leaders are still operating at a lower maturity level than many CEOs and leadership development specialists believe 21st-century organizations require. This means that leaders need to be supported to move towards the levels of Independent-Individualist and beyond as illustrated in Table 23.1.

The summary table (Table 23.1) sets out what might be expected of a leader at each of four maturity levels when demonstrating each Quality. We have found this a very helpful framework for stimulating those leaders on the cusp of a developmental leap, eg from 'Dependent' to 'Independent', or from 'Independent' to 'Interdependent'. This helps them to imagine their own future, and raises their awareness of the gap between where their attention currently is, and where it needs to be. The pointers given in Part Three regarding coaching questions to pose to those at a cusp between levels is also useful in this regard. Remember that Part Three also points out that each new level transcends and includes the level before. This means that a leader who matures to the next level has developed a new body-mindset which expands beyond the limits of the previous one, although they still have access to previous body-mindsets.

Table 23.1 Enacting the Five Qualities at each level of leadership maturity

Level of Maturity*	Dependent-Conformer	Independent-Achiever	Independent-Individualist	Interdependent-Collaborator
Focus	Self 1-3 months	Team and/or stakeholders 3-6 months	Business or Large Programme 1-3 years	Whole System 3-5 years
Tenacious Implementer	Executes jobs according to plan	Ensures timely/quality outcomes by driving progress	Lines everyone up to deliver – up, down, across	Continually tracks and anticipates change at multiple levels – seeing patterns and connections, and 'pulling' the right levers at the right time
Measured Connector	Communicates tasks clearly and supervises team	Clarifies accountabilities and helps sort conflicts/stuckness	Coaches individuals, teams and networks to build capability and resilience	Regularly convenes cross-boundary discussions that clarify purpose /intentions/ values / priorities + surfaces/addresses hidden agendas or anxieties in a non-anxious, non-defensive way
Visionary Motivator	Devises and sells solutions	Creatively motivates others to work towards clear goals, while seeking efficiencies and improvements	Engages own and others' passions in a way that inspires	Creates a picture of the change destination that engages and attracts followers across different levels of maturity and with different loyalties

(Continued)

Table 23.1 (Continued)

Level of Maturity*	Dependent-Conformer	Independent-Achiever	Independent-Individualist	Interdependent-Collaborator
Focus	Self 1-3 months	Team and/or stakeholders 3-6 months	Business or Large Programme 1-3 years	Whole System 3-5 years
Thoughtful Architect	Uses technical expertise to identify and solve problems, focusing on a week-to-week basis	Provides 3–6-month frame/plan with clear outcomes	Co-creates structured plans that allow for emergence and devises effective influencing strategies to support progress Spends time clarifying people's roles and interfaces	Offers elegant frames and structures to support complex change efforts and maintains long-range, system-wide view
Edgy Catalyser	Critiques the work of others against received professional standards	Spots and names resistance or poor performance, telling rather than probing	Gives astute feedback and probes to encourage reflection/ illuminate perspectives/ learn	Uses skillful inquiry to disrupt predictable/stuck ways of working/thinking

* These levels are similar to Torbert's Expert, Achiever, Individualist, Strategist.

Produced with permission of Integral Change Consulting Ltd. Please do not reproduce without requesting permission: esther@integralchange.co.uk.

Stop and Reflect!

Take a moment to reflect on your own mastery of the Five Qualities so far. Answer the following questions and then draw three clear conclusions:

- Which is the Leadership Quality you tend to use the most and in what ways has this served you and others well so far – at work or outside of work?

- Which Leadership Quality do you tend to ignore or under-value? How has this been awkward or disappointing for you or others?

- Which Leadership Quality is most important for you to develop right now, because of the current demands on you and the responsibilities you have at the moment – either in work or outside of work?

- What level of leadership maturity do you believe you are currently at? Note, it may be that you're at one level, and starting to show some capability at the next level. Do you see any urgency for you to develop vertically, given your ambitions or sense of 'calling' in the world? (In assessing your own maturity, try not to be judgmental with yourself, or conversely to inflate your capability in any way. Truthfulness is a very important quality for leaders to know how to bring!)

- What conclusions can you make from the above, and what steps do you now need to take to ensure that you continue to develop your leadership as you would wish? (Parts Three and Four may offer some helpful tips here.)

Combining the Qualities

The Five Qualities framework is deliberately set out as five distinct entities so that each Quality can be focused on. This way leaders can begin to

Figure 23.2 How the Five Qualities can be combined in a one to one performance conversation

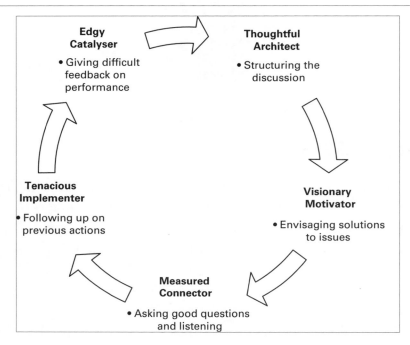

develop their relationship with each Quality so that it becomes more accessible and more refined. As leaders mature they discover that these Qualities, though distinct and individually recognizable, are interdependent and mutually reinforcing. The Qualities can then be used in all sorts of wonderful combinations in every moment of every day, and the more flexibly and skillfully they are used, the more deft and effective the combinations.

We offer some illustrations of this below by taking five particular 'leadership moments' or challenges in a leader's life and illustrating how all Five Qualities can bring value to each situation:

i) A one-to-one performance conversation (see in graphic form in Figure 23.2):

 – Thoughtful Architect: structuring the discussion.

 – Visionary Motivator: envisaging solutions to issues.

 – Measured Connector: asking good questions and listening.

 – Tenacious Implementer: following up on previous actions.

 – Edgy Catalyser: giving difficult feedback on performance.

ii) Running a weekly team meeting:

- Thoughtful Architect: framing the meeting in terms of current priorities and dilemmas.

- Visionary Motivator: making space to celebrate progress and offer appreciations for work done well.

- Measured Connector: facilitating the discussion in a way that ensures safety, and encourages participation.

- Tenacious Implementer: ensuring that decisions are made and actions agreed and documented.

- Edgy Catalyser: naming difficult issues in a way that can be heard.

iii) Restructuring the team:

- Thoughtful Architect: stepping back from the day-to-day to consider intent and options.

- Visionary Motivator: building an outline picture of the proposed new arrangements – what the team will be doing, how they will be feeling, what benefits this will have on customers; inviting the team to shape this.

- Measured Connector: sounding out individuals regarding your possible ways forward.

- Tenacious Implementer: planning a timeline and ensuring that the structure gets clarified, agreed, launched, monitored, tweaked, embedded.

- Edgy Catalyser: being clear about what problems the new structure is solving.

iv) Having a tough conversation with a stakeholder:

- Thoughtful Architect: framing the conversation clearly, eg 'I'd like to talk to you about how things have been going over the past few weeks. I have some particular issues concerning progress that I'd like your feedback on.'

- Visionary Motivator: offering a brighter picture of the future working relationship, eg 'I'd love it if we could start to meet monthly to sort this type of thing out.'

- Measured Connector: ensuring that a room is booked, turning your phone off, giving the conversation high-quality attention, letting others know if necessary that the conversation is taking place.

- Tenacious Implementer: referring to agreed plans and following up with a note that ties down next steps.

- Edgy Catalyser: pointing out the gap between your expectations and what appears to have happened.

v) Launching a new project:

- Thoughtful Architect: spending time understanding the project requirements and stakeholder needs; clarifying governance arrangements; mapping out project phases in accessible language; clarifying roles and responsibilities.

- Visionary Motivator: engaging the team in the top five project ambitions and what will be required of them during each phase.

- Measured Connector: establishing key meeting processes and how these will support project progress: 1:1; team; stakeholders; suppliers, etc.

- Tenacious Implementer: selecting and setting up a tool to track and share progress.

- Edgy Catalyser: setting clear expectations regarding people's time and commitment levels and being clear about any expectations which you sense others might find difficult based on past history.

Stop and Reflect!

i) Select three challenging leadership 'moments' that you have faced over the past month and reflect on these, using the above list as inspiration. Make some notes on how you brought each of the Five Qualities to that situation or context, using the cycles depicted above in Figures 23.1 and 23.2 to help you.

What went well, what didn't go so well, what might you have done differently and what needs attention now, given how things have played out since then?

Do you notice any helpful or unhelpful patterns in the way you tend to lead?

ii) Observe the leadership of someone you know well over the next few weeks – this could be your line manager, peer, a course tutor or someone outside work like a sports coach or a community, club or faith leader. What challenges do you notice them having to deal with and how do they handle them in terms of the Five Qualities? What maturity level do you believe they are leading from?

If you were asked to offer them some leadership feedback and pointers for the future, what would you say to them? What barriers might there be, and what support or suggestions would you offer?

Conclusions from Part Five

This section of the book has presented the Five Qualities framework in all its breadth, depth and facets. You should by now be feeling well-acquainted with the territory covered by this framework, how it was put together and validated, how you measure up against it, and what you need to do next to continue to develop yourself as a leader.

You should also be starting to develop a new language for observing, feeding back on and discussing leadership in all its component parts. This should help develop your ability to be aware of how you and others are leading, and to bring more clarity to your feedback, diagnostics and requests.

Pause for Learning Points

The Five Qualities Leadership Framework is derived from a synthesis of much of the leadership literature and has been validated through research and practice on the ground.

Each of the Five Qualities can be considered to be an archetype that represents a wide but coherent set of associated skills. Together, and with little overlap, they cover the territory that a leader at any level is required to master to be effective.

Each Quality has a particular focus:

- Tenacious Implementer on Delivery;
- Measured Connector on Connectivity;

- Visionary Motivator on Buy-in;

- Thoughtful Architect on Design; and

- Edgy Catalyser on Discomfort.

Each Quality can be developed by honing the fundamental skills associated with the Quality, as well as by thinking more imaginatively about how to play your role as leader and 'filling out' your own unique leadership 'recipe'.

The Tenacious Implementer, Measured Connector and Visionary Motivator qualities are good qualities to start with; the Thoughtful Architect and Edgy Catalyser provide increasing depth and edge as a leader progresses in all five.

The Five Qualities framework allows for different levels of leadership maturity (see Part Three for more on this). As a leader becomes more able to think longer term and hold more complexity, the use of each Quality deepens and expands, with more advanced skills and new body-mindsets coming into play.

Once individual Qualities are mastered, leaders become more flexible and adaptable in using them in combination in deft and highly effective ways.

Stop and Reflect!

Select three leadership figures you know well either personally or by repute, in business or public life. For each one, answer the series of questions below and draw conclusions.

What is the leader trying to achieve? What positive impact could this have on people/their organization/the world if done well?

How would you describe their overall style and impact in your own words?

Which one or two of the Five Qualities is most dominant in their leadership and how well is this working?

Which one or two Qualities do you believe they need to show more of, and how would this help them? What skills do they need to learn – either core or advanced?

What level of leadership maturity do you think they have attained, and what's your evidence for this? Would it be helpful if they matured a little more, and if so, how, and what might this enable?

What leadership development options and support do you think might help them to develop, or sustain the good work?

PART SIX
Leadership and Organizations

Overview

It's tempting to see leadership in a highly individualistic, and maybe slightly romanticized way (Meindl, 1987). In an organizational context, this can mean either believing that the leadership qualities of top leaders are completely determining of the company's success, or that success is simply down to each individual leader doing it in his or her own way as best they can.

Although there's truth in both these perspectives, when you enter an organization you may be aware that some invisible force is influencing how leaders think and act. In other words, each organization has its own 'culture of leadership' where the prevailing organizational culture impacts the way each leader operates. Leadership, viewed at an organizational level, is therefore not merely the style in which the CEO exercises his or her will, or the accumulation of a set of individuals bringing their different skills, but an interconnecting thread of the 'culture' that runs through an entire organization.

This part of the book explores this organizational dimension of leadership, which involves looking at the connections between leadership, culture and organizational effectiveness. Here we ask: what makes the culture of leadership the way it is; how can it be measured or compared in terms of effectiveness or outcomes; and what can be done to change or improve this in a sustainable way?

We also explore recent research into generational differences in leadership understandings and approaches, and the impact this may have on organizational leadership. Particular reference is made to Millennials (also known as Generation Y) who are currently bringing new, potentially transforming mindsets and sensitivities into the workplace. We discuss the latest research on this, including our own involvement in a recent series of surveys and interviews, and ask how these new leaders might need to be nurtured and challenged to enable them to bring their best.

The aims of the following chapters are therefore to:

- clarify the key components of leadership culture;
- discover what factors influence the formation of leadership culture;
- map out the relationship between leadership culture and organizational effectiveness;
- explain how the culture of leadership in an organization can be changed;
- explore recent research into the potential impact of Millennial leadership and the implications of this for organizations.

Reference

Meindl, J R and Ehrlich, S B (1987) The romance of leadership and the evaluation of organizational performance, *Academy of Management Journal*, 30, pp. 91–109

Defining leadership culture

24

This chapter sets out to define what leadership culture is, how it forms and what could support this culture to grow and develop. We ask whether particular leadership cultures are more effective than others, and attempt to offer readers a way of assessing the current level of leadership culture in their organization.

A failure of leadership culture?

Leadership culture is the invisible set of rules and beliefs that informs leadership behaviour in any organization and is often at the root of why so many organizations struggle with the complexities of today's world and end up ineffective or failing.

Typical signs of a failure of leadership culture are departments and projects becoming buried in bureaucracy and failing to deliver; the management team failing to act as a team and being resistant to change; decisions not getting made or constantly being overturned; too many rigid hierarchies and complicated processes; people finding their work stressful and even mind-numbing. So what is it that's going wrong here? And why are some forms of change, progress and newness so difficult for organizations to embrace?

These wonderings are central to many of our working lives, depending on where we find ourselves. Board members, CEOs, line leaders and HR professionals scratch their heads in relation to these questions, as does anyone with a stake in an organization as customer, employee, business partner, supplier or investor.

So if this sense of overload and stuckness is to do with a failure of leadership culture, what can be done about it at an organizational level, given that the work ahead isn't going to get any easier for any of us? How can leaders, or others, work together to create the type of organizations that can be valuable, adaptable and purposeful in today's world?

Research into the capacity for leadership to generate organizational effectiveness over the years has been inconclusive, perhaps due to the difficulty of untangling the impact of 'leadership' as a phenomenon from the impact of all the other contextual forces at play such as economic, social, political, etc. However, an interesting and thorough review of historic studies by Kaiser, Hogan and Craig (2008) points to a link between 'who's in charge' and the firm's performance.

Some of the studies reviewed indicate that the CEO's leadership accounts for about 20 per cent of the variance in financial performance. Although this figure is impressive at one level, it's clear that the CEO is not acting alone. It's also clear that financial performance is just one factor, and others such as productivity, quality, customer, human resources and level of innovation all have to be in balance for a sustained performance overall (Kaplan and Norton, 1996). If, at the end of the year, the financial performance of a company is good but their reputation is rock-bottom, the leadership cannot be considered to be effective. For an example of the latter, see two extracts from articles concerning Volkswagen's recent performance in the box below.

This example refers to the well-publicized discovery by the US Environmental Protection Agency that VW cars were appearing to automatically 'cheat' those attempting to measure the car's emissions by temporarily altering the way the engine was running. The incident, and its implications, show that even in a company that has all the hallmarks of success and efficiency, and prides itself on technological and engineering excellence, the leadership culture was clearly failing at some level. At least some leaders appeared to believe that cheating the environmental emissions testing was justified and in line with the company's intent. Or, perhaps, individual agendas were allowed to flourish. Whatever the reasons, the company's reputation in Europe took a tremendous knock and the discovery led to massive compensation payments exceeding $15 billion in the United States alone.

Corporate governance is a key part of the culture of leadership in an organization (Financial Reporting Council, 2016). This is the set of rules, regulations, structures and practices in place for directing and controlling the affairs of a corporation in service of its stakeholders, usually overseen by the board and carried out by the executive officers. The subject of corporate governance has attracted much attention following high-profile cases of accounting fraud in the early 2000s and gross financial mismanagement leading up to the 2008 crisis. It appears that even if structures and practices

The problem

In September, the Environmental Protection Agency (EPA) found that many VW cars being sold in America had a 'defeat device' – or software – in diesel engines that could detect when they were being tested, changing the performance accordingly to improve results. The German car giant has since admitted cheating emissions tests in the US (Hotten, 2015).

The impact

Volkswagen's share of the European car market fell to its lowest level since the financial crisis in the first half of this year, highlighting how the company has suffered a consumer backlash after the diesel emissions scandal.

The figures indicate that around 875,000 VW-branded cars were sold in the EU in the first half of 2016, which represents an increase of only 0.8 per cent compared with the year before, according to motor industry figures. This contrasts with a 9.4 per cent rise in sales of combined EU car manufacturers during the same period.

Abridged from *Financial Times* (2016)

are in place, they are not always used correctly or with integrity. Of course, care also needs to be taken to ensure that the corporation's executives have sufficient scope for innovation and autonomy, so as not to suppress new, valuable opportunities that serve the organizational outcomes.

Three levels of leadership

Our own experience indicates that leadership culture manifests in an organization through a community of leaders creating a 'context for performance', which can be more or less conducive to high individual and team performance (Schneider, 1998). This is done at three levels:

i) **Individual** – day-to-day exchanges between leaders and individual followers that encourage engagement and contribution to outcomes. See Chapter 5 on transformational and transactional leadership for some of the elements of this.

ii) **Team** – team leaders create a 'climate' that enables success, through focus on:

- goal clarity and support for problem solving (task);
- facilitated discussion and interconnection (relationship);
- see Part Two, Chapters 2 and 3 for a reminder of this territory.

iii) **Organizational** – through organization leaders establishing goals, strategies and policies and enacting these through a set of conscious and unconscious values, beliefs and behaviours. Board level and senior executive decisions regarding investment and other financial issues are also seen to be highly influential on company performance. CEOs, however, may have their own, narrow 'financial signature' which influences their habits regarding cost control and risky investments independent of the context or organization they are in. This can result in a top-down, blinkered leadership culture, in which leadership decisions are made because the boss says so rather than because it's the best decision (Prince, 2005).

There are many factors at play which impact the effectiveness of leadership culture. An example that many readers in Western-style organizations will be familiar with is that leaders get appointed or promoted for their ability to 'manage impressions' rather than for their ability to deliver outcomes through teams. This means promoting people because they come across as confident, engaging in a one-to-one situation, and effective at promoting themselves and their achievements. Sometimes this means that individuals claim a bit more than their fair share of the accolades for any success. This practice can lead to a culture where leadership competence is not respected (Kaiser, Hogan and Craig, 2008) and over time can have devastating effects on outcomes, as well as morale, safety and longer-term organizational health. An example of this is when a head of department is recruited because he is impressive in front of an audience and known for his directness, even though he doesn't have the right technical experience for the job.

This plays out in the political arena in the Unites States and the UK, where leadership elections are increasingly dominated by perceptions of a kind of super-human level of ability to 'fix things' rather than data about results and impact. This is perhaps because the latter is complex, involves sustained attention, and is inconclusive. This personality-oriented way of choosing leaders is often highly counter-productive, and even dangerous, for both nations and organizations. Sometimes it's the 'charismatically challenged' leaders who do not fit the 'super-human' mould, for example Eisenhower in the United States, who are seen to have been the most competent.

Defining the leadership culture in an organization

There are many ways to segment and describe what an organization is, and what part culture plays. Frederic Laloux's (2014) adaption of Wilber's (2001) 'integral' framework does a good job of mapping this out in a simple yet comprehensive way. He identifies four interdependent facets or dimensions of reality that need to be examined to see the reality of a whole organization. Illustrated in Figure 24.1, these cover the visible, the invisible, the personal and the systemic: 1) people's mindsets and beliefs; 2) people's behaviour; 3) organizational culture; 4) organizational systems (structures, processes, practices).

Laloux's framework reminds us how intertwined these four facets are, and how, if one of these changes, it has ripple effects on all the others. For instance, introducing a new reward system which privileges team rewards over individual rewards will have a potentially deep impact on people's beliefs and behaviours, and on the collective culture. How this works out depends on how it is done, and what beliefs and mindsets currently exist.

In our experience, the 'leadership culture' in an organization is a thread that runs through all four of the above quadrants, connecting mindsets, behaviours, systems and shared beliefs/values. This thread is heavily influenced at its inception by the founders and how they impose their own

Figure 24.1   The reality of organizations (Laloux, 2014)

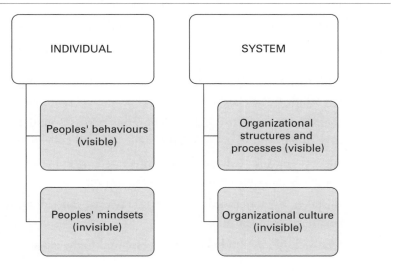

assumptions on a new group (Schein, 2004). As time goes on, other influences, including that of local leaders, start to play in.

Another way of looking at this is suggested by McGuire and Rhodes. They refer to a set of 'leadership logics' – a cluster of beliefs and interpretations that underlies the choices made by and through the leadership culture. This exists as a collective rationale through which leaders in the organization understand its situation and surroundings and its principles of operating. They define three types of logic and describe the prevailing leadership cultures. Note that these align with the leadership maturity levels outlined in Part Three. As you read the descriptions below (McGuire and Rhodes, 2009), you can probably fairly easily decide which type an organization you know well is closest to.

i) Dependent-Conformer:

- authority and control are held at the top;
- standards and rules take precedence over applying new learning;
- success depends on obedience to authority and loyalty;
- mistakes are treated as weaknesses and feedback tends to be negative and from above, and not sought or valued.

ii) Independent-Achiever:

- authority and control is distributed through the ranks;
- focus is on success, and adapting faster than competitors;
- success means mastery of one's own domain on behalf of the organization;
- mistakes may be seen as opportunities to learn;
- feedback is valued when it supports an individual's success.

iii) Interdependent-Collaborator:

- authority and control are shared, based on strategic competence for the whole organization;
- the mindset tends towards collaborating across boundaries so that new orders and structures can emerge through collective work;
- success means collaborative, integrated system mastery that produces outcomes now and into the future;
- mistakes are embraced as opportunities for individual, team and organizational learning;
- feedback of any kind is valued as essential for success.

It's possible to deduce from the above descriptions that the 'Interdependent-Collaborator' leadership culture, although perhaps hardest to envisage, is broadly aligned with some of the more multi-layered complexities of today's context. It's also possible to see how the journey from i) through ii) to iii) above might represent a cultural development journey. According to McGuire and Rhodes, most senior leaders say they need to create this new type of collaborative, learning-oriented culture. Few claim to have this right now.

Building on Schein's writings that founders have a huge influence on culture, Torbert (2004) says that organizational culture is more fragile than personal development. He asserts that individuals tend to maintain their developmental gains as a leader, rather than slip back, unless there is a big crisis in their lives. However, if an organization is sold, merges with another organization, or experiences a senior management 'clear-out' by the board, the culture may 'regress overnight'. Even if there are intentions to create a more progressive culture, this will take time and effort. Torbert uses the term 'Learning Organization' to describe a more evolved organizational system where feedback is continually sought at three levels of depth (see Figure 24.2): the results of behaviours, the effectiveness of goals and strategies, and the quality of ongoing awareness being brought to the first two levels.

Although the picture may not be consistent across the whole, an organization's structure, practices, values and habits tend to cluster around a 'centre

Figure 24.2   Three levels of organizational feedback required in learning organizations (Torbert, 2004)

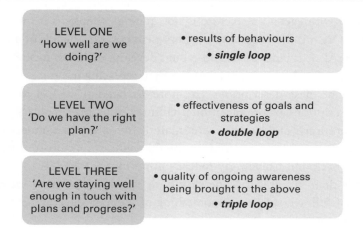

of gravity', even if there are differences within departments or across geographies. However, in larger organizations, certain units may have different centres of gravity depending on their history, ways of working and levels of interconnectedness (Laloux, 2014). These structures, practices, values and habits are put in place, consciously or unconsciously, by leaders in a way that makes good sense to them at the time and aligns with their own understandings of how things need to work to enable success.

How leadership culture evolves

Another, more demanding, way of viewing organizational systems is through the complex, layered work of Beck and Cowan (2006). They developed the work of Professor Clare W. Graves to describe a set of core values and intelligences that flow beneath what we believe and do as individuals, teams and organizations. This rich conceptual map, known as spiral dynamics, offers deep insights into why we believe what we believe and do what we do, how change arises and spreads, and how leadership plays its role in this. Using what they call 'value memes', Beck and Cowan mapped out the characteristics of organizations as they evolve culturally, together with the leadership assumptions associated with each. This body of work opens up insights into how to understand and work with complex system problems.

Seven evolving value memes, or cultural clusters, have been identified. These are relevant to a wide range of individuals, groups and organizations throughout history and beyond into the future. These value memes are described using colour codings and divided into two developmental tiers. To give a broad understanding, we list these in Table 24.1, in the order in which they are developed, together with a brief summary of the basic motivations associated with each. The picture is not quite as simple as it might look, however. Organizations are likely to represent complex blends of a number of memes. Also, as individuals and groups develop, each new meme includes and transcends the meme before, rather than replacing it.

Note that these descriptions are more 'archetypal' in feel than traditional descriptions of organizational cultures, thus they tend to open up bigger questions, and perhaps eventually offer a greater understanding of deeper themes at play. In terms of the leadership culture arising, or required, Beck and Cowan say that it's important for leaders to take care to match their culture of leadership with the developmental stage – or stages – of followers, bringing something of the next developmental stage when the time is right.

It's also important to note that the evolution from Tier 1 into the Tier 2 memes represents a considerable shift towards greater conceptual space, less compulsion, an ability to learn a great deal from many sources and a trend towards getting more done with less energy or resources. Table 24.2 shows the leadership assumptions core to each value meme, and examples of leadership tools in use.

Table 24.1 Brief outline of organizational cultural clusters, or 'memes', from the least to the most developed (Beck and Cowan, 2006)

Meme	Basic Theme
TIER 1:	
Purple	Keep the spirits happy and the tribe's nest warm and safe
Red	Be what you are and do what you want, regardless
Blue	Life has meaning, direction and purpose with predetermined outcomes
Orange	Act in your own self-interest by playing the game to win
Green	Seek peace within the inner self and explore, with others, the caring dimensions of community
TIER 2:	
Yellow	Live fully and responsibly as 'what you are' and learn to 'become'
Turquoise	Experience the wholeness of existence through mind and spirit

Table 24.2 Leadership assumptions of each value meme, and associated tools in use

TIER	Value meme	Leadership assumptions	Tools in use	Example organization
TWO	Turquoise	Work must make a meaningful contribution to the overall health of all life	Ecological thinking	Spiritual school
		The universe is a system of elegantly balanced, interconnected forces	Holistic structures	
	Yellow	Organizations are constantly evolving and changing – never static	Leader as facilitator	Some online networks, eg Wikipedia
		Meaningful work and self-development motivate people, rather than rewards or punishments.	Self-managed teams Integrated structures	Self-organized, interconnected care teams
ONE	Green	The organization is responsible for the wellbeing of all that depend on it	Interpersonal skills development	Cooperatives
		Collaboration and sharing resources lead to better results than competing	Values-led Large-scale, facilitated workshops	Culture-led organizations
	Orange	People are motivated by the chance to achieve and to be seen to gain rewards	Management by objectives	Multinational companies
		Competition improves performance and fosters growth	Strategic planning Situational leadership	

Blue	People need to be told what to do, and will learn the right behaviours through punishment for mistakes	Rewards and punishments	Army
	Employees owe the organization their loyalty in return for providing for them and their wellbeing	Moral education	
Red	People have urges that must be kept in check by a strong force	Correction unit	Tough love
	Those in power deserve their status just because they are who they are		Positive discipline Hands-on training
Purple	People willingly respect and follow leaders	Ritual	Street gang
	Employees owe their whole mind, body and spirit to the organization that looks after them	Harmony Superstitions	

(Adapted from Beck and Cowan, 2006)

Pause for Learning Points

Leadership culture is a pervasive and affective thread of organizational life. It impacts everything, although its connection with organizational effectiveness is complex and hard to pin down in a scientific way. Initiated by the founders, it's impacted and sustained through daily leadership actions at an individual, team and organizational level.

Organizational culture, and therefore leadership culture, is said to be fragile. Sudden organizational changes such as mergers and takeovers can have almost immediate negative effects, although this can be worked on over time, with effort.

Organizational culture and associated 'leadership logics' evolve over time in a way that can be mapped out. This evolution depends on the maturity or capacity for 'mental complexity' (see Part Three) of influential leaders.

Stop and Reflect!

Consider the example below of an organization that was investigated by the UK government. Find out a bit more about this case by searching online. Using the frameworks provided in this chapter to guide you, try to list the underpinning beliefs of leadership at this business and gauge the 'centre of gravity' of their level of evolution as a culture. Based on this, what moves would you advise the board and senior leaders to make to improve the situation?

Evidence of 'appalling' work practice at Sports Direct

- Every time an employee took too long in the toilet, took a break for a drink of water or took time off when a child was unwell they were awarded a 'strike'. After six strikes they were out of the organization.

- Shop employees were asked to clock out early despite having been asked to work overtime. This was to keep wages within budget.

- Warehouse staff were paid below the national minimum wage.

- Of 110 emergency service callouts to the Sports Direct's warehouse in Shirebrook, 50 of these were rated as 'life threatening', with one woman giving birth in the lavatory.

- Temporary staff were promised permanent contracts in exchange for sexual favours.

I can't be responsible for every single thing that goes on in Sports Direct. I can't be. I can't be! Mike Ashley, founder and deputy chairman of Sports Direct (Armstrong, 2016).

References

Armstrong, A (2016) Sports Direct: Mike Ashley turned blind eye to 'appalling conditions for staff', MPs say, *Telegraph* [online] http://www.telegraph.co.uk/business/2016/07/21/mike-ashley-turned-a-blind-eye-to-appalling-conditions-at-sports/ [accessed 12 August 2016]

Beck, D and Cowan, C (2006) *Spiral Dynamics*, Blackwell

Financial Reporting Council (2016) Corporate culture and the role of boards, *FRC* [online] https://www.frc.org.uk/Our-Work/Corporate-Governance-Reporting/Corporate-governance/Corporate-Culture-and-the-Role-of-Boards.aspx [accessed 12 August 2016]

Financial Times (2016) VW's share of EU car market falls to 10 year low, *fastFT* [online] http://www.ft.com/fastft/2016/06/16/vws-share-of-eu-car-market-falls-to-10-year-low/ [accessed 12 August 2016]

Hotten, R (2015) Volkswagen: the scandal explained, *BBC News* [online] http://www.bbc.co.uk/news/business-34324772 [accessed 12 August 2016]

Kaiser, R B, Hogan R and Craig, S B (2008) Leadership and the fate of organizations, *American Psychologist*, Feb–March

Kaplan, R and Norton, D (1996) *The Balanced Scorecard*, Harvard Business School Press, Boston, MA

Laloux, F (2014) *Reinventing Organisations*, Nelson Parker

McGuire, J and Rhodes, G (2009) *Transforming your Leadership Culture*, Jossey-Bass, San Francisco

Prince, E T (2005) *The Three Financial Styles of Very Successful Leaders*, McGraw-Hill, New York

Schein, E H (2004) *Organizational Culture and Leadership*, 3rd edn, Jossey-Bass, San Francisco

Schneider, B (1998) Executive selection in context, paper presented at the 13th Annual Conference of the Society for Industrial and Organizational Psychology, Dallas, TX

Torbert, B and Associates (2004) *Action Inquiry*, Berrett Koehler, San Francisco

Wilber, K (2001) *A Brief History of Everything*, 2nd edn, Gateway

Changing leadership culture

25

Beliefs about culture change

In our experience, various myths exist about how to develop the leadership culture of an organization towards greater effectiveness. Some say that only strong, 'larger than life' leadership from the top will do this; others believe that investment in training and education for middle leaders and incoming talent is the key; still others advocate structured, culture change programmes. A few believe, as we do, that more complex, multi-layered approaches work best, and that these are likely to include elements of all of the above.

Heroic myths about a CEO's ability to impact leadership culture through 'strong leadership' are unhealthy, and can create a leadership culture of dependence (see Red/Blue in the previous Chapter). Our experience indicates that CEOs who succeed in changing culture need themselves to be operating at the level of leadership maturity required and have an aligned mindset. High-quality support from board members and/or skilled 'change leadership' professionals can help.

Training and education programmes for leaders can have a positive impact on leadership skills levels (see Part Three, Chapter 12), but if a sustained development in leadership culture is required, there needs to be much more in place than just a well-designed programme of learning. These supports need to include:

- explicit board, CEO and senior leadership support for the programme;
- an agreed, measurable leadership improvement agenda;
- coaching and team development support for senior leaders;

- good links with existing HR systems of performance review and reward;
- confidential feedback loops to ensure that issues raised along the way are tackled.

See Figure 25.1 for an example of an effective middle leader development programme that was designed and run for over 50 middle leaders in organization ABC. Here you can see all the various elements of support required to enable a sustained development of the culture of leadership.

In our experience, one of the key difficulties with leadership training programmes is that senior leaders often lack the capacity and patience to coach newly trained team members through a period of leadership experimentation. Understandably, they become nervous about the potential loss of control, and impatient for results (McGuire and Rhodes, 2009). Additionally, leadership programmes often encourage behaviour that participants know to be counter-cultural, which requires new incentives and rewards to be sustainably embedded at an organizational level.

HR-managed 'culture change programmes' are very tricky to design and pull off, particularly if a move from Orange to Green or Yellow (see Chapter 24) is desired. This demands that any programme has to be conceived and led using the 'destination' mindset, which means that a series

Figure 25.1   Critical leadership programme supports

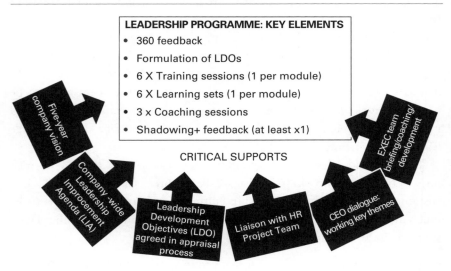

Reproduced by permission of Integral Change Consulting Ltd.
[For more about this work see www.integralchange.co.uk/casestudy/leadership-programme-sa-manufacturing/]

of consultant-run, one-day culture workshops is unlikely to work. Guiding and facilitating the culture of an organization is a complex rather than a simple problem (Snowden and Boone, 2007), and requires a highly adaptive 'body-mindset', involving head, heart and belly sensibilities, rather than an expert approach which attempts to follow a ready-made recipe (Chapters 13 and 14).

Strategic direction has a big influence on leadership culture, and any cultural work needs to be aligned with strategy. In Chapter 7 on Change Leadership, we introduced Schein's suggestion that it's only when strategy changes that the organization feels the need to shift its culture. He also says that leaders play a key role in forming the leadership culture via i) primary embedding mechanisms such as what they pay attention to, how they react to critical incidents, how they allocate resources and who they promote, reward and exclude, and ii) secondary articulation and reinforcement mechanisms such as organizational design, structure and processes, key rituals and symbols, stories and formal communications (Schein, 2004). Higgs (2006) indicates that up to 50 per cent of an organization's business performance can be attributed to leadership culture.

The leadership culture shift that many of today's CEOs and senior leaders are seeking is from Orange, the dominant culture in today's organizations, through to Green and then the more pioneering Yellow (see box; Beck and Cowan 2006). Laloux (2014) named the aspired-to, target culture 'Evolutionary – Teal' and has studied organizations at this level. He says that although the context and purpose of the organization drives the culture, there are a number of cultural traits linked to this developmental stage independent of sector or size. These can be summarized in the following adapted list:

Self-management:

– respect for the balance between freedom and accountability;
– open information systems and collective decision making;
– high levels of responsibility taking and holding each other accountable.

Wholeness:

– equal worth, yet distinctive contributions;
– use of words like care, love, service, purpose, soul…;
– an intent to be inclusive, interconnected, integral;
– learning from failure, feedback – and focus on strengths and opportunities;
– in relationship: inquiry, curiosity, integrity, reflection.

Purpose:

- listening to the collective, evolving purpose;
- sensing into one's own calling (not ego-centred);
- responsive to what's needed rather than 'controlling' when it comes to plans and strategies;
- focus on purpose and profits will follow.

Laloux gives a fascinating example of an organization that has made the move from 'Achievement – Orange' to 'Evolutionary – Teal'. This is Buurtzorg, a neighbourhood nursing organization founded in 2006 by Jos de Bok, which has been having considerable impact on this sector in the Netherlands and in the United States.

> The successful and growing Dutch neighbourhood nursing organization Buurtzorg is described by Laloux (2014) as an example of the move from 'Achievement – Orange' to 'Evolutionary – Teal'.
>
> It consists of many self-managed teams of 10–12 people, providing locally attuned nursing care, who have no 'boss'. These teams each use a very precise and efficient method for joint problem solving and decision making, and can ask for a regional coach or trained facilitator if they get stuck.
>
> There is no middle management and there are very few staff functions. Instead of regional managers they have 'regional coaches' who are not responsible for team results and have no decision-making power over them. Staff functions are kept to a minimum and 7,000 nurses are supported by only 30 people dedicated to serving the front line.
>
> There are no monthly, top-level 'executive' meetings, and the CEO meets with regional coaches only four times a year to deal with emergent issues, rather than launching initiatives without having the full picture. Coordination across teams is done elegantly and minimally when needed and information technology tools play a key role in helping to avoid unnecessary structures.

It's useful for those leaders interested in shifting the leadership culture of an organization to understand what they can do to support this development. Focusing on one's own leadership development and using the advice and frameworks offered in Part Three is a good start, particularly to grow your own leadership maturity and develop your body-mindset. Learning about the invisible dynamics of organizations as they evolve is also extremely

Journey from Orange to Yellow/Teal leadership practices

From: dominant practices (Orange):

Purpose: Self-preservation against the opposition.

Strategy: Strategy is set by the board and executive team.

Planning, budgeting and controlling: Monthly, six-monthly and yearly budget cycles dominate progress. Plans are there to be controlled against.

Change management: Projects and programmes are constructed to get the organization from A to B. Risk of failure is minimized.

Marketing and product development: The offer is defined through surveys, segmentation and/or client needs.

To: aspirational practices (Yellow/Teal):

Purpose: Organization has a clear sense of its own evolving purpose.

Strategy: Strategy is continuously emerging through collective and self-managed processes of sharing intelligence and making only necessary decisions.

Planning, budgeting and controlling: Budgets are radically simplified with longer planning cycles and continuous touching into progress in sensitive and responsive way.

Change management: Change is seen as continuous. Adaptability is seen as key.

Marketing and product development: The offer is defined by commitment to purpose and a sense of rightness and elegance

Adapted from Laloux (2014)

helpful when supporting culture change, although this takes dedicated work (see systemic leadership, Chapter 10).

Understanding the signs that indicate a culture is 'on the move' is also beneficial, as through spotting glimmers of progress, leaders can help to support and encourage these green shoots as they begin to show themselves. Here are a few helpful indicators, using the McGuire and Rhodes framework mentioned in Chapter 24 as a basis:

a) **Indicators of a move out of the Dependent-Conformer stage:**

   – a shift towards giving people some controlled autonomy or limited decision-making authority;

   – people start to critique authority and wonder about the wisdom of those in charge, and begin to voice this;

   – a belief that 'work is work' rather than play, and people demonstrate their moral commitment to produce disciplined output.

b) **Indicators of a move out of the Independent-Achiever stage:**

   – a new understanding that teams and collaboration can be useful as well as self-assertion, and signs of new networks and exchanges being set up;

   – people are less intimidated by complicated situations and there's an emerging competence in handling diversity and complexity;

   – improved empathy and interpersonal skills, and an increased capacity to understand and communicate with people who hold different agendas.

In their latest book, *An Everyone Culture*, Kegan and Lahey explain how organizations can unleash human potential by becoming what they call 'Deliberately Developmental Organizations' (or DDOs) and deliberately supporting adult development throughout. They offer three dimensions of this approach, all significant departures from familiar business principles, which they call Edge, Groove and Home. Edge is about putting adult development and human growth at the centre of the business. Groove is a set of non-traditional tools and developmental practices through which people work, build trust and grow. Home means establishing workplace communities where people belong, are valued and are continuously involved, engaged and held to account.

Central to the creation and sustainability of a DDO is the organization's leadership, say Kegan and Lahey. Leaders need to collectively commit to establishing workplaces where it's possible for people to grow. This also means making themselves vulnerable and open to continuous challenge and feedback, which takes courage and is extremely hard work. However, if you don't work in a DDO and yet sense that you buy into the principles behind it and want to work on growing your own leadership every day, these simple practices (abridged from Kegan and Lahey) might help:

● Find yourself a developmental buddy, and meet every few weeks to reflect on your leadership together.

- Ask people who you trust what they think your developmental challenges are, and commit to working on these.

- Actively seek regular feedback from trusted observers, eg after a meeting, presentation or other interaction.

- Involve your manager in your growth aspirations and ask him/her to help.

- Watch others who you believe role-model the above and talk to them about their approach

A good way of assessing the current leadership culture in an organization is to use a leadership diagnostic that helps pinpoint the dominant qualities and maturity levels of the leadership population. This can be done by asking individuals to self-rate and then discussing the resulting overall patterns as a group, perhaps with the interpretative help of an expert advisor. Table 23.1 in Chapter 23 offers a good starting point for this. It allows leaders to calibrate themselves roughly against our Five Qualities Framework and a set of maturity levels.

Table 25.1 shows an illustrative example of an improvement agenda for a company wishing to develop its leadership culture in line with strategic and cultural challenges being faced. Based around the Five Leadership Qualities, and a wish to consolidate leadership practice as well as develop maturity, this agenda is intended to be organization-wide, and can be self-rated by the leadership population at three- to six-monthly intervals to gauge progress, surface issues and plan next steps.

Table 25.1 Example of a leadership improvement agenda that supports the development of leadership culture over time (0–9 months)

FROM	TO*	Starting point +3m +6m +9m average score out of 10**
Resorting to fire-fighting and micromanagement	Owning problems, making strategic plans, managing solutions (TI)	2.5
Patchy people management and ineffective team meetings	Rigorous progress reviews; meetings that engage people and surface struggles; clearer decision making; personal accountability for next steps (TI/MC)	3

Table 25.1   (*Continued*)

FROM	TO*	Starting point	+3m	+6m	+9m
		average score out of 10**			
Unclear longer-term vision; lack of passion for improvement	Clear, agreed 'One Team' vision and strategy; productive focus and discussionre. longer-term initiatives and progress (VM/MC)	2.7			
Limited understanding of interdependencies across departments; silo mentality creating stuckness	Increased explicit linking of objectives across departments; novel teams and networks sharing information and addressing issues together (TA/MC)	3.1			
Tendency to avoid difficult issues or difficult conversations; feedback offered objectively against standards often by e-mail	Courage to ask for and offer feedback; increased transparency re. progress and performance; greater attention to learning and improvement (EC)	4			

*See definition of Five Leadership Qualities framework in Part 5, eg TI = Tenacious Implementer
**Scores are collected across the leadership population

Pause for Learning Points

Changing the leadership culture in a complex organization is likely to take careful work. The CEO's behaviour, the quality of education and the design of any culture change interventions all need to be in line with the aspired-to culture.

The shift from what's known as Tier 1 to Tier 2 leadership is much sought after by CEOs. Laloux recommends attention to self-management, wholeness and purpose. It's also helpful as organizational leaders develop their own maturity levels and become aware and supportive of the signs of a culture 'on the move'.

Creating a learning organization or Deliberately Developmental Organization (DDO), as proposed by Kegan, is a way of unleashing human potential. Kegan proposes a series of interconnected, non-traditional practices for companies to introduce, but suggests that individuals can start to build their own, emergent DDO even if the company isn't doing so!

Stop and Reflect!

Consider the case of VW, outlined in Chapter 24, and this abridged report from the *Financial Times* who attended the shareholder meeting in June 2016. Imagine you've been invited to interview Mr Pötsch on behalf of the employee stakeholder group. What questions would you ask him to uncover the truth about the leadership culture at VW and what needs to change? Be creative, curious and think broadly!

The shareholder meeting – what happened?

Mr Pötsch acknowledged that management did a poor job when independent tests in 2014 revealed that emissions by VW diesel cars on the road were far higher than those recorded in laboratory conditions. He said the issue was not given due attention because it was considered a technical problem.

VW's chief executive, Matthias Müller, however, was very clear that the company was doing its best to come to terms with the discovery and ensuing scandal. It wasn't only the resulting reputation damage that caused problems for VW, it was the costs related to fixing the cars with the wrongly adapted software. This has meant a fall in share price of around 20 per cent.

Mr Müller revealed a 10-year long-term plan of radical change, designed to leave VW much more profitable through cutting costs, becoming a leader in a new area: battery technology and electric cars.

Shareholders at the meeting focused, with some anger, on the implications for corporate governance, citing that the Institutional Shareholder Services have advised that VW's corporate governance has been awarded the lowest score of any company listed on Germany's DAX index.

The subject of governance was not tackled very convincingly by VW's leadership representatives at the meeting, with few signs of planned improvements.

Abridged from *Financial Times* (2016)

References and further reading

Beck, D and Cowan, C (2006) *Spiral Dynamics*, Blackwell

Financial Times (2016) VW's share of EU car market falls to 10-year low, *fastFT* [online] http://www.ft.com/fastft/2016/06/16/vws-share-of-eu-car-market-falls-to-10-year-low/ [accessed 12 August 2016]

Higgs, M (2006) Course materials prepared for MBA Henley

Kegan, R and Lahey, L (2016) *An Everyone Culture*, Harvard Business Review Press, Boston, MA

Laloux, F (2014) *Reinventing Organisations*, Nelson Parker

McGee, P (2016) Volkswagen shareholders vent anger at chairman, *Financial Times* [online] http://www.ft.com/cms/s/0/12789d2e-388e-11e6-9a05-82a9b15a8ee7.html#axzz4H7XO196F [accessed 12 August 2016]

McGuire, J and Rhodes, G (2009) *Transforming your Leadership Culture*, Jossey-Bass, San Francisco

Schein, E H (2004) *Organizational Culture and Leadership*, 3rd edn, Jossey-Bass, San Francisco

Snowden, D J and Boone, M (2007) A leader's framework for decision making, *Harvard Business Review*, November, pp. 69–76

The implications 26 of Millennial leadership

Who are Millennials?

There is currently a great deal of research and public interest in the way social or cultural generations evolve and behave. There seems to be a hunger for some clear distinctions to be made, in an effort to make sense of the rapid changes we're going through. It seems we've become increasingly interested and fluent in discussing this territory of values and behaviours, perhaps because it's clear that the current value system adopted by the developed world isn't working for everyone. Many argue that a new set of cultural values is critical to our future, which at the moment feels uncertain and volatile. As is often the case, the younger generation appears to bring new hope.

There are differences in exact dates used, but according to Pew Research (Pew, 2016) the recent generational timeline is as follows:

Generation (US/UK perspective)	Birthdate	Significant influences
Greatest	Before 1928	Great War/Depression
Silent	1928–1945	WWII
Baby Boomer	1945–1964	Post War, Cold War
Gen X	1965–1980	Latchkey, sexual revolution, MTV
Gen Y or Millennials	1981–1997	Internet and World Wide Web
Gen Z	Post-millennial	

In this chapter we focus on the characteristics and potential of Millennials as the new, incoming leaders of the early 21st century. By 2020 this generation will comprise over half the global workforce (Catalyst, 2015), although, depressingly, it is predicted that as many as one in three will be unemployed. The proportionate picture is different in different geographies, with Millennials increasing in proportion overall, but US, Japanese, Canadian and European populations increasingly dominated by older workers and retired people. Conversely, in India a talent shortage is predicted as half the population will be under 25 by 2020.

According to Pew's US-based research (Pew, 2010), data from interviews with over 2000 Millennials indicates they can be lacking in work ethic, difficult to manage, more likely to quit without notice than other generations, and unwilling to ask for permission. They also appear, in the same research, to be well-educated, technologically savvy, socially conscious, confident, good communicators, open to change, welcoming of diversity and liberally minded. Financially, those in work are likely to be still receiving support from their families, living at home or in shared accommodation, perhaps managing education loans and with the prospect of earning less than their counterparts in previous generations. It's important to note that the popular media in the United States (such as *Time*, *Huffington Post*) has latched onto this generation with some vigour, labelling them variously as narcissists, selfish, generation 'me', entitled and 'special snowflakes'. This has probably coloured many people's attitudes globally towards this generation.

Research by Inkling in the UK, also based on data from Millennials themselves, aligns with much of the US research, additionally describing this generation as: wanting to enjoy their work; focused on earning rather than volunteering; conscious of their mental health (even more than physical health); valuing experiences over possessions; preferring crisp and authentic exchanges; and particularly concerned about the state of the NHS.

Millennials as leaders

The leadership aspirations and talents of this segment of the population are more unknown and less proven given their age, though of great interest to organizations, for whom they represent the talent of the future. A recent report from Deloitte (2016) based on the responses of nearly 8,000 college- or university-qualified, private sector-employed Millennials from all over the world shed some light on this subject. The headlines of their research are:

- they like and benefit from mentors, community service, job rotation and cross-functional projects;

- two in three expect to leave their current job by 2020;

- over 60 per cent say their leadership skills are not being fully developed;

- personal and business values matter a great deal – with employee satisfaction and ethics high on the list;

- they appreciate receiving good-quality feedback, being communicated with regularly and receiving recognition;

- they prefer to work core hours and deliver on outcomes rather than be measured via a timesheet;

- they want to be trained as leaders and considered seriously for promotion.

An understanding of what leadership is, from the perspective of Millennials, is starting to emerge; it may be quite different in flavour from the leadership that currently exists in the organizations that recruit them. This is exemplified by CIO magazine (Brousell, 2015) whose report on Virtuali's recent research claims:

> Millennials say they don't care about money, legacy or hierarchy, and instead aspire to be collaborative, empowering and transformational leaders. However, many Millennials also say their organizations lack the necessary corporate training programmes to get them there.

The Virtuali research (2015) involved interviews with 412 US Millennials and pointed to the growing sense that Millennials see organizations in a less hierarchical way than previous generations. The majority of participants aspired to be leaders, but were seeing this in more expansive terms than aspiring to be CEO or department head. They value their own advanced communication skills and worry more about their gaps in technical knowledge and industry competence. Reservations about committing to leadership roles include fears of a poor work-life balance (28 per cent) and fear of failure (19 per cent). Their biggest problems with their companies' leaders appears to be their lack of ability to develop others (39 per cent) and poor communication (50 per cent).

The above research has a heavy US bias, and it's helpful to see how these patterns of response differ when you look at Millennial populations across the globe. According to INSEAD's survey of 16,637 18–30-year-olds from

43 different countries, reported in the *Harvard Business Review* (Bresman, 2015), several key patterns exist in terms of attitudes to leadership:

- High future earnings are a consistently attractive benefit of becoming a leader across all geographies, although this ranges from 50 per cent of Central/Eastern Europeans to 17 per cent of Africans.

- African Millennials seem to care most about gaining opportunities to coach and mentor others (46 per cent), whereas this features lower down the list of attractions elsewhere.

- The opportunity to influence an organization is attractive to nearly half of Central/Eastern Europeans and North Americans, but to only around 25 per cent of those in Asia-Pacific locations and the Middle East.

- In Northern Europe and the United States, Millennials want to work for empowering leaders whereas in Central/Eastern Europe, functional and technical expertise are seen as more helpful.

Results of our own Millennial leaders research

In 2016 we partnered with Integral Change Consulting Ltd to investigate Millennial leadership in the UK (see **www.integralchange.co.uk/uk-millennial-leadership-report** for the full report). The aim of this research was to offer insights and recommendations to UK talent managers and line leaders about how best to nurture the transformative potential that we believe young Millennials can bring, while enabling them to quickly overcome their leadership skills gaps and blind spots. The research also included a question about the type of effective, flexible leadership development solutions that could be created for this group.

We surveyed 124 'young Millennials' aged 20–30, in paid or unpaid work in the UK, with some interest in leadership. Some were alerted to the survey by their organizations while others came to it via peers, friends or parents. The survey group was 60 per cent female, aged 25 on average, 91 per cent employed and from a very wide range of sectors including finance/banking, media/arts, fashion/retail, manufacturing, science and technology, transport, sustainability/energy, public sector, charity sector, health, education, sport and management consulting.

All participants completed a 20-minute, online questionnaire and 26 volunteers were confidentially interviewed via skype or phone, which enabled a more intimate understanding of their experiences, survey responses and wider perspectives. The following headline patterns emerged, some aligning with previous research, and some offering startling new insights.

There was a high level of enthusiasm for becoming a leader and developing the relevant skills, with an average score of 8 out of 10 being given. This interest was further evidenced by 70 per cent claiming to have found the survey enjoyable or stimulating and 42 per cent volunteering to take part in interviews. Many were already in roles where they were required to influence others with varying levels of responsibility and authority. Participants were asked to offer alternative names for the role they aspired to if the word leader didn't quite fit and a third choose to do this. Descriptions most often offered were process manager, collaborator, creative designer, catalyst and enabler/facilitator.

Emerging capacities

Participants were invited to agree or disagree with current hypotheses about this 'young Millennial' generation gathered from recent research. They indicated ambivalence about the 'we're special' tag, and accepted that in many ways they are just like other generations at this age. Despite this, they do see themselves as bringing something new and fresh to organizations. They rated themselves as particularly good at spotting patterns and trends, collaborating with others while enjoying some autonomy, being flexible and willing to adapt to new realities or changes of plan, being willing and able to process multiple inputs and leading through interpersonal skills and empathy. This is a significant finding, as this cluster of capacities aligns with higher levels of leadership (see Chapters 12 and 14).

They didn't see themselves or their peers as particularly work-shy or lacking in resilience, although many agreed that they struggled with negative or harshly delivered feedback given that school and university experiences had been broadly encouraging, and feedback given in skillful ways. Pushing for promotion and wanting to 'be someone' was seen as a reasonable thing to pursue, given that salaries for this group can be quite low and it pays to progress up the ranks.

The search for meaningful work is important to this group and once passions are engaged they say they work extremely hard, and some even found themselves articulating their own passions in an inspiring way during the interview. However, in interviews, several also spoke about how this need has to be tempered with the need to make money and gain experience, given that 'entry-level' jobs are so hard to come by.

All sorts of skills and particularly sector knowledge gaps were acknowledged, with half of all participants saying that developing themselves was the highest priority for them right now, while only 15 per cent chose making money and 14 per cent making an impact.

Experience of work

Regarding their current work, things looked on the surface to be going well for this group, with many survey participants saying they appreciated quite a bit about their role. This included learning a lot (68 per cent), being able to bring their skills and insights (61 per cent), being given a lot of responsibility (52 per cent) and working as part of a highly collaborative team (48 per cent). However, only a third said that they were receiving good encouragement and having a decent level of influence.

Frustrations seemed manageable, with the most common work difficulties named as squeezed resources/everything done in a rush (33 per cent), seeing wrong or ill-informed decisions being made (29 per cent) and experiencing stressful working practices (27 per cent), with 17 per cent saying that everything was great!

Interviews revealed a rather different picture, perhaps because of the more personal and private conversation this offered. Many were already working in roles involving leadership responsibility and yet there were several quite shocking stories about the lack of regular, decent-quality performance discussions with line managers, even from those who were part of a graduate programme. This generally meant a lack of regular one-to-one time with the immediate boss, an absence of even the most broad-brush career plan, zero discussion about the type of leadership and influencing skills they need to learn and little indication of the sort of leadership development options they might get if they're keen to lead. Many said how much the research interview had helped them to reflect on their leadership and some even committed to asking for improved line manager contact and feedback.

As aspiring leaders, interviewees mostly felt competent in basic interpersonal skills, which was demonstrated by their emotionally intelligent responses in the interview. A few had already attended some simple team management training workshops and although they seemed grateful for the contact it offered, much of it appeared to be a bit too simple for them.

Everyone surveyed wanted to get better at the 'next level' leadership skills offered on the survey, although in interviews few had a clear idea of what these really involved. High on the list of valuable topics for this group were having tough conversations, managing dialogue, holding others to account, and thinking and acting strategically. In interviews, additional needs expressed were learning how to process difficult feedback, influencing upwards/across, and engaging others in your ideas.

Participants in interviews spoke eloquently about their frustrations around bringing even the smallest of new ideas or suggestions to their colleagues. Most had been exposed through their studies to new ways of working of significant use to their employers, and could articulate their process innovation ideas clearly to the interviewer. The phrase 'we've always done it this way' was mentioned by many as a familiar 'blocker', although some working in more flexible and innovative environments were clearly being listened to.

In interviews, many spoke about old-fashioned-sounding work practices, with either rotas and plans that appeared to be overly restrictive given the task, or line managers who gave vague directions and then became unavailable. This age group is more used to working flexibly in collaborative teams and being responsible for individual or joint outcomes. Autonomy and clarity of direction were also valued.

Support for development

Participants were asked what leadership development supports they would most like to have more of, if money was no object, and the results were startlingly consistent. The most popular choices by far were:

- high-quality feedback against a clear framework (81 per cent);
- good-quality, regular coaching from line manager (81 per cent);
- advice from a good-quality industry mentor (56 per cent);
- the opportunity to attend leadership training (41 per cent).

As with the Deloitte research cited above, there was a very strong wish for better-quality interaction with line managers, and for much better-quality feedback. Some talked about rarely having a structured performance session with their line manager, if at all. Day-to-day conversations and patchy bits of direction were the norm for many, even for some of those enrolled on graduate training schemes. Mentors were often senior leaders with little insight into the individual's actual performance and often with what sounded like rather outmoded ideas of what leadership is.

In terms of structured leadership development, there was almost unanimous interest in live, personal or group interactions as opposed to reading online or watching webinars, which only attracted 20 per cent of votes. Most admitted, however, that the material they had already experienced via webinars and online learning was extremely dry, not particularly relevant, poorly structured and delivered in an uninspiring, detached way. If this was to be improved and made more engaging and interactive, they said they might well be interested and could see the value in such a flexible, cost-effective approach.

Implications for organizations

The research above creates a rich picture of both the leadership potential that Millennials can offer to organizations and the type of resistances they meet as they try to bring this. Our sense is that there is great, transformative potential in the type of approaches and capacities that young Millennials already have when they start work. Given the aspirations to greater organizational maturity and effectiveness that many senior leaders have (see Chapter 24), the pattern-spotting, collaborative, complexity-friendly, interpersonally acute abilities of this group need to be nurtured and welcomed rather than resisted or ignored and left to wither.

For *talent managers*, this implies the need to:

- get very clear about the particular skills and insights each young Millennial is bringing, and find a ready outlet for this;
- provide training for line leaders in how to nurture and coach new recruits, particularly those with leadership interests and potential;
- identify a map of leadership that supports the development of young Millennials and provide engaging skills training beyond the basics to help close their gaps;
- find ways of cross-pollinating ideas about how to lead and manage core processes between senior leaders, team leaders and Millennials;

For *line managers*, this implies the need to:

- brush up on your coaching and teambuilding skills!
- commit to a structured, high-quality one-to-one conversations with every team member every month;
- get familiar with an up-to-date map of leadership that fits with the aspirations of your organization;

For *millennials interested in leadership*, this implies the need to:
- ask your line manager for a regular one-to-one discussion about the work you're doing every month, including some coaching feedback;
- work on your openness to critical feedback – try not to take it personally, even if you sense a little aggression or impatience from the other person;

- commit to taking responsibility for your own leadership, making time to reflect on your progress and clarifying the type of support you need to get in place.

Pause for Learning Points

Millennials have been widely researched and talked about, perhaps because they bring hope and much-needed inspiration to organizations and society at a challenging and complex time.

As leaders, Millennials want to learn about their sector and organization, develop themselves as leaders, and bring their passions in a collaborative and inspiring way. To enable this, they need good-quality feedback from their line managers and a good-quality, trusting relationship.

In the UK, the implications for talent managers and line managers are about nurturing this group more explicitly, helping them to address their skills gaps and drawing more on their insights and passions.

Stop and Reflect!

Imagine you want to build a small, vibrant business that is powered by Millennial employees. What would be the key difference between the way this new enterprise runs and the organization you currently work in? Consider aspects such as structure, core processes, relationships with stakeholders, management and leadership style, performance management, education and training, etc.

If you are a Millennial, invite your line manager to read this chapter. Then ask to have a focused discussion about how the research findings resonate for each of you, what feedback and/or requests you have for each other, and how you wish to carry on from here. Likewise, if you manage a Millennial, invite them to do the same thing, but ensure that the conversation feels genuinely two-way.

References and further reading

Bresman, H (2015) What Millennials want from work, charted across the world, *Harvard Business Review*, February

Brousell, L (2015) How Millennials challenge traditional leadership, *CIO* [online] http://www.cio.com/article/2956600/leadership-management/how-millennials-challenge-traditional-leadership.html [accessed 11 August 2016]

Catalyst (2015) Generations: demographic trends in population and workforce [online] http://www.catalyst.org/knowledge/generations-demographic-trends-population-and-workforce [accessed 11 Aug 2016]

Deloitte (2016) The Deloitte Millennial Survey 2016 [online] http://www2.deloitte.com/global/en/pages/about-deloitte/articles/millennialsurvey.html [accessed 25 October 2016]

Inkling (2016) UK Millennials Report, *Inkling* [online] http://www.thisisinkling.com/inklingreports/2016/1/21/inkling-report-no-1-uk-millennials [accessed 25 October 2016]

International Labour Organization (2013) Global employment trends for youth, *ILO* [online] http://www.ilo.org/wcmsp5/groups/public/---dgreports/---dcomm/documents/publication/wcms_212423.pdf [accessed 25 October 2016]

Pew Research (2010) Millennials: confident, connected, open to change [online] http://www.pewsocialtrends.org/2010/02/24/millennials-confident-connected-open-to-change/ [accessed 25 October 2016]

Pew Research (2016) Demographic research definitions [online] http://www.pewresearch.org/methodology/demographic-research/definitions/ [accessed 11 Aug 2016]

Stein, J (2013) The Me Me Me Generation, *Time*, 20 May

Virtuali and Workplacetrends.com (2015) The Millennial Leadership Study, *Workplace Trends* [online] https://workplacetrends.com/the-millennial-leadership-survey/ [accessed 25 October 2016]

Conclusions from Part Six

Although leadership culture within organizations is an invisible and elusive entity, there are some useful frameworks to support increased understanding of how leadership culture is formed and evolves over time.

Leadership culture is a fragile thing that can be impacted suddenly by changes in ownership or status, as well as influential personnel. It grows and is sustained in various complex ways, but mostly through the values, beliefs and behaviours of the organization's leaders.

The effectiveness of an organization depends to a great extent on the quality of its leadership, and this has to be well-attuned to the needs of the context. Many CEOs and HR leaders aspire to change the leadership culture of their organization, particularly from Tier 1 to Tier 2, which is a tricky move to make. This involves introducing new ways of thinking and behaving, which demand in turn that leaders themselves need to become sufficiently mature in their capacity to deal with high levels of complexity and collaboration.

The potential of Millennials to bring more complexity-attuned ways of working and thinking seems promising. This is likely to have a positive effect on organizational cultures if these new, young leaders can be welcomed and nurtured sufficiently. The danger for larger, more slow-moving organizations is that they lose out on this talent and miss opportunities to reform and innovate their core processes as well as their leadership culture.

Appendix: The original research

In 2007 we set out to discover how much these Five Leadership Qualities are being used by effective organizational leaders, how independent the use of these five Qualities is, and how people view these Qualities in terms of their effectiveness, attractiveness as a Quality model and the level of difficulty experienced in mastering the Quality. This is a record of our research write-up, which offers readers more details than we had space for in the body of the book, and lets you into some of our early thinking.

Research group

In January 2007 we invited experienced organizational managers to complete a questionnaire which formed the basis for our investigation into the Five Leadership Qualities, and how the Qualities manifest themselves in organizational life. Eighty-three people completed the questionnaire; some online, and some paper-based. The questionnaire attempted to uncover to what degree each of these Five Leadership Qualities is used by successful leaders, and how participants see the Qualities demonstrated within their own leadership work. It also investigated peoples' thoughts about which leadership Qualities 'suit' which contexts.

The population who responded was a mix of public, private and voluntary sector managers with around half of the respondents working in the public sector, 40 per cent in the private sector and 10 per cent in the voluntary sector. The vast majority of respondents live and work in the UK, and a small percentage live and work outside the UK. Seventy per cent of the respondents were male and 30 per cent were female.

We asked people to describe the changes in their current work situation by choosing any number of situations from a range of options. The five most popular selections were:

- need to work with a range of partners and stakeholders – 39 per cent;
- cultural change – 33 per cent;
- working towards a new five-year strategy – 33 per cent;
- complex whole organizational change – 29 per cent;
- restructuring – 25 per cent.

Qualities used by effective leaders

We invited people to think of two effective organizational leaders, and to analyse the way these leaders operate by telling us how much each leader demonstrates each of the Five Leadership Qualities. It's worth mentioning that at least two people declined to fill the questionnaire in because they couldn't think of any leaders that they had known throughout their working lives who they would describe as effective.

In Figure A.1 below, you can see the average proportions in which each leadership Quality was used by the effective leader described. This was derived by adding up all the proportions given for all the leaders described. It's clear that when all the analyses are added together it looks as if, on average, all Five Leadership Qualities are used in equal quantities by successful leaders. Further inspection of the data revealed that 80 per cent of the leaders described by respondents used all the Qualities to some extent.

We wanted to identify any particular leadership patterns; for instance, is there a specific combination of Qualities that appears to work well in a specific situation? We noticed that leaders of successful turnarounds seem to use the Measured Connector Qualities a little less than they use the other four Qualities, whilst leaders of successful complex whole organization change use the Measured Connector Quality more than the other Qualities. No other obvious patterns emerged, indicating that combinations of Qualities appear to work well in all sorts of situations.

The spread of use of different Qualities is interesting (see Table A.1). It's interesting to note that just about all of all successful leaders described by survey participants use the Measured Connector Quality to some extent, making this Quality appear to be a fundamental requirement for leaders to master.

Figure A.1   Use of qualities by effective leaders

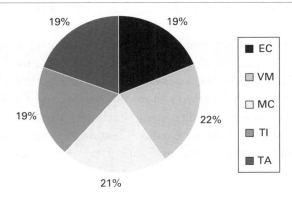

The Visionary Motivator Quality was also extremely widely used. Nearly 30 per cent of the successful leaders described use the Visionary Motivator Quality a great deal, with only 15 per cent using any one of the other Qualities a great deal. It appears that the Visionary Motivator Quality is one that can be used successfully in large quantities, and is less likely to be used (or spotted) in small quantities. Perhaps this Quality can make up for inadequacies in the other Qualities.

The Quality that was most often missing was the Edgy Catalyser. Eight per cent of the leaders described didn't use the Edgy Catalyser Quality at

Table A.1   The spread of use of the different leadership Qualities – percentage of total number of leaders described using each Quality in the various different strengths

	Never (1)	Little (2)	Some-what (3)	Much (4)	A great deal (5)	Weighted av. use of each Quality
Edgy Catalyser	8%	23%	31%	23%	15%	**19%**
Visionary Motivator	3%	13%	28%	29%	27%	**22%**
Measured Connector	2%	19%	28%	37%	14%	**21%**
Tenacious Implementer	4%	25%	30%	26%	15%	**19%**
Thoughtful Architect	4%	21%	31%	29%	15%	**19%**

all. The next most absent were the Thoughtful Architect and the Tenacious Implementer Qualities, neither of which were used by 4 per cent of the leaders described.

Was there more information to glean about the strength of usage of each Quality? Only 38 per cent of the leaders described in the survey appeared to be using the Edgy Catalyser Quality either 'much' or a 'great deal', compared to 56 per cent using the Visionary Motivator Quality and 51 per cent using the Measured Connector Quality either 'much' or a 'great deal'. This might indicate that the Edgy Catalyser Quality is best used in slightly smaller doses, as are the Tenacious Implementer and Thoughtful Architect Qualities.

Are the qualities independent of each other?

We looked for correlations between the use of all five Qualities to see whether the use of one gets in the way of the use of another, or if two Qualities appear to work well hand in hand. This analysis would also tell us if the Qualities we have proposed are in some way overlapping.

Table A.2 shows the correlations found between the use of different Qualities. The correlations that are starred once are low, and those starred twice are medium-level correlations (according to Cohen (1988)). There were no strong correlations identified in the data collected. Experienced statisticians tell us that only the medium-level correlations are of any real significance, although the other lower correlations are interesting and worth commenting on.

The most significant correlation is between the Edgy Catalyser and the Tenacious Implementer Qualities. This is a medium-level positive correlation, which implies that there might be a connection of some sort between the levels of use of these Qualities. This means that if a leader is a heavy user of the Tenacious Implementer Quality, it is quite likely that he or she will also be a heavy user of the Edgy Catalyser Quality, and vice versa. Likewise, if a leader doesn't use the Tenacious Implementer Quality very much, it is quite likely that he or she does not use the Edgy Catalyser very much either, and vice versa.

It could be that either the Edgy Catalyser Quality and the Tenacious Implementer Qualities are overlapping, or maybe they simply work together well. Both are associated with a sense of urgency and clear boundaries which could be the link. Some might argue that the two Qualities could be combined. However, we believe that it's important to distinguish the Edgy

Table A.2   Correlations between the Qualities: * = low correlation, **=medium level correlation. [no star= no correlation]

	Edgy Catalyser	Visionary Motivator	Measured Connector	Tenacious Implementer	Thoughtful Architect
Edgy Catalyser		0.18 *	–0.08	0.373 **	–0.27 *
Visionary Motivator			–0.13 *	0.07	–0.089
Measured Connector				–0.11 *	0.19 *
Tenacious Implementer					0.09
Thoughtful Architect					

Catalyser Quality as we have seen careful use of this Quality making a big difference to organizational change efforts, and yet the key behaviours associated with it are missing from many management competence lists.

A low positive correlation exists between the Edgy Catalyser and the Visionary Motivator Qualities, implying that there might be a slight connection between the level of use of these Qualities. This may be to do with emotional connection and energy levels. The Visionary Motivator and the Edgy Catalyser are more extraverted, heart-oriented forms of leading, and require passion to be expressed, so it's possible that leaders who can master one Quality might find it easier to master the other.

Likewise, the Measured Connector and Thoughtful Architect Qualities have a low positive correlation, which implies that there is a slight connection between levels of use of these two Qualities in any one leader. This may be because they are both calmer, less interventionist ways of operating.

The Measured Connector and the Tenacious Implementer Qualities are slightly negatively correlated, which means that if a leader is a heavy user of one, it is likely that he or she is a low user of the other. This could be because the Measured Connector Quality is about divergence. It involves opening up discussions and including people. The Tenacious Implementer is by contrast a convergent Quality in which the leader encourages people to follow the agreed plan and complete tasks on time. One can imagine that doing both would take some juggling. The Tenacious Implementer Quality seems to be focused on moving things forward in a very purposeful, linear way whereas the Measured Connector is ensuring the linkages are made across the whole organization and beyond in a more networked or spatial way.

The Edgy Catalyser and the Thoughtful Architect are also slightly negatively correlated. Again, this means that if a leader is a heavy user of one it is likely that he or she is a low user of the other. This makes some sense, as these Qualities are quite different in nature. The Edgy Catalyser points out problems and raises issues with people very directly, whereas the Thoughtful Architect is more inclined to find a solution to something offline and tackle issues in a more considered way. This might be why use of the Edgy Catalyser Quality doesn't sit very easily with the use of the Thoughtful Architect Quality and vice versa. They seem opposite in nature.

None of the correlations that arose from our research were high, which indicates that the five Qualities are reasonably independent from each other. This suggests confirmation of our belief that each of the five Qualities can be used independently, developed independently. This also suggests that each Quality is likely to have a different use, and therefore a different organizational effect.

What type of leader are you?

Everyone who completed the questionnaire has been a manager within organizations at some point in their career. We asked them to choose which one of the Qualities was most like their own style as a leader or manager. The most popular selection was Measured Connector. Nearly half of those asked said they operated most frequently as a Measured Connector, 26 per cent as Visionary Motivator, 18 per cent as Thoughtful Architect and only 8 per cent as Edgy Catalyser and 6 per cent as Tenacious Implementer.

Was this as we expected? Maybe the Measured Connector is the most frequently found Quality in our respondents because it is the most prevalent managerial profile in today's organizations. Or perhaps it's the most natural profile for the type of population that is willing to fill in such questionnaires! The Quality is calm, unhurried, but purposeful and focuses on people and connections between them. The least prevalent Qualities in our respondent population were the Tenacious Implementer and Edgy Catalyser Qualities, which are by contrast a little more directive and task focused in approach; in extremes, these can be more reminiscent of the traditional command and control manager. As we had asked people to select only one Quality, it's possible that the Tenacious Implementer and Edgy Catalyser Qualities are used by respondents, but just less frequently.

Figure A.2   Participant self-ratings

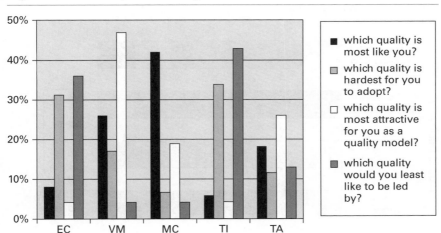

We wonder whether organizations have a natural limit on the uptake of the Edgy Catalyser and the Tenacious Implementer Qualities. Perhaps organizations which have too many people performing these Qualities develop disconnected and unsupportive cultures, lacking in connectivity or sense of purpose, or any real overarching thought processes.

Which of the five Qualities do you find hardest to adopt?

We then asked people which Qualities were hardest for them to adopt. The Edgy Catalyser and the Tenacious Implementer came joint top of the list. Both of these Qualities were selected by around 30 per cent of the participants apiece as the hardest Qualities to adopt. Seventeen per cent of participants named the Visionary Motivator Quality as the hardest to adopt. The Measured Connector was selected by only 6 per cent and the Thoughtful Architect selected by 12 per cent. These last two Qualities seem much easier for most people to access.

Given that all five Qualities appear to be required for successful leadership, it is intriguing to discover that two of the Qualities that are regularly used by successful leaders seem to be hard for one-third of the leadership population to access. What might this mean for the development of successful leaders? This research would indicate that many leaders need to learn how to manage and direct complex projects, how to move into and handle

Figure A.3   Relationship between self-perceived 'natural' Quality and 'hardest' quality to adopt

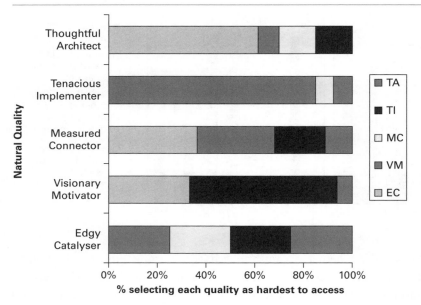

difficult situations and how to find their work passion or vision and express this. On the other hand, it might indicate that people tend to underestimate the importance of the Thoughtful Architect and Measured Connectors Qualities, and what's required to demonstrate these well.

We wanted to investigate the relationship between the participant's natural Quality and the Quality he or she found hardest to access. See Figure A.3 for this data. On close inspection of the data, it appears that the hardest Quality for Visionary Motivators to perform is the Tenacious Implementer Quality, while the hardest Quality for Tenacious Implementers to perform is the Visionary Motivator Quality. Perhaps these Qualities are somehow opposites; the Visionary Motivator works with others to create an attractive future state while the Tenacious Implementer is constantly looking to see what's not being done to reach an already agreed set of deliverables. They are very different approaches to leading, although it's possible to see how a project or change initiative might well require both Qualities to be present in the leadership team.

Thoughtful Architects tend to find the Edgy Catalyser Quality the most difficult to access, whereas the Edgy Catalysers in our questionnaire found a variety of Qualities hard to access. Measured Connectors tend to find the Edgy Catalyser and Visionary Motivator Qualities most difficult to access.

Which of the five Qualities is most attractive as a role model?

The Visionary Motivator was selected by respondents as the most attractive role model. This Quality was chosen by 47 per cent of participants. The very nature of the Visionary Motivator Quality is to energize and motivate people, so it's not surprising that in the UK and US context, it provides a very attractive role model for nearly half of those asked. We wonder whether this Quality is so popular, or even so respected in other populations or cultures. In other cultures, senior figures are more likely to occupy Thoughtful Architect Qualities, or perhaps to use a less extraverted version of the Visionary Motivator Quality.

The next most attractive role model for our respondents was the Thoughtful Architect, selected by 26 per cent. What is interesting is that stereotypically leaders are often seen as action-oriented, so perhaps it comes as a welcome surprise to see that over a quarter of people valued this Quality so highly. We imagine that there is some kudos or prestige associated with the Thoughtful Architect Quality. Perhaps it is linked with a high IQ or a well-developed analytical brain, which we value highly in the UK and the United States. Or perhaps there is a real belief that cognitive, strategic, offline thinking will solve organizational issues and enable survival.

The Measured Connector was selected as the next most attractive. It was chosen by 18 per cent of participants. However, the Edgy Catalyser and the Tenacious Implementer Qualities were seen as the most attractive role models by only 4 per cent of participants apiece. It's possible that leaders are influenced in their choice of role model by popular leadership literature and by models purveyed by leadership training courses. Perhaps they are also influenced by what they notice is lacking in their own organizations. As respondents themselves appear to recognize that all five Qualities are being used by successful leaders, it's curious to note that their choices of role model don't appear to reflect this spread. Perhaps this is more of a subjective choice, based on current myths of what a leader 'should' be like, such as those who are strongly promoted as successful leaders. The Edgy Catalyser perhaps is the Quality which is least likely to win friends and most likely to need an emotional resilience, if not a thick skin! The Tenacious Implementer on the other hand may be associated with the more prosaic and potentially 'dull' aspects of leadership, the project management side of change, although it is nonetheless critical to successful leadership.

Figure A.4   Relationship between self-perceived 'natural' Quality and choice of role model

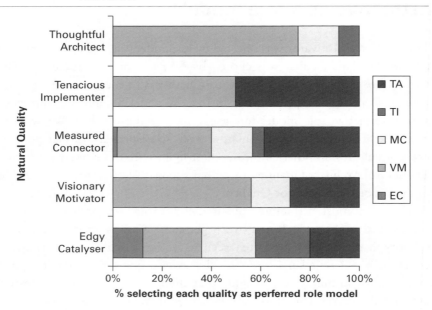

We also looked through the data to see whether there were any patterns that emerged from looking at the relationship between an individual's natural Quality, and the Quality they chose as a role model. See Figure A.4 for this data. We were intrigued to find that 56 per cent of the Visionary Motivators found Visionary Motivators most attractive as a role model. Only 28 per cent of the Visionary Motivators found Thoughtful Architects attractive role models and 16 per cent found Measured Connectors attractive. Is the Visionary Motivator a narcissistic Quality perhaps, or just self-sufficient?

We also found that 75 per cent of the Thoughtful Architects completing the survey found the Visionary Motivator Quality the most attractive as a role model, with only a small interest in the Measured Connector and Tenacious Implementer Qualities. Around a third of the natural Measured Connectors found the Visionary Motivator the most attractive and a third found the Thoughtful Architect Qualities the most attractive. Only 15 per cent of all natural Measured Connectors that participated found the Measured Connector the most attractive Quality.

Tenacious Implementers were evenly split between admiring the Visionary Motivator and the Thoughtful Architect Qualities, whereas Edgy

Catalysers admired all different Qualities to some extent. Maybe Tenacious Implementers realize that to demonstrate their Quality really well, they also need to incorporate some of the Visionary Motivator Quality and the Thoughtful Architect Quality. Note that the Edgy Catalyser Quality was the least attractive role model.

Which of the qualities would you least like to be led by?

When participants were asked which Qualities they would least like to be led by the Tenacious Implementer came top at 43 per cent, with the Edgy Catalyser a close second at 36 per cent. The Thoughtful Architect was third in the list with 13 per cent of those asked naming this Quality as the one they would least like to be led by. This suggests that the Tenacious Implementer and Edgy Catalyser Qualities are less likely to meet the support needs of their staff when used in isolation from the other available leadership Qualities. The Visionary Motivator and Measured Connector Qualities are more likely to provide supportive, steady relationships for people.

Figure A.5   Use of Qualities in participant organizations

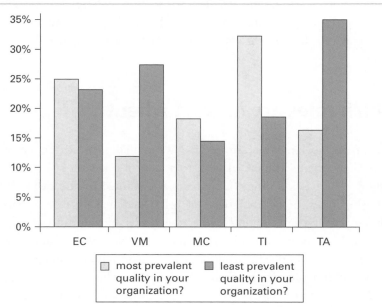

Again, some patterns emerged here. Nearly half of all the Measured Connectors didn't want to be led by Edgy Catalysers. Eighty per cent of the Edgy Catalysers didn't want to be led by Tenacious Implementers and two-thirds of the Visionary Motivators felt the same way. Most Thoughtful Architects don't like to be led by Tenacious Implementers or Edgy Catalysers.

Which are the most and least prevalent styles in your organization?

Figure A.5 illustrates the responses to the questions we asked about the most and least prevalent styles used within participants' organizations. The Tenacious Implementer Quality is the most frequently observed style, with the Edgy Catalyser a close second. Maybe this result reflects the level of urgency and haste present in many organizations, with much chasing of actions and kicking-off of new projects. In our experience, a great deal of this activity is ineffective because the projects tackle surface issues rather than deeper systemic issues, usually because they are conceived too quickly and without the use of a Thoughtful Architect. In a high-pressure, delivery-conscious environment, Thoughtful Architects can be seen as slow and laboured; too focused on details or problems. However, sometimes that is what is needed.

Least frequently observed styles are the Thoughtful Architect and the Visionary Motivator. We often hear staff yearning for vision from senior managers, with an accompanying yearning to have this backed up with sound rationale. Sometimes leaders are so busy taking responsibility for everything (and becoming a bottle neck) that they have no time left for crafting a well-thought-through vision that takes an organization into the future.

Which roles are needed when?

Which roles work in which situations? We invited our research participants to use their organizational wisdom to select the roles they thought would be most effective in a range of contexts. We wanted to find out if different leadership roles, or combinations of roles, matched up to any particular contexts. This type of insight could enable leadership teams to spend time in consciously choosing which leadership roles need to be carried out by team members, for example to progress a particular type of change initiative. This research might also help shed some light on the selection, recruitment and development of leaders, in the sense that it might be more desirable to

Figure A.6 Participant views about the most effective Qualities to employ in a variety of contexts

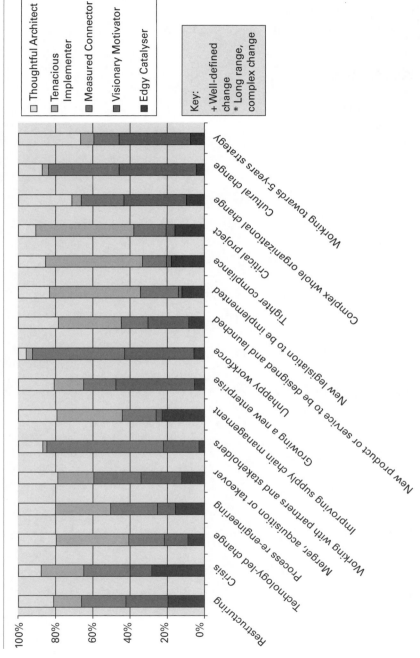

Key:
+ Well-defined change
* Long range, complex change

Legend:
□ Thoughtful Architect
▨ Tenacious Implementer
▨ Measured Connector
▨ Visionary Motivator
■ Edgy Catalyser

Contexts (along horizontal axis):
Restructuring
Crisis
Technology-led change
Process re-engineering
Merger, acquisition or takeover
Working with partners and stakeholders
Improving supply chain management
Growing a new enterprise
Unhappy workforce
New legislation to be designed and launched
New product or service to be implemented
Tighter compliance
Complex whole organizational change
Critical project
Cultural change
Working towards 5-years strategy

recruit a leader who excels in one type of role if you are recruiting into a particular context. Our questionnaire therefore asked people to select the one or two leadership roles that they thought would work best in each of a range of organizational contexts.

The summary of results appears in Figure A.6 below.

Reference

Cohen, J (1988) *Statistical Power Analysis for the Behavioural Sciences*, Erlbaum, Hillsdale, NJ

INDEX

Italics indicate a figure or table in the text.